VIYYUKKA

THE MORNING STAR

Stories by Indian
Women Revolutionaries

(Translated from Telugu)

EDITED BY

P. Aravinda · B. Anuradha

Daraja Press

Published by
Daraja Press
https://darajapress.com

© 2025 P. Aravinda and B. Anuradha

ISBN 978-1-997742-13-5 (soft cover)

This book is available for sale worldwide except South Asia
where it is available from Aakar Books https://aakarbooks.com

Book prepared by Kate McDonnell

Library and Archives Canada Cataloguing in Publication

Title: Viyyukka = The morning star : stories by Indian women revolutionaries (translated from Telugu) / edited by P. Aravinda, B. Anuradha.
Other titles: Morning star
Names: Aravinda, P., editor. | Anuradha, Bi., editor
Description: Includes bibliographical references. | In English, translated from the Telugu.
Identifiers: Canadiana 20250331020 | ISBN 9781997742142 (softcover)
Subjects: LCSH: Women revolutionaries—India—Fiction. | LCSH: Revolutionaries—India—Fiction. | LCSH: India—History—20th century—Fiction. | LCSH: Telugu fiction—20th century—Translations into English. | LCSH: Telugu fiction—21st century—Translations into English. | LCGFT: Short stories.
Classification: LCC PL4780.57.W65 V5813 2025 | DDC 894.8/273010835854—dc23

Table of Contents

Introduction

Viyyukka, a word in the Gondi language meaning morning star, is an anthology of stories written in Telugu by Maoist women revolutionaries over the past four decades. This anthology, published by *Virasam* (Revolutionary Writers Association) in 2023, consists of six volumes and features 316 stories written by nearly fifty authors. Around a hundred stories from these 316, written with armed revolution as the subject and covering various aspects of life in the movement, have been selected for translation into English and are being published as the *Viyyukka* series.

The *Viyyukka* series represents a rare and compelling collection of stories penned by women revolutionaries from India's Maoist movement. These narratives are not works of fiction in the conventional sense – they were penned while the authors were leading the life of a guerrilla soldier and often under conditions of extreme duress. They are lived experiences written from within the movement, reflecting the intertwined realities of revolutionary struggle, gendered participation, and engagement with Adivasi communities. At their heart, these narratives are about survival: of people, forests, rivers, and a way of life. They capture how struggles against exploitation and dispossession evolved from local rebellions into a wider revolutionary movement that challenged the Indian ruling classes, the state, and global Capital alike.

The women writers of these stories a(we)re engaged in armed struggles and documented tactical and ideological engagements. Apart from these, they also documented the political climate, the cultural and emotional realities of life under repression, as well as intimate experiences such as love, loss, camaraderie, and everyday life in the squads. These narratives offer a rare glimpse into the human dimensions of armed struggle, highlighting the agency, resilience, and moral consciousness of the women participants. Their works cross language and geographical boundaries, offering a collective testimony of resistance.

The effort to bring these stories into the public domain has not been easy. They were written in hiding, smuggled across regions, and preserved against all odds. This introduction seeks to situate the stories of 'Morning Star' within the broader history of revolutionary and Adivasi resistance movements in India.

Revolutionary Movements in India

The Naxalbari uprising of 1967 in West Bengal marked a significant turning point in India's political history. 'Naxalbari' – the name of a village in North Bengal in the Terai region near Nepal – is the place where, on 24 May 1967, peasants resisted police repression with bows and arrows, killing one officer. They had been fighting for their right over the land they were cultivating. The next day, police opened fire on a gathering in Naxalbari, killing 11, which included eight women with their two suckling babies. That's the start of the Naxalite/Maoist movement. People's Daily of China hailed that as 'a peal of spring thunder' that 'crashed over the land of India'. This struggle – unique and of great historical significance in many ways – was led by Charu Mazumdar and a group of revolutionary activists who then belonged to the Communist Party of India (Marxist) (CPI(M)), against the leadership of which they revolted. 'Naxalbari', as its leader explained, was 'not a struggle for land, but for political power.' It represented not only an armed rebellion but also a profound call for justice, self-determination, and structural change. Since then, the movement has come to be known in history as the Naxalbari movement, and its followers are referred to as 'Naxalites'.

As Arundhati Roy described it in 'Walking with the Comrades':

> If nothing else, from the time of the Telangana movement, which in some ways was a precursor to the uprising in Naxalbari, the Naxalite movement, for all its faults, sparked an anger about being exploited and a desire for self-respect in some of the most oppressed communities.

In 2008, an expert group appointed by the Planning Commission submitted a report called *'Development Challenges in Extremist Affected Areas'*. It said,

> (I)n its day-to-day manifestation, it [the Maoist movement -ed] is to be looked upon as basically a fight for social justice, equality, protection and local development.

Naxalbari shattered illusions about the Indian state, independence, the Constitution, and Gandhian politics. It declared 1947 a mere "transfer of power," called the ruling bourgeois comprador classes, analysed the Indian society as semi-feudal and semi-colonial and declared the State character to be so. It rejected peaceful transition and emphasized the agrarian revolution led by peasants under the working-class leadership. Elections were declared meaningless, and the protracted People's War became its chosen path.

Influenced by the Naxalbari struggle, an uprising occurred in Srikakulam, Andhra Pradesh, from 1967 to 1970. The movement spread to many places throughout India. It inspired thousands of students from all over the country to abandon their studies and join the revolutionary transformation of India. It left no field untouched and inspired new forms of art, literature, cinema, and more. The Indian economy and history were written in a new light.

In November 1967, the All-India Coordination Committee of Communist Revolutionaries (AICCCR) was established, which undertook political work on an all-India level. This continued until the CPI (Marxist-Leninist) was formed in April 1969, with Charu Mazumdar as its general secretary. Meanwhile, a parallel effort had been going on, with some other revolutionaries forming themselves into a group and uniting around their mouthpiece, Dakshin Desh. These activists formed the Maoist Communist Center (MCCI) in October 1969.

During this period, thousands were killed by the police, security forces, Congress lumpens and CPI (M) cadres, while a large number were imprisoned on charges of sedition, etc, and also detained without trial under the oppressive law called MISA (Maintenance of Internal Security Act). Charu Mazumdar died in police custody in July 1972 after torture. After the death of Charu Mazumdar, the CPI (ML) fell into disarray, as most of the central committee members were either jailed or martyred. Following his death, three trends emerged in the movement. One trend adhered to the adventurist line, and another trend completely repudiated the Naxalbari line in the name of correcting it. There was a third trend, particularly represented by the COC (Central Organizing Committee), which upheld the essence of the CPI (ML) line, but sought to rectify the 'left' errors. The COC comprised state units from Punjab, West Bengal, Andhra Pradesh and Bihar. The Punjab unit later merged with the Unity Organization to form the CPI (ML) Party Unity in 1978, and the Andhra Pradesh unit developed into the CPI (ML) People's War in 1980 under the leadership of Kondapalli Seetharamayya.

Some among the Communists belonging to the Andhra Pradesh Committee were the first to appreciate the significance of the Chinese Revolution. In the Telangana region of central India, the revolutionary peasants in the late 1940s raised the slogan 'China's Path is our Path', built their own guerrilla units, fought against the feudal forces of the Nizam and Nehru's army, and set up their own organs of power in the countryside. Ten thousand villages were 'liberated' from the clutches of the landlords, and land was redistributed to the people. That struggle was crushed by military means and disowned by the then CPI (Communist Party of India) leadership. The movement in Telangana heralded the emergence of revolutionary Communism in India. Due to this background, there was heavy recruitment from Andhra Pradesh (now divided into two states, Andhra Pradesh and Telangana) in the revolutionary movement.

Following this self-critical evaluation, a powerful revolutionary movement emerged in Andhra Pradesh, Dandakaranya, Bihar, and Tamil Nadu, among other regions. The CPI (ML)

Party Unity and the People's War parties merged in 1995 and continued as the CPI (ML) People's War. MCC independently built a strong revolutionary movement and Party, especially in Bihar and Jharkhand. Later, The MCC and the Punjab-based Revolutionary Communist Centre of India (Maoist) (RCCI(M)) merged to form the MCCI in January 2003.

In 1980, thirty-five CPI (ML) People's War armed activists from the Karimnagar and Adilabad peasant struggles split up into groups. They entered the Gadchiroli, Bastar, Adilabad, and East Godavari forest areas of Andhra Pradesh to spread the message of revolution among the Adivasis. This forest was also intended to serve as a rear area for the revolutionary movement in the event of intense repression. The struggles and activities undertaken by the revolutionary movement in Dandakaranya (DK) represent a significant attempt by the CPI (ML) People's War and later the CPI (Maoist) to create an alternative model of development rooted in agrarian revolution, anti-feudal struggle, and resistance to comprador capitalism and imperialism.

DANDAKARANYA

Spread across the states of Chhattisgarh, Maharashtra, Telangana, Andhra Pradesh, and Odisha, DK covers 1,10,000 square kilometres, rich in forests and minerals, inhabited by nearly twenty million people from diverse Adivasi communities. It is a vast, sparsely populated forest area dependent on shifting cultivation and collective land ownership, where the Maoist movement took root in the early 1980s when armed squads from Andhra Pradesh entered Gadchiroli and Bastar.

In the initial months, the Adivasis were highly suspicious of them and wouldn't let them into their homes. No one would offer them food or water. The police spread rumours that they were thieves. There was an enormous amount of repression.

The perennial problem in the lives of the Adivasis was the Forest Department. The forest department officials harassed and prevented people from ploughing their fields, grazing their cattle, collecting firewood, plucking leaves and picking fruit from the forests. People would be beaten, arrested, and their crops destroyed.

Revolutionaries began to organise the Adivasis to fight these atrocities and excesses, and to demand a rise in the price they were being paid for collecting *tendu* leaves (used to make a local variant of cigarettes), cutting and collecting bamboo for paper mills, and other similar activities. They mobilized to assert their right over their land. It wasn't easy for them to organise people entirely unfamiliar with this kind of politics, to lead them on strike. Eventually, the strikes were successful and the price was doubled. However, the real success for the Party was to demonstrate the value of unity and a new approach to conducting political negotiations.

Emboldened by the people's participation in the various struggles, the Party decided to confront the Forest Department. It encouraged people to take over forest land and cultivate it. The Forest Department retaliated by burning newly established villages in forest areas. In 1986, it announced the establishment of a National Park in Bijapur, which meant the eviction of sixty villages. The People's War Party demolished the construction going on for the park and stopped the eviction of the remaining villages. It prevented the Forest Department from entering the area. Between 1986 and 2000, the Party redistributed 300,000 acres of land for cultivation by the Adivasis.

On the other hand, very intense anti-feudal struggles were waged in the plain areas of Telangana, mobilizing hundreds of thousands of peasants. Tens of thousands of workers, students, and various sections of the population relentlessly waged struggles on multiple issues. Hundreds of intellectuals and writers organised into democratic rights organisations, revolutionary writers' associations, and other groups. A powerful revolutionary cultural movement was also built.

Terrified by this, the ruling classes instigated the State to launch intense repressive campaigns to root out the revolutionary movement. The revolutionary Party was then forced to launch armed resistance against the State. Thus, the guerrilla war started in the late 1980s.

Since then, the Maoists have built guerrilla zones in Telangana, Bihar, Jharkhand and across districts in Maharashtra, Chhattisgarh, and Odisha, establishing both armed structures and mass organisations such as Revolutionary People's Committees, Adivasi Peasant Organisations, Women's and Children's organisations, and village defence forces like Peoples Militia, etc. By 2000, the Party also launched the People's Liberation Guerrilla (PLGA) and gradually grew in strength to form company- and battalion-level units.

Women and Caste Questions in the movement

The impact that the Telangana armed struggle, Naxalbari, and Srikakulam struggles had on the people of the Telugu states (Telangana and Andhra Pradesh) was immense. It was, in fact, the revolutionary movement that gave women in India the greatest hope for liberation. In March 1967, with the slogan "Advance on the path of armed revolution," peasant struggles erupted like a storm. Oppressed people, with their traditional weapons, participated in these land struggles on a large scale.

With the participation of women, these struggles gained sharpness. Taking lessons from the sacrifices of women, the revolutionary movement gradually developed a clear understanding of women's liberation, refining it further, and arrived at the conclusion: *"A revolution without women cannot succeed."*

The parliamentary Communist parties of India failed to develop the correct perspective on the struggle against patriarchy. Their view at the time was that patriarchy, as a reflection of the exploitative class basis of society, operates on the surface – in the ideological sphere, religion, culture, traditions, customs, laws, and family. Therefore, until the economic base was fundamentally changed, they thought there was no need to consider fighting patriarchy. They believed that once the economic base was transformed and a socialist economic base established, patriarchy would automatically disappear.

The CPI (ML) People's War Party was the first (in 1995) to attempt to formulate an understanding of women's liberation into a perspective document. The Maoist party further developed this understanding in its first Congress, held after the merger in 2007, as follows.

"The struggle against patriarchy and for women's liberation must necessarily be waged as part of the anti-imperialist, anti-feudal people's war. The struggles for a new democratic revolution open new doors for women's liberation from patriarchy, and likewise, the struggle against patriarchy strengthens the new democratic revolution. Between the two, there is a continuous, living, dialectical relationship."

The writers of these stories, as well as many of the characters within them, are individuals who are engaged in such struggles and practices. As their social consciousness developed through these struggles, the writers came to understand many aspects of society and were able to capture, with sensitivity, how discrimination and patriarchy manifest even in what seem like small matters, shaping them into stories. Their stories contain observations drawn from their practical activity in the midst of ordinary people's lives. Every one of the writers first began as an activist.

To combat patriarchy in Adivasi society and draw women into the revolution, the CPI (ML) PW party established the Adivasi Mahila Sangathan (AMS) in 1986, which later evolved into the Krantikari Adivasi Mahila Sangathan (KAMS). At its peak, KAMS had 90,000 enrolled members and could well have been the largest women's organisation in the country. It campaigns against the Adivasi traditions of forced marriage and abduction, the custom of making menstruating women live outside the village in a hut in the forest and against bigamy and domestic violence. Women are encouraged to participate actively in various developmental activities, the people's militia, and to join the squads. As police repression had grown in Bastar – a part of Dandakaranya – the women of KAMS had become a formidable force. They rallied in their hundreds, sometimes thousands, to physically confront the police. The very fact that the KAMS exists has radically changed traditional attitudes and eased many of the traditional forms of discrimination against women. Many young women joined the People's Liberation Guerilla Army (PLGA), and women make up 45 per cent of its cadre.

Another major challenge before the revolutionary movement is the caste question. Caste is a specific social problem confronting India in the form of a hierarchical ladder. In India, land ownership has been caste-based, and this system remained essentially unchanged until the British colonial conquest. Certain reforms under British rule – such as the spread of education, the establishment of railways, and the recruitment of Dalits into the army – shook the caste system to some extent. Yet the advantages the exploiting classes derive from the caste system are immense. Assigning "degraded" work to the lower castes seems natural not only to feudal society but also to capitalist society, and this proves highly profitable to both. For these economic benefits, capitalism, though expanding, continues to sustain caste. Caste being an all-pervasive phenomenon in India, it is also intrinsic to Capital. It is not surprising to see that most of the big capitalists belong to the upper castes.

Moreover, caste serves as a crucial tool for politically organizing and dividing people along caste lines in order to exploit labor, and hence it is preserved. To strike at it and uproot it is the greatest challenge before the revolutionary movement.

Declaring their standpoint on caste, the then People's War Party in 1995, and later in 2004, the Maoist Party, formed from the merger of two major parties, published documents in which they stated:

> The caste system has immensely aided feudalism in extracting huge surplus value from the oppressed, especially from those pushed into a state akin to slavery and branded untouchables. For the New Democratic Revolution to succeed, the caste-based feudal system that forms the foundation of caste must be overthrown, along with the comprador bureaucratic capitalism and imperialism that support and sustain it. A genuine democratic socialist culture, free from Brahmanical caste domination, feudal, and imperialist cultures – one that leaves no room for untouchability and caste oppression – must be established.

In 1967, Charu Mazumdar gave a direction to the revolutionary activists to stay in the houses of the 'untouchables', eat with them, learn from them about the landlords' oppression and annihilate the class enemy. While acting in compliance with this directive, the activists also led struggles against caste discrimination. This praxis naturally attracted the 'untouchable' community, and a large number of Dalits joined the movement, fighting for self-respect with its help. Due to the large number of Dalits associated with it, the Party itself was heckled by the landlords as an 'untouchables' party. Many inhuman practices and cruel treatment of Dalits by the upper caste people ceased due to the intervention of the movement.

Adivasi Resistance movements – *jal, jangal* and *jameen*

Adivasi, meaning original inhabitant, refers to the tribes residing in various dense forests of India. Their resistance to colonising powers has deep roots in India's history – from the Ho, Oraon, Santhal, Munda, Kol, and Gond uprisings against British colonialism to the continuing struggles against post-independence State and corporate encroachment. These movements have consistently fought for the defense of *jal* (water), *jangal* (forest), and *jameen* (land). The Adivasis always sought a collective way of life, living simply in harmony with nature. They have been waging an unrelenting struggle for the right to self-rule. They never considered land as private property, but viewed it as a collective asset belonging to the community in which they lived.

The Constitution of India too ratified colonial policy and made the State custodian of Adivasi homelands, thus turning the entire Adivasis into squatters on their own land. They were denied their traditional rights to forest produce, fined for using the forest land or forest produce in their traditional ways and harassed endlessly by forest officials.

Contemporary struggles extend the legacy of Adivasi struggles against the British and the Indian government. At Kalinganagar (Odisha), police firing on protesters against a Tata Steel project in 2006 killed 12 Adivasis. In Niyamgiri, the Dongria Kondh people successfully resisted Vedanta's bauxite mining project, securing a landmark Supreme Court judgment in 2013 that affirmed the village council's rights to approve or reject projects in their area. In Jharkhand state, the Pathalgadi movement reasserted constitutional guarantees of autonomy, only to be met with repression. These struggles exemplify the ongoing fight of Adivasis against destructive development paradigms.

Convergence of Adivasi and Revolutionary movements

Due to India's vast geographical expanse, Maoist revolution-aries, who had to confront the largest standing army of the state, opted for a protracted people's war and employed the strategy of guerrilla warfare. The dense forests in various parts of the country provided the most suitable terrain for this. The Adivasis living in the forests inevitably joined hands with the revolution-aries. The aspirations of the Adivasis bore a remarkable resem-blance to the goals of the Maoists. Therefore, in Dandakaranya, which became one of the Maoists' strategic regions, the local Gonds, Koyas and other Adivasis not only supported them but also participated *en masse* in the movement, rising to leader-ship positions. In Bihar and Jharkhand, the Santhali, Mundari, Oraon and other Adivasis joined the revolutionary movement. The Santhals, being one of the largest Adivasi communities, not only joined in significant numbers but also rose to leader-ship positions at the Central Committee level. Similarly, when the movement was strong in the Nallamala forests of Andhra Pradesh, the local Chenchus joined in. During the Srikakulam struggle, the Savara, Jatapu, and other Adivasis actively partic-ipated in the movement. This is in total contrast to the notions that the media propagates and the intellectuals and literati in mainstream society parrot regarding the Adivasis being misled by the Maoists or being sandwiched between the Maoists and the Indian State. As Arundhati Roy put it in 'Walking with the Comrades':

> ... It's worth keeping in mind that the Adivasi people have a long and courageous history of resistance that predates the birth of Maoism. To look upon them as brainless puppets being manipulated by a few middle-class Maoist ideologues is to do them something of a disservice.

The central achievement of the DK struggle is the emergence of a new society in which previously voiceless people have gained dignity. Unlike famine-stricken regions of India in 1997, DK reportedly saw no deaths from hunger due to collective developmental efforts. Dandakaranya was administered for nearly two decades by an elaborate structure of *Janatana Sarkars* (people's governments) formed by the revolutionary movement. The organizing principles came from the Chinese Revolution and the national liberation struggle in Vietnam. Each *Janatana Sarkar* is elected by a cluster of villages whose combined population can range from 500 to 5000. It has nine departments – covering defence, finance, agriculture, trade, justice, education and culture, health, forests, and public relations – most devoted to welfare rather than war, countering the State's portrayal of Maoists as only violent. A group of *Janatana Sarkars* falls under an Area Committee, and three Area Committees comprise a Division. There were ten such Divisions in Dandakaranya. Built through decades of struggle, these institutions are projected as the foundation of a future People's Democratic Federal Republic of India. These alternative forms of governance had taken up a number of developmental works that had aided the Adivasi community, such as mobilizing community labour for farm ponds, rainwater harvesting, and land conservation works in the Dandakaranya region.

The synergy between the Adivasi and revolutionary movements has created a formidable challenge to both State repression and corporate land grabs. It has enabled villages to defend forests, practice self-rule, and resist displacement on a scale unmatched by any other movement in independent India.

Dandakaranya represents one of the most sustained experiments in Adivasi self-rule and revolutionary partnership. The *Janatana Sarkars* not only reclaimed land and ensured food security but also redefined social relations. They fought patriarchal practices, challenged casteist incursions (such as Hindutva's attempts to impose Brahmanical norms), and fostered collective production and ecological preservation.

Iron Heel of the Indian State

The forests of Central India are rich in mineral resources, with estimated deposits of 70 billion tons, including iron ore, graphite, limestone, bauxite, and uranium. The bauxite reserves of Odisha alone are valued at trillions of dollars, attracting multinational corporations such as Vedanta, Essar, and POSCO.

The Indian government, in order to transfer this rich mineral wealth to the imperialists and their compradors, is trying to displace Adivasis by all means. In the past four years alone, the government has signed 104 agreements with corporate entities for mining these minerals. Behind the State repression of Adivasis lies the logic of global capital. Counter-insurgency serves as the ground-clearing operation for neoliberal "development" that benefits corporations while displacing indigenous communities.

Adivasis are resisting displacement, insisting on their rights over water, forests, and land, as recognized by laws such as the Forest Rights Act. The government believes that if it can eliminate the Maoists, it will be easier to displace the Adivasis and hand over their land and mines to corporations.

Therefore, for the past twenty years, the government has made several attempts to suppress the Maoists and render the Adivasis helpless and displaced. In 1990, Mahendra Karma, one of the region's largest landlords, rallied a group of village chiefs and landlords and initiated a repressive campaign, deceptively called the *Jan Jagran Abhiyan* (Public Awakening Campaign), in two phases. The Maoist movement successfully defeated this campaign.

In June 2005, again under his leadership, they mobilized and rallied young Adivasis, armed them and launched another campaign of repression with the complete aid and abetment of the State in the name of the *Salwa Judum* (Purification Hunt) initiative. It sought to uproot the Adivasis from their homes, villages and forest and encamp them in faraway makeshift camps to cripple the support base of the Maoists. As Arundhati Roy put it in 'Walking with the Comrades':

The *Salwa Judum* was a ground-clearing operation, meant to move people out of their villages into roadside camps, where they could be policed and controlled. In military terms, it's called Strategic Hamleting.

During the *Salwa Judum* campaign, just staying at home and living an ordinary life became a dangerous activity for Adivasis in Bastar. Between June and December 2005, the campaign burned, killed, raped and looted its way through hundreds of villages of south Dantewada. The centres of its operations were the Bijapur and Bhairamgarh blocks near Bailadila, where Essar Steel's new plant was proposed. Not coincidentally, these were also Maoist strongholds, where the *Janatana Sarkars* had done a great deal of work, especially in building water-harvesting structures. The *Janatana Sarkars* became the special target of the *Salwa Judum*'s attacks. Hundreds of people were killed in the most brutal ways. About 60,000 people moved into the camps, some voluntarily, most of them out of terror.

Thousands of Adivasis and Maoist guerrillas resisted *Salwa Judum* heroically and practically defeated it. The Supreme Court also struck down this unconstitutional method of creating an untrained armed force, declaring it led to civil war in 2009. Subsequently, the old *Salwa Judum* SPOs were reappointed as District Reserve Guards (DRG) through a backdoor approach. In 2009, the government initiated "Operation Green Hunt," in three phases of "clear, hold and build", aimed at eliminating the Maoists and terrorizing the Adivasis to force them to flee their lands.

When results fell short, new drives like Operation *Samadhan* and Operation *Prahar* began in 2017, setting up hundreds of camps in the name of carpet security, burning villages, displacing farmers, labeling Adivasis as Maoists, and committing abuses, including against women and children.

In this context, during a meeting held by the current ruling party of India, Bharatiya Janata Party, in Surajkund in 2022, it was decided to make the country free of Maoists, not to spare even pen-wielding Naxals, terming them as *Urban Naxals*.

Gandhians and liberals working among the Adivasis in Chhattisgarh, advocating against the exploitation of national wealth by corporations, were also labelled as Maoists and harassed.

Union Home Minister Amit Shah announced plans for a new strategic attack, Operation *Kagar* (the "final assault"), which was launched on 1 January 2024. The Central Armed Police Forces, consisting of the Border Security Force (BSF), Central Reserve Police Force (CRPF), Indo-Tibetan Border Police (ITBP), and Sasastra Seema Bal (Border Security Force at the Nepal Border) prepared for an attack on Maoist strongholds in Dandakaranya and the attacks are continuing to the present with increasing intensity and tremendous loss of Adivasi lives. They are resorting to aerial bombing, the use of grenades and rockets, drone attacks, etc. Nearly 600 Maoists have been killed since January 2024 during Operation *Kagar*, including the General Secretary of the CPI Maoist Party, Namballa Keshava Rao (aka Basava Raj), and three authors whose stories are part of the Morning Star anthology.

Conclusion

The revolutionary and Adivasi movements in India have reshaped the political, social, and cultural terrain of the country. They defended and continue to defend not only land and livelihood of people but also dignity, equality, and ecological survival of all.

Their resonance extends beyond India. Just as Adivasis in India are resisting corporate mining and displacement in the name of development in various places of India, Native Americans in the US are opposing oil pipelines across their sacred lands, Palestinians are fighting for their survival against the Zionist takeover of their homeland, and Amazonian tribes are resisting the deforestation of Amazon rain forest by multinational corporations.

All these struggles share a common thread: they are struggles against capitalist and colonialist forces seeking to control land, labour, and life itself. They remind us that the future depends on the survival of those who still know the secrets of sustainable living. Victory for imperialism may mean annihilation for Adivasis, but it will also carry within it the seeds of planetary destruction. To quote Arundhati Roy again from 'Walking with the Comrades':

> India has a surviving Adivasi population of almost one hundred million. They are the ones who still know the secrets of sustainable living. If they disappear, they will take those secrets with them. Wars like Operation Green Hunt will make them disappear. So victory for the prosecutors of these wars will contain within itself the seeds of destruction, not just for Adivasis, but eventually, for the human race. That's why the war in Central India is so important.

> Resistance, therefore, is not just political – it is existential, for all humanity.

References:

1. Amit Bhattacharyya. (2016). *Storming the Gates of Heaven.* Setu Prakashani
2. Arundhati Roy. (2011). *Walking with the Comrades.* Penguin Books

Tender Hands

Anala

It was the courtyard of a police station, unlike the current ultra-modern hi-tech police stations with bright colours and high impenetrable walls. We are talking of a time before it was blasted with bombs by somebody with a heartburn. It was an old building with a tiled veranda and mud coloured walls. The courtyard was surrounded by a four-foot-high compound wall.

Chitti, who had been thrown into a face-down position and was in a daze, moved a little and lifted his head up and looked around. For a while, he couldn't even recognize where he was. He regained consciousness as the sand, heated by the afternoon sun, burned his skin. As he heard the moving buses, rickshaws, cycles and people over the compound wall, he figured out he wasn't 'encountered'[1]. As soon as he thought of 'encounter', he shivered in fright. He wanted to get up from there and shout loudly to the people passing outside – 'The police caught me'. Forget about shouting, not even a whimper came out of him. There was no strength in his hands and legs.

'Okay, now tell us what happens if the shops don't respond to your "shut down" call?'

'You became heroes eating the government food?'

'Come on, tell me. Who is training you to be like this?'

'Speak up'

The *lathis* (batons) of the police interrogating Chitti danced on his young five-foot body.

Maybe because Chitti heard so much about 'torture', he didn't find any of this new, and he felt as if he had experienced all these before. The only clear thought in his mind was that he shouldn't reveal anything, regardless of what the police did.

The constable got tired of thrashing Chitti. The SI (Sub Inspector) told the constable, 'Throw him outside and I will take care of him.'

'You take lunch boxes for them; do you feed them rice?'

The brutal dance of booted legs on the tender fingers spread on the sand continued.

'The government is feeding you for free in the hostels. You are being overfed.'

As he heard these words, Chitti thought of the masoor dal sambar[2] and the food cooked with rotten rice that were served in his social welfare hostel. On the rare days that they made Dal with fresh vegetables or curry with fresh leafy vegetables in the hostel, they would put it in a lunch box and go to the bank of the canal.

'I wonder if they brought Ramulu and Sankar also. Sankar will never say anything, even if they beat him to death. *Anna* said he would go only after making sure everyone left after the meeting. Who knows where he is,' thought Chitti.

Nobody bothered to check if the boy who was lying motion-less was dead or alive. Chitti lifted his head and looked at the road. The people were walking hurriedly as if something was pursuing them. In any case, who would like to walk leisurely in front of a police station? Chitti imagined that some of the people going on the road might have stopped and looked over the wall and then, pretending not to have seen anything, hurried away from there.

It had been four hours since they had brought him to the station. They may leave him alone now.

'Why are you still keeping him there?' the SI asked while leaving the station. Chitti's whole body felt like a big wound because of the way the police beat him black and blue all over. The constable who came to lift him up was as old as his father. 'Are you Lakshmaiah's younger son?' he asked. Chitti nodded his head.

'Which class are you in?' asked the constable.

'Seventh class,' replied Chitti.

'If both of you brothers take this path, what will happen to your parents?' thought the constable, though he didn't say it aloud. He gave water to Chitti and said, 'Ask your brother if he will surrender'.

What had they done to Sadanandam, who surrendered to take care of his mother? They had picked him up from the shop right in front of his mother and then declared him 'missing'.

The twelve-year-old Chitti learnt his political lessons from the police *lathis* and boots. The police used to raid their hostels at midnight, break down the doors, drag whoever they could find by their hair and question them – 'Who is there inside your rooms? Who is teaching you these things? Which of you is going to meetings outside?' At that time, Chitti didn't really know anything.

When the children from the hostel came to know that the Radicals[3] had intercepted the ration rice that was being pilfered away and distributed it among the people, they ran to see the spectacle. They saw the happiness of the people who crowded around the cart carrying rice sacks, filling their baskets with rice. 'Hey! Isn't your brother also there among the Radicals?' asked his friends, and he didn't respond. He wasn't even sure if what they were doing was a good or a bad thing.

When he came to know that his brother was caught by the Police in Gollapalli, but was rescued by the women there who also chased away the Police, he started thinking about the situation. When they protested in the hostel against insect-infested food and for an increase in the ration quota, his thoughts took a step forward.

He came out of his hostel and went to all the other hostels. All of them discussed the problems and issues in the social welfare hostels.[4] They started an agitation in the school too about the dilapidated state of the classrooms and school building, lack of benches and chairs, the absentee teachers and the increased syllabus.

They started boycotting classes and holding *dharnas*[5] on the road, demanding the reduction of syllabus, proper supply of notebooks and the construction of class rooms. In the evenings, the students would meet again in their houses and discuss the next steps in their program which moved into a higher gear.

This continued till the high school students were arrested. Then, they started the agitation to get them freed by putting up posters, writing copies of 'Radical Voice' through the night using carbon paper and sticking them on walls early in the morning before anybody got up.

He was once caught by the patrolling police while he was distributing pamphlets. The police thought he was too young to be doing this of his own volition, and somebody must have tempted him with chocolates to do this work. So, they asked him to get into the jeep and show them who gave him the pamphlets. After the jeep went some distance, he asked them to stop it in front of a house and showed them an old woman and said, 'This *amma* gave me the pamphlets'. His friends and he had a good laugh about it for many days after the incident.

They wrote posters demanding that those arrested must be presented in the court within twenty-four hours after arrest and put them up in the bus depot. At 5 in the morning, while it was still dark, the RTC (Road Transport Corporation) drivers somehow figured out that there were people in the depot waiting to stick posters. Every one of the drivers parked their bus in the depot, got down, lit cigarettes and loitered around, giving them time to stick the posters on the buses. Only after they were sure that the posters were stuck on the buses did they move out of the depot.

It had become dark, and mosquitoes started buzzing. Chitti could hear some familiar voices outside. He felt nauseated by the smell of urine in the lockup. He suddenly felt hungry because he hadn't had anything to eat after the sambar rice in the hostel in the morning. They told the hostel warden they were going to school, but they roamed around distributing pamphlets which exhorted the people to boycott elections.

'Boycott the fake elections'

'Beat the leaders coming for your votes with your slippers'

These were the contents of the pamphlets that applied to the entire spectrum of politicians from the red-shirt parliamentary communists to NTR[6], who had started a new party and claimed that Naxalites were the true patriots.

Suddenly, the entire station became alert due to the SP's (Superintendent of Police) visit. The CI (circle inspector) stood in front of the SP and told him, 'They make four folds of the pamphlets like this in order to throw them easily into shops and houses'.

While looking into the case files for the day, the SP told the CI "Let go of the girls and the minors, we are getting a lot of phone calls about them."

'Yes Sir, just now civil liberties activists also came to demand the same,' said the CI.

'In their view, these are the only citizens and they are the only ones who have rights,' said the SP in an annoyed tone.

The CI pointed in Chitti's direction and said, 'He is P.K's brother Sir'. The SP merely said 'Ahh', looked in Chitti's direction and left. Chitti mentally prepared himself for a night of beatings.

'Who are all the people who come to the hostel?'

'I don't know'

'Show us your brother's shelters'

'I don't know'

'If you don't assist us in capturing him, we will 'encounter' you'

So, the interrogation of Chitti in the lockup went on.

The morning dawned and the station was all abuzz with a combing party in which the CI was also a member. They were talking about the areas to be combed in shortened forms – RC, BG, Kottur .....

Chitti was alarmed when he heard Kottur, because the shelter where he met his brother was there. Sweat broke out all over his body and his face became pale. He asked a constable what the time was and the constable told him it was 9.15. He felt very relieved and could breathe easily. He had an appointment with his brother at 9 and it was now past that time which meant his brother would no longer be in that place. Chitti looked proudly at his crushed fingers.

(Chitti is his real name, so is his brother's. I didn't change the names as their family, which had provided four members to the revolutionary movement, has no one else left for the police to 'encounter'.)

Translation of 'Chitti chetulu'. (First published in *Arunatara*, July 2006)
Translated by P. Aravinda

Notes:
1. Encounter: So many fake encounters took place in the revolutionary movement areas that over a period of time the word encounter became synonymous with 'police murder' and is used as a verb.
2. Masoor dal sambar: stew made with red gram and vegetables, to be eaten with rice.
3. Radicals: Radical Student Union and Radical Youth League members popularly known as Radicals.
4. Social welfare hostels: a government run residential facility that provides free or subsidized accommodation, meals, and support services to vulnerable groups, such as students from low-income families or marginalized communities, to ensure they have safe housing and access to educational resources.
5. Dharna: A sit-in protest.
6. NTR: N T Ramarao, a Telugu actor who entered the political scene of the state of Andhra Pradesh in 1982, won a landside victory in 1983 and became the Chief Minister.

Diku

B. Anuradha

As the dawn broke, the fragrance of Mahua flowers wafted intoxicatingly from the forest adjoining the village. Reelamala, Maini, and Budhini, activists of the women's organisation, finished their meeting and had to go to another village for the next task in their planned program. They quickly completed their morning routines, packed their bags, and set off. These were villages mostly inhabited by Adivasi people in Jharkhand, located either within or adjacent to the forest.

They held a meeting to discuss the expansion of the organisation. Activities had been stagnant for some time due to the arrest of women's organisation activists and leaders in charge of various districts. Over the past month, they had been warmly welcomed by people wherever they went. The area in charge, Budhini, and Maini had planned the villages they needed to visit in the meeting. Since they were going out after a long break, the state secretary Reelamala came along to assist Budhini and Maini.

They walked slowly along the forest path after crossing the village. To reach Purnadi, they had to pass through two villages, so they hurried to avoid the sun. Forest paths were familiar to them. From childhood, the locals roamed the forest for various tasks like collecting Mahua flowers, leaves, firewood, and grazing goats and cattle. These women had also roamed the forest as children. The path was strewn with Mahua flowers that looked like jasmines, fallen under the Mahua trees. Children and adults were gathering them into baskets. They would dry them and sell them or ferment them to make Mahua liquor.

The houses were spaced apart rather than clustered together. Here and there, some people were working in the fields. Even before dawn, small children were driving goats and cattle into the forest. Some young women, with babies tied to their backs, were also heading into the forest.

Within an hour, they approached the first village. At the village's edge, a structure with half-built walls and a thatched roof caught their attention. 'What is this? It seems like something new has been built,' Reelamala asked in surprise.

'I had mentioned that they were coming. This is Saraswati Shishu Mandir[1],' Budhini said, barely finishing her sentence before the board and the saffron flag fluttering on it became visible. Reelamala fell silent, seemingly trying to digest the sight. Deep furrows of thought appeared on her forehead. Generally, emotions do not appear quickly on the faces of many Adivasi people. It is only among those who work in organisations and travel to different areas that some emotions are visible. Otherwise, it is hard to understand what they had in their minds.

'After crossing Purnadi, Serang is on the other side near the road. There's also a Vanvasi Kalyan Kendra[2] there,' Budhini continued. 'It seems Purnadi is somewhat influenced, as it is close by. There is some interaction back and forth. But the women there are very supportive of us. I visited recently. Some issues might need our immediate attention. I told them we would come today. Since you were coming, I thought we could handle it together,' Reelamala nodded. They remained lost in their thoughts until they reached Purnadi.

Six-year-old Chutku set out with his grandfather to gather bamboo shoots, which grow abundantly there. The tender inner shoots of the bamboo are harvested, cut into small pieces, and cooked as a curry. Even pickles are made. These shoots are known as "Karil" in Santhali speaking areas and are a favorite among the Adivasis. Mushrooms that grow in the bamboo thickets are also a special treat, prized for their unique taste.

Chutku was eager to go with his grandfather because that day the women from the organisation were expected to visit. He wanted to help prepare a nice meal for them. Chutku's task was to gather the mushrooms. His elder sister Lalmuni had assigned him another job too – after finishing with the bamboo shoots, he was to keep an eye out for the arrival of the organisation women and inform her as soon as they appeared.

After completing his task, Chutku went to his sister. Lalmuni took a potato that was roasted, mashed it and mixed it with onion, chilli, and salt. She added a little bit of raw mustard oil, forming it into a ball for her little brother. She washed a leaf, shaped it into a bowl, and placed the mixture in it before giving it to Chutku. Chutku happily sat on a rock under a tree, eating slowly, while watching the forest path.

In the distance, someone was approaching. At first, Chutku thought it was the women from the organisation, but it turned out to be Manglu, from his village who had been acting strangely lately. Manglu was well built. He had started applying a red powder on his forehead, which no one else in the village did. When Chutku asked his sister about it, she said Manglu was possessed and advised against talking to him. Now, Manglu was coming closer, and Chutku, terrified, couldn't move. Manglu smiled and said something, but Chutku didn't hear it out of fear. Suddenly, Chutku jumped up, shouting 'ghost, ghost' as he ran away. Manglu left with a disappointed look on his face.

Lalmuni's name was given by her father. She was his first child, born while he was working with the Peasants and Agricultural labourers' organisation and he fondly named her that. After Chutku was born, their mother died of illness, and Lalmuni had raised Chutku like a mother. There was a considerable age difference between them. During a protest against displacement, their father was beaten up by the police, leading to his mental instability. The three of them were living under their grandfather's care.

Even though Lalmuni was doing her work mechanically, she was preoccupied with the thought of when the women from the organisation would arrive. Knowing they were coming soon gave her a sense of relief.

When Chutku came running and shouting, Lalmuni dropped her work in alarm. He clung to her legs, and she saw Manglu in the distance. He grinned at her saying 'the days are not long' and left, laughing mockingly.

Soon after, the women of the organisation arrived, much to Lalmuni's relief. They greeted everyone warmly. Budhini, who had worked in the village for a long time, introduced the two other women, and they mingled with the villagers. In the past, when the revolutionary movement had a strong presence, even armed squads used to visit the village. The villagers were familiar with these organisations, although they hadn't been able to come around for a while due to repression. Many members were in jail. So, seeing the women, the villagers came out of their homes to greet them. Children were especially excited, and the village elders also joined in. This went on till afternoon.

Chutku enthusiastically invited the women to have lunch at their home. After the meal, Lalmuni and the women washed the dishes outside. Reelamala noticed that they were still using soil to clean the dishes, so she went to the hearth and got some ash. When they used ash instead of soil to clean, Lalmuni was surprised and said, 'They will shine like new, if you clean them with soil'.

Reelamala responded saying that ash was preferred because it didn't harbor germs and their eggs like soil did, preventing diseases. Lalmuni, impressed, agreed to use ash from then on. Maini went to fetch water. They quickly did the dishes and placed them on a table like structure erected with bamboo.

The village mostly used bamboo for construction. This hamlet was also big. The houses were relatively close to each other. Whenever there was a wedding in a family, a new hut was built for the newly wedded couple.

Lalmuni suggested they talk privately and led them to a tree, spreading a sheet of plastic under it for them to sit.

These sheets, sold at local weekly markets, were often used by villagers. Even T-shirts are sold in these markets. The young men wore T-shirts with English writings they didn't understand and carried axes, which looked amusing. Of late, young men started wearing more of such colorful clothes along with accessories such as chains of beads around their necks and applied face powder in thick layers and tied their curly hair with hair bands or ribbons.

Women traditionally wore saris in the Bengali style, but young girls had started wearing *Salwa*r kameez. They roll up their *Salwa*r legs to their knees for convenience when crossing rivers, washing clothes, or fetching water. These trends were now common in the village.

Lalmuni discussed with Reelamala and others about an incident that happened exactly a week ago. That day, Lalmuni woke up before dawn, while it was still dark, grabbed a basket, and went into the forest to collect mahua flowers. Usually, two or three people would go together, but that day she went alone as her friends were not available. Because it was dark, she couldn't see far. Suddenly, someone grabbed Lalmuni from behind. A strong hand covered her mouth. She was startled and struggled to free herself.

'It's me, it's me. Don't be afraid. I am Manglu,' he said without letting go. Lalmuni, struggling hard to free herself, kicked with her feet. Without removing his hand from her mouth, he forcefully held her and, with his right hand, took some vermilion from his pocket and smeared it on her forehead to the parting of her hair. She didn't understand what was happening. She pushed him hard and freed herself from his grip. As soon as his hold loosened, she screamed loudly. Her face was covered in vermilion, and her eyes were burning.

'Now we are married,' said Manglu. For a moment she was confused and stopped screaming. Manglu had been after her for a long time, but Lalmuni liked Karu. Marriages in the

Adivasi community do not happen in this manner. They don't know about sindoor[3]. Lalmuni didn't know either.

But once, when she went to Mahua Tand, she saw a TV there. It was the first time she watched a movie. From that movie, she learned that applying sindoor in the parting of the hair is part of the Hindu marriage ritual. Later, when she went to Ranchi on March 8 (International Women's Day), she saw many women on the streets with sindoor in their hair. Otherwise, she wouldn't have understood this action. Moreover, she didn't like him. The party had been working in that area for many years, so the younger generation didn't even know about the custom of abduction[4] to get married.

While these thoughts were buzzing in her head, Manglu said that since they were now married, it wasn't wrong for them to be together and he pushed her to the ground, grabbing her saree. Hearing the sound of footsteps and voices a little distance away, he got scared and disappeared into the darkness. After a while, she recovered from the shock, slowly got up and walked towards the stream. Despite the cold, she entered the water and bathed. She washed her head for half an hour. She didn't even have soap. She took mud from the bank of the stream and scrubbed her head repeatedly.

Manglu's family were not originally from this village. They had come here from another place. They had lands in Serang. Manglu's father was a contractor. In Purnadi, no one else has as big a house or as much land as they did. Their family was very different from the rest. They also went to Ranchi often. Manglu had many friends in Serang. Some of them are also in 'Van Kalyan'. Manglu learned many new things from them.

'We are also Hindus. Krishna[5] married Rukmini, who belongs to our lineage. She was an Adivasi, which is why Krishna had to abduct her to marry her. Since she joined a Hindu family and we are her descendants, we are also Hindus,' Masterji (the teacher) said. That's why he started wearing a tilak[6] now. He was also doing *Shakha*[7] in Serang. Manglu wanted to abduct Lalmuni, just like Krishna did.

Manglu also liked Ram[5] a lot, but the teacher said he was an Aryan God whereas Krishna being a non-Aryan God was closer to them. He thought he should somehow bring Lalmuni around and even change her name. 'Lalmuni, what a disgusting name!' thought Manglu. He had many thoughts racing through his mind. That's why he went to Serang and discussed this with his friends. They encouraged him. 'You can bring her to the village council and claim her. Once you put *sindoor* (vermilion) on her, no one can stop you because it will be considered as marriage. It won't be considered abduction since you tried only after putting *sindoor* on her. If needed, we can come with you,' they said. But Manglu didn't have the courage. He thought he shouldn't rush without knowing if his father would agree.

When Manglu was coming back from Serang, he was puzzled to see Lalmuni's younger brother shout at him for no apparent reason. He went home in surprise. When Manglu told his mother the day before that he wanted to marry that girl, she got very angry. Lost in thoughts, as he stepped inside, his mother anxiously pulled him into a room. 'Today there is a people's court being held by the organisation here. They are talking about something with Lalmuni's family. If you...' she paused, looking at him suspiciously. Manglu didn't understand. 'Which organisation?' he asked. He didn't know much about these matters since there hadn't been any activities of the mass organisation for a while.

Manglu's mother didn't know the details either, but since her son mentioned marrying Lalmuni, she had been a bit anxious. She knew her husband wouldn't like a girl from such a poor family. It could also be because of Lalmuni's family background. Added to that fear, these people from the organisation came again! She knew about "them," which made her very nervous. She tried to reassure herself that it might not be about them. She had various doubts and fears.

Meanwhile, Manglu went outside to see the organisation people and then came back inside, laughing. When his mother got annoyed, he teased her a lot. 'What's this? They! Holding a people's court? Are they even twenty-five years old? Are these women going to hold a people's court? Are you afraid of them?'

Reelamala called Budhini, and asked, 'Did you inform Karu?'

'He has come,' she replied.

As Maini took a drum from her bag and began to beat it rhythmically, Budhini sang, 'Nari Mukti Jhanda Hum Lehray-enge... Soshon Mukti Jhanda Hum Pehrayenge' (We will raise the flag of women's liberation! We will raise the flag of liberation from oppression!) While she sang 'come all friends, mothers, and sisters... join', some young men and Adivasis joined in with 'Mandar' (large drums) around their necks, stepping gracefully and rhythmically as they accompanied the chorus. Suddenly, the entire atmosphere became electrified. The whole village moved to gather under a tree. This tree was like a public square for the village. All the village meetings happened there. The elders fondly remembered the old days. Manglu felt an unknown discomfort looking at the scene.

The meeting began. Reelamala first spoke about the current situation. She briefly explained the organisation's relationship with the village and its activities, then said, 'Let's solve our problems ourselves. Let's rebuild our mass organisations. Some of us are facing certain issues. Today, let's discuss an important matter. Let's list the names of those who must be present in this people's court. It would be good if they could come forward.' She looked at Budhini, signaling her to begin. Budhini called out Lalmuni and Manglu's family members. Manglu wasn't present, nor were his family members visible. The young men who had sung earlier quickly went and fetched those who were sitting inside their houses. Only Manglu and his mother came, grumbling, and stood nearby.

'Go ahead, Lalmuni,' Budhini said. Lalmuni courageously stepped forward and narrated everything that had happened. 'What is your response?' Budhini asked, looking at Manglu. Manglu didn't understand anything. Lacking courage, he remembered his friends' words and said, 'I married her.'

'Whom did you ask before marrying her?' Budhini asked calmly.

'I was doubtful if my parents would agree.'

'So, it's okay if they agreed?'

'.....................................'

'Speak up.' He remained silent. An elder from behind asked, 'Don't you have parents or grandparents? Are we not here?'

Budhini felt a surge of frustration for a moment. 'That's not what I'm asking. Did you think you alone could decide on the marriage?' Budhini raised her voice.

Lalmuni, who had been silent and composed until then, became extremely angry. 'Aren't you ashamed to touch a woman without her consent? Shame on you!' she exclaimed.

Budhini continued, 'Wanting to marry her without her consent is the first mistake. Forcing her secretly and applying *sindoor* to marry her is even worse. The practice of abducting and marrying has long been abolished here. A marriage only happens if both the boy and girl agree. If you continue such actions, no one will accept it. And where did these *sindoor* traditions come from? Don't try to deceive us like the *dikus*,' she said in a stern tone. Adivasis use the term *'Diku'* to indicate hostility towards outsiders who historically exploited Adivasis in various ways. Calling an Adivasi a *'Diku'* is akin to treating him as an enemy.

Manglu's mother intervened, saying, 'He likes Lalmuni. We were planning to ask. Please don't separate them. It is a sin.'

'There's nothing like sin or virtue. There's only good and bad. Do Adivasi marriages happen like this? If someone did this to your child, would you tolerate it?' Budhini was furious. There were arguments for a long time.

Then, Budhini warned everyone again and asked Lalmuni, 'You tell us who you wanted to marry. Do you accept what Manglu did as a marriage?' Although she knew the answer, she asked in front of everyone.

'I wanted to marry Karu. This Manglu followed and harassed me,' Lalmuni couldn't speak as she was extremely angry. Manglu looked around, but the village youth were standing around him like a circle. They appeared to be standing nonchalantly, but Manglu understood their intention.

'Karu, will you marry Lalmuni?'

Karu stepped forward and said looking at Lalmuni, 'I will. I like her.'

'Manglu, do you admit what you did was wrong?' she asked. He remained silent again. 'It would be better for you if you admit your mistake,' said Budhini. Manglu looked up and saw some women standing behind Budhini holding women's organisation flags. He was not looking at the flags but at the sticks they were tied to. They were looking at him without any expression. He had never seen village elders not intervening in a panchayat like this before. For the first time, he realized this matter was not as small as he thought, and he felt a chill down his spine.

'It's wrong,' he said abruptly.

'Tell Lalmuni, not me.'

Manglu's mother said, 'He didn't do anything wrong. Why should he say so? He got married, didn't he? Is that wrong too?'

Lalmuni felt like hitting her, but Maini was standing next to her, holding her hand tightly. 'Ok. Let us decide what is right and wrong now,' said Budhini.

'Now tell me, was what Manglu did wrong or not?' Many voices shouted that it was wrong, mostly women's voices. The elders remained silent.

'So, what punishment should we give him?'

Various proposals came up: to tie him up and beat him, to fine him, and to banish his family from the village. There was a discussion on these matters for a while.

Reelamala and Budhini consulted each other quietly. Then Budhini said, 'On behalf of the organisation, we are putting forward some decisions taken by this people's court. It considers what Manglu did as not a marriage but a rape. As punishment for his actions, Manglu must bear the expenses of the celebrations and feasts during Karu and Lalmuni wedding in the village. He must also buy the materials and personally build a hut for them to live in at his own expense. Since his family supported his wrongdoing, no one should work in his family's fields or house for a year. Manglu's punishment must be implemented within a month, and the village committee members must ensure they do not leave the village during this period. After this panchayat, let's revive the village committee with an equal number of women and men in it.' Reelamala quickly wrote these decisions on a paper. 'Now, if you approve these decisions, clap your hands. If you have objections, speak up.' There was loud applause. Drums also sounded. The youth stood up slowly. Budhini announced, 'This people's court is now concluded.'

Chutku ran and hugged his sister. He was very happy even though he didn't fully understand. Lalmuni's grandfather came and shook hands with Reelamala and Budhini, raising his fist in salute. 'Long live the Women's Organisation' shouted the youth. As the drums beat rhythmically, everyone started stepping in a circle, congratulating Lalmuni and Karu. That dance would continue through the night.

Translation of 'Diku'. (First published in Arunatara, March 2021) Translated by the author

Notes:

1. Saraswati Shishu Mandir: These are schools established by the Rashtriya Swayam Sevak Sangh (RSS) to indoctrinate young children with the Hindu religious perspective. Rashtriya Swayam Sevak Sangh is an extremely conservative and nationalist paramilitary Hindu ideological organisation. One of the main objectives of the RSS is to indoctrinate young children with its supremacist Hindu ideological perspectives and learn to reject their own Adivasi culture and traditions as 'primitive' and 'backward'.

2. Vanvasi Kalyan Kendra: A voluntary organisation established in Adivasi societies by the Akhil Bharatiya Vanakalyan Ashram affiliated to RSS in order to co-opt Adivasis into the Hindu religion. The RSS deliberately uses the word 'Vanvasi' as a way to denigrate Adivasis as simply 'backward forest dwellers'.

3. Sindoor: vermillion or kumkum, a traditional cosmetic red powder that is worn by married Hindu women in the parting of their hair.

4. Custom of Abduction: In many Adivasi communities every young man has the customary right to abduct a young woman of his choice in order to get married. The only condition is that he should pay the bride price demanded by the bride's parents. Consent of the young woman is not taken for marriage. If the parents of the bride and groom come to an understanding and drink traditional liquor together that itself is an agreement. If the woman refuses to marry him, the groom can abduct her and marry her forcefully. In some places even if the bride and groom marry with mutual consent they enact a scene of abduction just as a ritual.

5. Krishna and Rama: Hindu Gods, considered avatars of Vishnu. Rama is considered an Aryan God and the Aryans are considered supreme. The caste system in India has a hierarchical structure and divides the people into castes according to the hierarchy. So to keep that hierarchy intact even the Gods are assigned caste in their avatars. Krishna is considered a Yadav by caste and Yadavs are inferior to Brahmins, Kshatriyas and Vysyas. So by suggesting that Krishna is closer to the Adivasis they are trying to absorb them but at the same time keeping them in the lower rungs.

6. Tilak: vermillion mark applied by Hindu men on their forehead

7. Shakha: A branch of the Rashtriya Swayam Sevak Sangh, whose organisational work is done through the coordination of the various shakhas, or branches which involve the gathering of male RSS members to train in martial arts, physical fitness through yoga, exercises, and games.

Bali

Nitya

In the winter when nature's beauty bursts forth, the cold can freeze your bones. A camp fire was lit in the front yard of the house. In the backyard of the house, there was a girl tied to a mango tree. That girl was Bali.

Her body was cold as ice... She was wearing a *salwar kameez* made of synthetic cloth, which made the cold even worse. Both her hands were tied behind her back and the rope was twisted tightly around her wrists and then tied to the tree.

Her father was repeatedly bringing water to wet the rope. His body was seething with anger.

'I raised her, taught her how to understand things. I sent her to school to study, and she dares to defy me. The arrogance from her education must be beaten out of her. Let's see who stands up for her. Let's see who dares to oppose me,' Ramji ground his teeth.

Both of Bali's hands had gone numb. Her whole body was like an open wound. The injuries to her mind hurt Bali more than the ones on her body. Her eyes have dried up. Is he really her father, who gave birth to her? This was the question that was tormenting Bali.

He beat her as if she were a beast. He beat her till the staff broke. Why such rage? she was not a stranger... She was his own child. Her father's hisses rang in her ears.

The blood was clotted, and her pale body had turned black and blue.

Why did he even send her to school?

She was not a lump of flesh, but a human with a brain.

An animal that doesn't want to go to an unwanted place runs back to the home where it was born and raised. Was her life worse than that of an animal? Was her crime that of being born a girl? Why this punishment? Why must she endure it?

Her mind rebelled.

Even if she were to die, she would not submit. What more could they do? The humiliation she had endured was enough.

Her friends always admired her hair. She loved her silky, flowing hair so much. How could her father think of treating such beautiful hair so mercilessly... Her friends would laugh if they saw her with a shaved head... How could he have done this!

She hadn't eaten for two days. Early in the morning, her grandmother had given her hot tea without anyone noticing her. Her grandmother was terrified that her son would cause a ruckus if he found out. It was with fear that she had come. The son she had given birth to... the son she had helped take his first steps holding his finger... yet he was her son. She had to live her life in his shadow. That was why even she was afraid of him.

Finally, she couldn't bear it anymore. She made up her mind for the sake of her granddaughter. It was night. Everyone had fallen asleep. She got up quietly and untied Bali. Holding her by the wrist, she led her into the room, put her to bed, and covered her with a blanket.

Bali slept fitfully.

The village of Tekala was deeply traditional. The *Panchayat raj* power in the village lay in the hands of those with white caps, while the Adivasi power rested with those in black caps. The Ahiri royal family split into two factions: one merged with the Congress party, and the other merged with the Naga Vidarbha Samiti in the parliamentary system. Congress supporters wore white caps, and Naga Vidarbha Samiti supporters wore black caps in the villages. The revolutionary mass organisations had always been weak in this village. The formation of revolutionary people's governments was still in the prospective stage.

Bali was the beautiful flower that bloomed in that village. She represents a generation free from old customs. In the Adivasi society, girls grow up freely until they reach marriageable age. Unlike in feudal societies, there are no restrictions on attire, speech, behavior, or manners. They have friendly relations with their parents. Boys and girls mingle freely, participating in games and songs with their arms over each other's shoulders without any hesitation. Bali grew up in such a free environment.

When she was young, her father enrolled her in the Lok Biradari School established by Baba Amte, three kilometers away from their village. Bali was an active student, intelligent and disciplined. She was well-liked by her teachers and always completed her homework on time. She never gave her teachers a chance to scold or punish her.

Baba Amte started the Lok Biradari Institute near Hemalkasa in 1975. The primary aim of this organisation was to provide medical services to the Adivasi people. They also ran a school. His son, Prakash Amte, is revered by the people of Bhamragad *taluka*[1] as a god. Despite having plenty, the Amtes led a life of simplicity which greatly influenced Bali. Growing up in such a school environment shaped Bali's character.

Unlike other girls, Bali had no interest in lipstick, face powders, colorful bangles, or other ornamental items. She would comb her hair and braid it once and wouldn't bother with it again until the next day. She didn't enjoy looking at herself in the mirror and grooming herself multiple times a day like other girls.

In her free time, Bali read books. She read about Savitribai Phule and Jyotiba Phule[2], who fought against traditional customs and paved the way for girls like her to get an education. She admired them greatly. She also read about other social reformers. Having seen Prakash Amte and Baba Amte immersed in social service every day, Bali matured into a young woman with a strong character.

※

The school was closed for the summer holidays. Suman, her cousin studying in Etapalli, also came home for the holidays. Since they were of the same age, they were very close friends. That Sunday, Bali went to her uncle's house to watch TV. Bali was not too keen about movies. She usually didn't watch other movies. But that day, "Chak De India" was on, which is an interesting story of a women's hockey team that emerged as champions. Almost everyone was engrossed in the movie.

Suddenly, from the backyard of the neighboring house, there was a sound of something being hit with a stick. They thought it might be some venomous creature.

'Don't stay in my house... Go away... this is my house... my wish...'

It was a man's voice, shouting.

'This is my house. I carried mud and bricks for it, I helped build it... I carried the plough and tilled the land, harvested the crops... I have worked just as hard as you did to build this house,' a woman's voice responded, equally strong.

The old man hadn't sobered up from his toddy. He stood there swaying, clutching his stick.

'Hey, old man! Why are you hitting that woman?'

Someone asked softly from the darkness...

'She's my wife... It's my wish...' he replied firmly. The entire scene disturbed Bali. She turned off the TV and prepared to sleep. She lay down on the bed but couldn't sleep. Thoughts clouded her mind.

Is this the situation for all grandmothers and mothers? A woman has no value. No matter how much she toils, she is considered insignificant. If she was driven out of the house, where would she go and live? She poured all her blood and sweat into keeping that house running. In the end, what does she get? Whether it was her husband who was angry or she was angry, it was the woman who had to leave the house!

'My wife, my wish...' Where did he get such authority from? Who gave him that power!

He is the one who drank the toddy... and swayed in drunken

stupor... He is the one that hit her with the stick as if she is a beast... And then he is telling her to get out of the house.

Even those who gathered there were just watching. Why isn't anyone saying that it was wrong? Why aren't they speaking up!

While a thousand questions troubled her mind, Bali shut her eyes tightly and tried to sleep.

Her younger sister told her that the squad had asked her to come and meet them. A shiver ran down her spine and spread throughout her body. Why would they call her? Even before she was born, the squad had been coming and going in their village. Since she had been going to school from a young age, it always happened that the squad never came when she came home during holidays or they came when she was out of the village on some work. She had mostly heard about the squad indirectly, so she had many questions.

She saw the squad once when she was young. Their close relative, Joga Gavade, who was called Lalsu in the squad, gathered her close. Their squad sang songs. The women in the squad wore frilly skirts like frocks and draped sarees over them. They tied red bands around their heads and waists and held red scarves in their hands. There was a symbol on the flag that looked white, but Bali couldn't understand it in the dark. The combination of green and red colours was beautiful.

Rhythmic dances, songs inviting people to join, beats of the drums and tunes that stirred the soul made even those who were asleep to wake up and come for the meeting. The place was in an uproar with children, elders, young men, and women all milling around. The programs continued until midnight at which point the commander announced, 'Let's wrap it up.' From the crowd, there were shouts of, 'One more song, Shankaranna!' It was past midnight by the time everything ended.

The meeting ended. The young men and women hummed their favourite tunes as they headed home. Little Bali was particularly moved by the song:

"Youth in the prime of their lives, let's sing a battle song and dance to the drums. The red sun is rising, the whole forest is red. In that forest, the red flag is flying high. Let's go into battle."

Since the start of Operation Green Hunt, the frequency of the squad's visits to the village and the meetings had decreased. The squad wouldn't let the entire village know about their visits. Bali read in the papers that development work was not happening in the Gadchiroli district because of the Naxalites, and as a result, the Adivasis were being left behind. She also read that if people disobeyed the Naxalites and voted to elect public governments, the Naxalites would cut off the fingers that bore the ink mark indicating they had voted. She heard the elders in the village discussing that the Naxalites wouldn't let people accept the schemes offered by the government. She heard that the Naxalites destroyed schools. When she was in the school's administrative office, she heard that the Naxalites burned the computers sent to their school that year. Do Naxalites consider computers as enemies? Are they really against education? If they are working for the people, why are they obstructing things that benefit the people? If she asked them these questions, would they get angry? Should she go or not, considering that they had called for her? She debated within herself and finally decided to go and see what they had to say.

Someone came to their school and distributed a Marathi book with the title 'Mala surrender vyaycha. (I will surrender).' The book had the following story: "There was a squad commanded by a man. He held a meeting in the village and ordered the young men and women to join the squad. Some young men and women joined the squad. After a few days, the squad faced gunfire and a woman got injured. Somehow, they managed to carry her with them. She cried out, unable to bear the pain. The commander got angry about her cries, thinking that the police would come if they heard her cries. Yet, she moaned in pain. Losing his patience, the commander ordered a member to shoot her. When the member hesitated, he shot her himself. They dug a hole to bury the body. But the hole was not big enough. So, they cut the body into four pieces, buried it, and left. Shocked by this incident, a member decides to go home and surrender to the police."

There were heated discussions about this story in their school and hostel. At the same time, their classmate Priyanka suddenly went missing. The news spread like wildfire that she joined the squad, got injured in the firing, and was killed and buried by her companions.

What happened after that, Bali did not know. This was one of the doubts that plagued Bali's mind. Do they really shoot and kill their fellow comrades in the squad like that? Are the people who do such things really human? How can such heart-less, callous people serve society?

Bali couldn't sleep for most of the night thinking about all these things.

By the time she woke up, it was already six o'clock. They had asked her to come by seven o'clock. She was worried they might get angry if she was late. She hurriedly got up, finished her morning chores, took a bath, and got ready.

Her sister, who was all ready to go, made some hot tea and gave it to her. When she reached the squad, they welcomed her with smiles. Everyone stood in a row and shook hands.

Bali couldn't immediately tell the difference between the women and the men. 'Come, sit here...' said a person pointing to a *jhilli*. The person had short hair and was wearing a cap. Bali wondered if the person was a woman or a man. The person was fair, chubby, and delicate with a voice that sounded like a woman's. Is this the terrorist that the government had been publicising? She hadn't seen such a person before. A small fear kept haunting her.

Still uncertain, she went and sat quietly in a corner, shrinking into herself. It seemed as if some of the students from nearby villages were already familiar with her. They gathered around her, asking her affectionately, 'How are you, *akka*?'

All the students were girls. After chatting casually for a while, the commander began to speak slowly and thoughtfully.

She spoke about the education system and explained how the Adivasis have been discriminated against since the times of kings. After listening to the story of *Ekalavya*[3], Bali was astonished to realize there was such a conspiracy in the name of reverence to a teacher. Teachers shower so much love on us... they show *Ekalavya* as an ideal for us, don't they? But is there such a malicious conspiracy hidden behind that ideal? It felt as if the layers of clouds that blocked her vision were dissipating and she could finally see clearly.

'Today, we are fighting for equal access to food, shelter, and clothing for everyone. We are fighting for the gap between the rich and the poor to disappear. We are fighting for equality among men and women. Our adivasi men and women are being discriminated against. They enacted many laws to turn the people born and raised in this forest into strangers in their own land. Their goal is to use these laws to turn us into outsiders and loot the wealth of the forest. They are using the guise of Adivasi development to prevent us from understanding this grand loot.

They need roads, trains and electricity to transport the mineral wealth hidden in our land. They need dams to provide water for their facilities. We will lose our lands, homes, and forests and become beggars when the mining starts. This is what our party is opposing. That's why they see our party as a thorn in their side. That's why they bear a grudge against our party and are spreading false propaganda about us...'

Bali listened intently. It seemed like there was some truth in what they were saying. She was deep in thought.

Diwali[4] tournaments were taking place at the school. Bali was actively involved not only in studies but also in sports. Excelling in volleyball, she was selected for the district team. Her team was even selected for the state-level sports competitions.

They travelled to Nagpur for the tournaments by bus. The bus from Bhamragad to Nagpur departs at seven in the morning. Bali, not used to bus journeys, fell asleep due to the rocking motion of the bus. While she was asleep, the bus crossed the borders of Gadchiroli. Due to a sudden jolt of the bus, she hit her forehead on the seat in front of her, causing her head to spin. Bali was annoyed with the Naxalites. She had heard that Naxalites don't allow roads to be laid and they dig holes in the tar roads. What business do they have with roads? How do they benefit from troubling the people? She thought that she should talk to them the next time she met them. She observed the surroundings outside the window and realized that they had crossed Gadchiroli and they were no longer in a Naxalite area. Bali laughed to herself for getting annoyed with the Naxalites for no reason.

Arrangements were made for them to stay at a school. Behind the hostel, there was a slum area... on one side there were high-rise buildings reaching the sky... on the other side, dirty slums. On one side was affluence, and on the other side, extreme poverty and starvation. There were roads, bridges, electricity, and all facilities... Yet, why were the people here so miserable? She had heard propaganda that in their area, the benefits provided by the government to the poor were not reaching them due to the Naxalites.

With many unresolved questions troubling her mind, she had dinner and went to bed. Perhaps due to the fatigue of the journey, she fell into a deep sleep.

In the middle of the night, loud cries were heard from the slum houses across the wall. In the illumination of the street lights, men in khaki uniforms were seen beating someone with sticks.

'Bitch... I will pour petrol on you and set you on fire.' She came to know later that it was a brothel, and the women there had to regularly pay bribes to the police. The day they didn't pay up, they had to face beatings by the police.

Oh... women can't escape troubles wherever they go... Bali thought that violence against women existed only in her society.

But here, it was even worse!

Is being born a woman a curse... do they have to endure all this? Bali was pained by what she saw and couldn't sleep a wink. She spent the rest of the night in fear.

The Gadchiroli team won the tournament. Bali received a medal as a state player and returned. The exams were over. Being in 9th grade, it wasn't very significant, but Bali worked hard and studied diligently for the first rank.

The Holidays were over. That year, Bali had worked day and night to prepare for the tenth grade public exams. She would be able to secure a seat in the science stream only if she scored well. Aiming for a high rank, she had immersed herself in her books.

Bali's father came to take her home after getting permission from the teachers. He said her mother was not feeling well and was serious, so he got permission. Bali took a day off from school and set off with her father.

When they reached home, some distant relatives from Chhattisgarh were sitting on the cots in front of the house, drinking tea. She went inside, washed her hands and feet, and then sat down near her father.

Her father explained the reason for their visit.

'Look, Bali, I don't have any sons. Daughter or son, it's only you for me. You are the eldest child in the family. You understand the responsibilities. We don't have anyone else to support us. Your sisters are still young. While searching for a *lamde*[5] for you, we found this boy. He is intelligent. Your mother and I have given our word to them. Today, they brought the engagement gifts. If you serve them the engagement drinks with your own hands, according to our tradition, the agreement will be finalized.'

'They are saying there is no rush for the wedding. They want you to continue your studies,' he added.

Bali's right eye twitched, a sign she felt something was wrong. She sensed a trap closing in around her. 'You are okay with this, right? No matter how much you study, you have to get married someday. It's not like we depend on your job to make ends meet.'

'I don't want to get married now. I want to study. Even if I do get married, I won't marry him. I don't like him,' Bali said firmly.

'Who said we are getting you married off today? It's our tradition to serve drinks to the visiting relatives. Serve the drinks in the cup.'

Bali refused outright, and her father didn't force her.

The next day, he dropped her off at school. Her father was still serious. Bali was happy thinking she had won.

She wrote her tenth grade exams.

The school declared holidays, and Bali returned home. As soon as she arrived, her parents started pressuring her to get married. They wanted her to accept the boy they had chosen for her.

'I don't want to get married now,' she said clearly.

But society doesn't respect the opinion of a girl... a girl has to agree to everything that her parents propose.

She didn't want to give in but she couldn't see any support coming from anywhere. She wondered if there was anyone who would stand by her.

She remembered her close friend Minko. She needed her advice and help.

She told her family she was going to visit a friend and left.

Minko advised her that meeting the squad might provide a solution to her problem. It had been a long time since the squad had come to their village. Sarita was the only one who had come to their village, spoken with the women of the village, and then left. After that, no one came.

Upon inquiry, they learned that the squad had come to the neighboring village. She went there with her friend and came to know that the squad held a meeting and then left the place.

※

The revolutionary movement in Gadchiroli district has endured ups and downs and spread. Many people and revolutionaries shed their precious blood and planted the seeds of struggle.

Organised in struggle committees fighting for increased wage rates, the people declared, "All powers to the committees," and "Only the Adivasis have rights over the forest." The women and men who shouted these slogans organised themselves into the Dandakaranya Adivasi Kisan Mazdoor Sangathan and the Krantikari Adivasi Mahila Sangh.

Overcoming various stages of repression, the movement continued to progress. The UPA-2 (United Progressive Alliance) government, led by Manmohan Singh, declared Operation Green Hunt[6], labelling the Naxalites the biggest threat to the nation's internal security. To escape the economic crisis plaguing the world, America set its sights on the raw materials of third-world countries. The Adivasi areas, rich in these raw materials, were protected by the Maoist party, which the exploitative ruling classes could not tolerate. They declared war on the Adivasi people under the guise of Operation Green Hunt.

With the aim of hunting down the Adivasis and wiping them out, the ultimate goal of Green Hunt was to hand over their lands and minerals under the lands to companies like Mittal, Jindal, Essar, Niko, Lloyds, and Vedanta.

Special commando forces, known as C-60[7], were unleashed on the people. CRPF (Central Reserve Police Force) battalions were deployed to augment them. This was a multifaceted attack on the people. One aspect of this multifaceted attack was psychological warfare. This created fear and panic among the people.

The squad was coming and going in secret which is why Bali did not know about their arrival. When she saw food being gathered that day, she understood the squad had come. So, along with her friend Pungati Baby she followed those carrying food and water in the darkness.

Voices could be heard faintly from the edge of the field. It was raining lightly. Both of them were getting drenched. Yet, they sat still, waiting for the villagers to leave. Bali hoped that explaining her plight to the squad might yield a solution.

Carrying empty water pots and bowls of food, the villagers left. It was pitch dark. Bali and Pungati Baby could hear people moving. When they went closer, no one was there. They searched for footprints to find out where the squad might have gone. Following the direction where the grass was trampled, they could go a little distance and then, they lost their way.

Still, they did not lose hope. They searched until two in the night but to no avail. It was pitch dark, and nothing was visible. They were exhausted from the search. They were hungry and cold due to the damp clothes. Just then, there was lightning that lit up the surrounding areas. In that light, they saw a hut some distance away. The two friends went to the hut. The fire, lit during the day, had not yet cooled in the hut. They rekindled the fire. Searching for something to eat, they found wild beans hanging from the vines around the hut. They plucked them, roasted them over the fire, and ate. They spread out a torn gunny sack next to the fire and went to sleep. Before dawn, they got up and headed back to their village. Bali was very despondent.

Without going home, Bali went to her grandmother's house. She spent the whole day there. She had dinner and slept beside her grandmother near the fire. Her family came to know this.

Her father got furious. He drank alcohol and with the help of a torch light, he came to where Bali was sleeping. He beat her repeatedly with the torch light.

'Where did you go? Who is there to stop me? If you go again like that, I will break your bones... What do you think?' he shouted, shaking with anger. In his drunk condition, the torch slipped from his hand and fell far away. He picked up a firewood stick and came to beat her.

'Are you going to kill this innocent child? If she doesn't want to get married, why do you torture her!' shouted her grandmother.

Her father backed off. Her aunt came, helped Bali up, took her to their room, and put her to sleep there. Morning came, but Bali had no appetite for food. She felt disgusted with life and stayed in bed all day. Despite her aunt's many pleas, she did not touch even a morsel of food. At dusk, she climbed the hill at the village boundary. She sat there under a mahua tree. She considered her options and felt that all the possible paths before her were closed. She decided that there was no point in living, and it is better to die.

She threw her saree over a branch of the mahua tree to make a noose. As she was about to put the noose around her neck, she remembered the party. 'No! I shouldn't die like a coward. If I meet the comrades, I will go and work with them. Dying for the people is so noble. Death is inevitable anyway. If I give my life for a good cause, I will be remembered forever.'

This thought revived her dying hope. She decided she must meet the party somehow. That's where she would find her path. That's where she would find her liberation.

During her classes, Jainakka spoke about the hardships she had endured. She also spoke about how much freedom she now had since joining the party. In the party, no one forces or coerces anyone about marriage. Whether to marry or not is purely a personal choice.

'No, she should not die. Even if she dies, it won't change the evil customs oppressing our society! Somehow, she must meet the comrades', Bali thought to herself.

'Even if she can't meet them, she could write a letter...', she debated with herself. But what if the letter falls into her father's hands? That would be hell.

She decided not to write a letter.

As dusk fell, she came home. Everyone had eaten and gone to sleep. She lay down in a corner in the dark room, thinking about the unknown paths ahead, and drifted into sleep.

Someone was dragging Bali forcefully by the hair. As she woke up, Bali realized it was none other than her father. He dragged her and threw her into a room, locking the door from the outside.

They got their son-in-law drunk on palm wine until he was completely intoxicated. 'Here is your property... yours to do as you please,' they said, handing over full control over her to the son-in-law.

In the Adivasi society, men were given the authority to forcibly take ownership of women who opposed a marriage arranged by the elders, even before the wedding. Men were allowed access to the rooms where the woman was locked up. If the woman still resisted, even the man's brothers and male relatives were given the right to force themselves on her. This kind of violence was officially implemented as a right to coerce the woman into marriage. These rights were abolished as the mass organisations under the leadership of the revolutionary party gained strength in Gadchiroli. However, the roots of this system still lingered. Operation Green Hunt provided the needed ingredients for these roots to flourish again.

Bali found herself in the room with someone she didn't like, with people guarding the room all around. When the prospective groom put his hand on Bali's shoulder, she gathered all her strength and pushed him away. Stunned by the unexpected resistance, he staggered.

In the darkness, she groped around and found a sickle near the wall. 'See what happens if you touch me,' she threatened. Shocked by her unexpected defiance, the groom didn't dare to step forward. Seizing the opportunity, Bali slipped out through the back door, but her uncles guarding around the house quickly surrounded her. Her father bent her down and started punching her.

Using the cover of darkness, she jumped over the backyard fence and hid in the cornfield. At dawn, in the dim light, she went to her grandmother.

With a hand on Bali's head, her grandmother advised, 'Listen to what your father says, child! You can live peacefully. You're bringing unnecessary troubles upon yourself. As a daughter, you grew up under your father's care; now, as a grown woman, you need the shadow of a husband. Even if you refuse marriage, they won't leave you alone... they won't spare you...' and then fell silent.

Her grandmother remembered her own turmoil for not being able to marry the man she loved in her youth.

Can't a woman live without a man's support? She also has hands and feet. She works alongside men, doesn't she? Doesn't she have strength? Isn't she the primordial mother, the embodiment of power, as the schoolbooks say? No, she doesn't need a man's support. She must stand on her own feet. Bali thought for a long time, sitting there in silence.

Following her grandmother's advice, Bali went to her uncle in Etapalli. She poured out all her grievances to him.

'Your father is a fool, Bali! Does one beat one's child as if she is a beast?' her uncle said soothingly.

Bali heaved a sigh of relief that her uncle understood her pain. A week passed. She assisted her aunt with all the household chores. Seeing Bali's diligence, her aunt praised her, calling her a 'capable girl'.

Bali lacked the life experience to understand the secret meanings in her uncle's words and his behind-the-scenes consultations.

There are women who 'hypnotize' young women who resist such forced marriages. They are called *moose asu*. Bali was taken to one such woman. It is believed that she would put girls in a trance with her words and convince them to agree to marriage. The neighboring women who listened to Bali's woes, warned her sympathetically, 'Look, Bali! Be careful when you eat. She might even drug the tea.'

Even the *moose*'s attempt on Bali failed.

One morning, the *Kotwal* (village officer) announced that everyone should gather near the *gotul*. Drums were also beaten to summon everyone.

The *gotul* was in front of Bali's uncle's house. The whole village gathered.

Women do not usually attend *gotul* meetings.

A woman was sitting in the *gotul* with her head bowed. There was nobody near her. She was accused of being *Vode* (a witch). There lived a family called Naitam in her neighboring house. Recently, two children in their house died of illnesses and a cow died due to snake bite. A child was scalded by hot water. All these were considered bad omens.

Naitam Amulu said, 'This is definitely witchcraft. It is none other than her... She has devoured my children. If not for witchcraft, why would we face so many troubles? The neighboring priest pointed to her. She has ruined my family. I will not let her go, I will kill her.'

He was seething with anger.

A silence fell around. *Vode* is a terror in the Adivasi society. No one has the courage to deny and refute it. Nagging doubts linger in everyone's minds that there might be some truth to it. Such meetings of villagers have overwhelming public support.

Amulu gained courage from that silence.

He stood up, took off his sandal, and began to beat the woman mercilessly. He dragged her by her hair and kicked her with his feet.

'Tell me, confess... If you don't, I will kill you right here and bury you,' he shouted.

The woman's husband and sons sat helplessly in a corner with their heads bowed. A family accused of witchcraft is treated as outcasts in the village.

When it happens to others, the depth of this pain is not understood. Only when it happens to us, do we understand the severity of the wound. There have been instances where husbands, unable to abandon their wives accused of witchcraft, left their villages. There are families who lived in isolation in the fields, far from the village. This is only possible with the support of the husbands.

There were no other women at the *gotul*. Generally, women are called to the *gotul* only when a woman is accused of being *Vode*. In Adivasi society, being beaten with a slipper is considered very shameful. There have been many instances where women beaten with slippers at the *gotul* have taken refuge in poison.

'You have to prove it somehow, or else the consequences will be severe,' the meeting at the *gotul* ended with the warning.

The next morning, Bali woke up, brushed her teeth, and came to the courtyard. Groups of people were gathering and talking in the market.

'She must have done something wrong, that's why she took her own life. If she had nothing to hide, why would she kill herself? She could have proven her innocence...'

'What happened, aunt? Did someone in the village die?'

'Didn't they hold a meeting at the *gotul* yesterday? It seems that the woman consumed poison.'

Bali felt darkness descend before her eyes. Her stomach churned. Was it sorrow... or distress? Bali couldn't eat that day. Is this the life of women? Do they really possess witchcraft? She had heard at school that witchcraft was a superstition. However, their society had strong belief in this superstition. This superstition claimed the lives of so many women.

Bali shuddered with fear and insecurity. All day, she wandered around restlessly, like a cat on a hot tin roof.

Bali's father had complete information about her. He got the wedding invitations printed and sent them to all the neighbours and relatives in the nearby villages.

Only when her sister-in-law told her did Bali come to know that the preparations for her marriage were going on.

The marriage preparations were going on at a brisk pace in her village. Her parents fed the entire village to bring firewood. This act of feeding everyone is called '*aro tehat*'.

Her uncle came on a motorcycle to take Bali away. She stubbornly refused to go.

'The wedding has been announced to the entire village. Now if you refuse to come, our honor is at stake. If you don't come, we'll tie you to the vehicle and drag you there,' he threatened.

Bali got on to the motorcycle silently. Another person sat behind her so that she is in the middle, making it impossible for her to escape.

The women of the household applied turmeric to her body and gave her a bath. Bali bowed to all the things they did, but she did not accept defeat. The wedding ceremony concluded.

She busied herself with household chores, living in harmony with everyone and maintaining friendships with her friends. However, she could not bring herself to look at her husband Manguru. She could not accept him as a person, let alone as her life partner.

It is not that she loved someone else either. This bitter experience, happening at a time when she had no thoughts of marriage, had turned into distaste for marriage in her. Despite her education, Bali did not shy away from physical labor. She did not see farm work as beneath her dignity. She tilled the land with a plough, harvested with a sickle, and levelled fields with a spade, working as hard as any man.

After sowing seeds, during the growth stage of the paddy, farmers stay in the huts in their fields. Elderly folks guard the fields at night, while the entire family spends the day working in the fields and returns to the village by evening.

They remain in the fields until the harvesting is complete and threshing is done.

One day, Bali, along with her younger sister, slept in a hut in the field. They hadn't been home for two days. Her father came to the hut drunk in the middle of the night. The sisters, exhausted from working in the field all day, were fast asleep.

'Bali... Bali!' her father yelled, waking her up and making her sit up. He placed a bottle of poison in front of her and said 'Either drink this and die or start living with your husband as a wife. Choose between the two.'

Bali wasn't a coward to choose death, hence her ongoing struggle. She sat silently with her head bowed. Her father, boiling with anger, picked up a stick and started beating her. The sticks were breaking from the force of the blows. Hearing the commotion, the neighbouring farmers ran over, thinking her father was beating her mother and fearing she might die from the blows.

When they arrived, they saw him beating his own daughter as he would beat a beast. 'Isn't she your own child? Why are you beating her like this? She is a good and intelligent girl. How can you beat her so mercilessly?' they asked.

'My child, my wish. I gave birth to her, I raised her. She is defying me and tarnishing my honour. Killing her wouldn't be enough to wash away my shame,' he raged.

Bali's white *Salwar* suit was stained red with blood. She had decided she would rather die than compromise. As long as there was breath in her body, she would not give in.

She kept searching for ways to escape. Her classmates were studying in Ahiri and Aalapalli. She thought that she might find some help if she went to them.

She went to her friends' hostel in Ahiri and shared her woes with them. With their help, she went to work as a labourer in a building construction site. Some young women from her neighbouring village of Bejjuru also came there for labour work, and a week passed without any worries. Once the payments were completed, those young women went back to their homes.

Bali's troubles started again.

'Our headmistress is very kind... we will talk to her. If you bring your transfer certificate (TC) and rejoin, you can study like us,' her friends advised.

To get the TC, she had to go back to Hemalkasa. If she went there, someone from her village might see her and inform her father. She would end up back in that hellhole. Bali's heart rebelled against the idea.

She couldn't stay in the hostel for long either. Without any destination in mind, she stepped out of the hostel and went from Ahiri to Aalapalli. She sat at the bus stand alone, thinking for a long time.

She remembered her friend Baby Naroti in Etapalli. Thinking that Baby might help her, she boarded a bus to Etapalli. She searched and searched for Baby's place, and just when she was about to give up, she found it.

'Is Baby here, aunty? We are friends. I came to see her,' she said.

'Baby is not here, dear. She went out on some work and said she won't return for a week,' Baby's mother told her.

Bali's heart sank, but she decided not to lose courage. After having a meal, Baby's mother asked Bali her story and she spilled out her entire story.

'Well, you can stay at our house, dear,' Baby's mother comforted her. Another week passed this way.

One afternoon, as Bali washed her hair and was drying it out, Baby's mother slowly began,

'You said you don't like your husband. Our son Rakesh is a good match for you. If you like him, we will inform your family.'

Bali, unsure of what to say or where to go, stared blankly. Her silence was taken as acceptance. They informed the village elders that they found a bride for their son.

The news reached Bali's father, but she was unaware of this. A Tata Sumo SUV stopped in front of the house. Her uncles came, grabbed her by the arm, and dragged her into the car. They took her back to her village, where the entire village gathered, both men and women.

Bali's father twisted her arms behind her back and tied them. He went inside, brought a pair of scissors, and chopped her hair unevenly. It was neither a proper haircut nor a complete shave – just a disfigured appearance.

She realized that she was going to become a "*Kerde*[8]". Bali shuddered. She remembered hearing from her grandmother about the sufferings of the *Kerde* women.

She recalled the tragic stories of young women who sought refuge in poison to escape the disgrace. Bali resolved not to let her story become another tragic tale of a *Kerde* woman.

✳

When Bali fled to Etapalli, her father filed a complaint at the Bhamragad police station saying, 'Our child is missing.'

For that reason, Bali now had to be taken and presented before the station head. Bali had already been given warnings. She was instructed to say, 'I lost my mind and went somewhere, and as soon as I came to my senses, I returned home. No one harmed me.' After giving this statement, Bali was sent home.

From there, she was quietly taken across the Indravati River and dropped off at her in-law's house in Karmavada. The elders washed their hands of the matter, saying, 'Here is your daughter-in-law, you take care of her.'

Two months went by and they felt like two aeons. Bali kept finding excuses to avoid her husband. Her nature rebelled against sharing a marital life with someone towards whom she had no feelings. There was a cold war going on between the two. Every night, she found some excuse to avoid entering the room.

She was waiting for a way to break her bonds. She was seeking freedom and people who would respect her individuality.

One day, she was washing dishes in the yard. At that time, two women came into the village. One of them was named Mangi.

Later, Bali learned that Mangi was the commander of that squad. Seeing them, Bali felt as if life had returned to her. She ran up and shook hands with them.

She greeted them warmly, full of affection. Bali, who had been spending each day like an age, felt she had found a lifeline.

She was not worried about what her in-laws, sisters-in-law, and relatives would think.

'*Akka*, I want to talk to you for a while. Will you listen?'

'What is it? Tell me,' Mangi said, sitting on the house's veranda.

Both sat down.

For two hours, Mangi listened to Bali's anguish without blinking. After thinking for a while, Mangi consulted with the President of the local revolutionary *Janatana Sarkar*.

Information was sent out that the *Janatana Sarkar*'s village council would be meeting. The women's organisation members were also given special notice to attend the meeting.

The next day, by noon, everyone had gathered. The President of the Revolutionary *Janatana Sarkar* started the meeting with a brief introduction.

'Today, we are facing terrible oppression. The central and state governments have declared an unjust undeclared war against our Adivasi people. We must defend the existence and identity of the Adivasis through an uncompromising struggle. Despite any internal disputes, we must stand united. This is a conflict between the ruling classes and the oppressed. This can only be resolved through a fierce class struggle. We all agree on this. Within our Adivasi society, this class struggle appears as a conflict between the old powers and the new ideas in the villages. It seems like a conflict between the elders and the organisation members. In reality, it is a clash between the old and the new. Without this conflict, society cannot move forward.'

'Our society has imposed certain restrictions on women. 'They should not sow seeds,' 'a girl should not enter the granary,' women should stay in the '*kurmalonu*[9]' during their menstruation and should not be seen by priests,' 'they should not refuse to marry a cousin,' 'they should not oppose a marriage approved by elders even if they don't like it,'; women opposing such marriages are tortured, branded as witches, ostracized, sentenced to death, or forced into marriage without consent. All these customs are torturing women. Before the Party came, all of us, including me, followed these customs and practices. We lost many of our sisters and mothers. With no one to support them, they took refuge in poison.'

'Take Bali's case, for example. Her father has three daughters. Since they have no sons, it's not wrong for them to hope that their son-in-law would live with them in their house and take care of them in their old age. But they must also consider their daughter's wishes. He tortured his own daughter saying it's his way or no way. She brought her issue to us. She clearly said she doesn't want this marriage.'

The legal committee gave Bali the opportunity to speak. Bali presented her plight before the assembly.

The president of the women's organisation came forward and promised to stand by Bali. Bali wanted a divorce from her husband, and the women's organisation supported her decision.

The Committee ruled that Bali doesn't need to live in a marriage she doesn't like, she can leave her husband's house and marry a young man of her choice. The Committee ruled further that nobody should be forced into marriages against their wishes.

Bali's bonds were broken. She wanted to dance in ecstasy. She packed her belongings into a small bag. As she was about to step out of the house...

'Bali, Bali, where are you going?'

Bali turned around. The parrot in the cage was silently watching. Bali lovingly called it Mittoo.

Holding Mittoo in her hands, she hugged it to her chest. 'I am leaving, Mittoo... to break our cages and for the freedom to fly in the sky, Mittoo...'

Now she is a bird in the sky, a little bird teasing nature with her beauty. Saying *'Lal Salaam'* (Red Salute) to everyone, the squad bid farewell to the villagers and moved on to another destination...

'Akka! I too am with you...' Bali said to Mangi, who was looking at her in amazement.

Her life blossomed with new hopes.

Translation of 'Bali' (First published in Arunatara, August 2021)

Translated by P. Aravinda

Notes:

1. Taluka: A taluka is an administrative unit in India, a subdivision of a district. It comprises a group of several villages organised for revenue purposes. The taluka is called tehsil in northern India.

2. Jyotiba and Savitribai Phule: The Phule couple were influential social and educational reformers in 19th-century Maharashtra. They championed female education by establishing the first school for girls in India in 1848 and worked to eradicate caste- and gender-based discrimination through their initiatives, including the Satyashodhak Samaj (Truth-Seeker's Society).
3. Diwali: A Hindu Festival of Lights
4. Ekalavya: Mythological character in the epic Mahabharata. As a youth, Ekalavya approached Drona and requested him to teach him Archery. But Drona rejected him as he was a forest dweller who didn't belong to the Hindu Varna system and was considered as being of inferior caste. Ekalavya then made a statue of Drona and deeming the statue as his guru, he taught himself archery over many years. When Drona came to know about his talent in archery, he asked Ekalavya to give his thumb as *Guru Dakshina* so as to eliminate competition for Arjuna. Ekalavya cut off his thumb and paid his *Guru Dakshina* (remuneration given to a teacher as demanded by him).
5. *Lam*: Typically, after marriage, daughters move to their in-laws' homes. However, families without male heirs often prefer to marry off their daughters and bring their son-in-law to live with them. This practice is known as Lam and such a son-in-law is referred to as *Lamde*. The family hopes that the son-in-law will take on the responsibilities usually borne by a son. *Lamdes* are not respected in the Adivasi society so young men who cannot afford a bride price often agree to such marriages.
6. Green Hunt: an operation launched by the central paramilitary forces and state police forces to root out the Maoists. This was launched in 2009 with three phases: Clear, Hold and Build.
7. C-60 or Crack-60: The C-60 commandos are a special police unit in Maharashtra, India that fight against Naxalites in the Gadchiroli district.
8. *Kerde*: When parents force their daughters to marry young men they do not like, those young women run away and return to their parental homes. In such cases, parents beat them and send them back to their husbands. Consequently, some of these women choose to flee and live as orphans, surviving on wild fruits and berries found in the forest. Among the Koya Adivasis, such women are called "Kerde". These individuals are considered communal property by society. To make them easily recognizable, their heads are shaved, and they are made to look unattractive. Men pursue them and harass them sexually. Many young girls branded as *kerde* often try to take their own lives.
9. *Kurmalonu*: hut built far from the village inside the forest for women to stay in isolation during their menstrual cycle. These women are not supposed to be seen by men during that time, especially the priest. If by mistake the women are seen, they are stoned as punishment. Food is given to them by their families only once a day, at night.

Why I became a guerrilla
Budri

The greenery of jackfruit, mango, and tamarind trees enveloped the entire village as if in a warm embrace. Rising higher than these trees were the towering hills and above them the boundless blue sky, holding everything together in its expanse. Amidst all this natural beauty lay our small village – Peelbari – situated in Narayanapatna block, Koraput district, Odisha. We were a part of the majority Kuyis, an Adivasi community of poor families.

My *Soyi* (grandfather) had worked hard to earn the land, but a large part of it was taken away by the village head (the *Munsab*), and non-Adivasi people. Whatever remained, my *Aba* (father) cultivated to sustain us. We lived solely on agriculture. My father's assets were twenty cows and fifteen goats. We survived on rice, *ragi* (finger millet), and the vegetables we grew along the canal's edge – potatoes, radishes, peanuts, peas, and various other vegetables. My *Iya* (mother), my siblings, and I would help with the fieldwork every day.

My parents had five children – two elder sisters, one brother, one younger brother, and me. My *Bai* (grandmother – father's mother) named me Budri because I was born on a Wednesday. Everyone called me by that name. My father had four sisters and two younger brothers. His sisters had been married off by the time he was old enough to be aware of the world. Due to the *Munsab*'s constant threats, my grandparents took the younger sons and left for another village. My father, however, chose to stay back, enduring the intimidation.

The villagers endured many hardships under the *Munsab*'s

authority, but no one dared to question him. Over time, families from our seven neighboring households were scared away, leaving only our family behind. Despite being alone, my father wasn't frightened by their threats; he continued his work courageously. The *Munsab*'s people, however, plotted to drive our family out. They threatened him frequently, saying, 'What do you think you'll achieve by staying here alone? All the other families have left, and you should, too. Leave before things escalate – you don't want to bear the consequences.'

My father, always adamant, would say to my mother, 'Why should we leave just because they're threatening us? Let's live our lives here. It's not like we rely on them.' Two or three months passed like this, and then one night, seven men came to our home and confronted my father. They demanded, 'Are you too arrogant to leave when we tell you to? You have no respect for us. Leave now, or else your life will be at risk.' They then beat my father mercilessly. Although everyone saw the incident, no one stepped forward to help. My mother tried to intervene, but they shoved and kicked her aside. Somehow, my father managed to break free and ran into another house. Despite chasing him, the *Munsab*'s men didn't find him as he pleaded with the homeowner to hide him, and she didn't reveal his whereabouts. Later, she helped my father escape from her house in secret.

It wasn't until a month later that we learned my father had fled to a village called Gorkajala that very night. The *Munsab*'s men had vandalized our house tearing it apart out of rage. My mother painstakingly tidied up the broken roof and scattered belongings, restoring our home as best she could. Since they couldn't get hold of my father, they took out their rage by ruthlessly slaughtering our goats and cows with an axe, and destroying the little we had. Even after this, my mother didn't confront them about our livestock; she was just relieved they had let us live.

The pain my mother endured in those thirty days, worrying about what had become of my father, is indescribable. Yet even after all this, the *Munsab*'s men did not leave us alone.

Mother completely stopped going to the fields. The *Munsab*'s family and their workers took over our fields. She thought, 'If I confront them and work in the fields, will they let me live? If something happens to me, what will become of my children who have already lost their father?' So, she avoided any direct conflict. Whenever she went towards the forest, she would look at the field, reminiscing about the days she worked hard alongside father. She would feel deeply saddened, and during those times, even food would feel intolerable to her.

Mother tended constantly to the small vegetable garden behind our house. During her free time, she'd take us into the forest. We would gather tubers, bamboo, and sticks from the forest. One day, as usual, we went into the forest and found our father waiting for us there. It had been a long time since we had seen him, though he said he came looking for us several times. But somehow, we never crossed paths. When we saw him, we all ran and hugged him tightly. My older sister and brother cried, begging him not to leave us again. I didn't miss him as much, as I was young and spent most of my time with my mother. My mother told father about all that had happened since he left.

Mother served him some gruel she had brought for us, leaving just enough for us to eat. Just then, a large herd of goats and sheep belonging to the *Munsab* appeared in the distance. Father quickly said, 'We'll meet again another time,' and disappeared. After he left our village, we met him two or three more times in the forest.

During the days when father wasn't with us, even the neighbouring villagers, fearful of the *Munsab*, avoided talking to us. Mother spent her time solely with us five children. When father left, we still had a little grain and rice stored at home, but within three months, it was all gone. After that, mother would give us mangoes, jackfruit seeds, and boiled bamboo shoots she had saved. Before long, even these were finished. Not a day went by without us crying for food. Unable to bear our tears, mother would go alone into the forest, bring back two or three types of tubers, and feed us. No one would hire her because of their fear of the *Munsab*. Our land was now in their hands. With no other option, we relied on the forest for survival. But even now, those six months of hardships endured by our mother remain etched in our memories. Thinking back to those days still makes my stomach twist in pain.

After exactly six months, news came from our father. We didn't know what the messenger told our mother, but that evening, we set off on our journey. By nightfall, we reached a village called Gorkajala, where father was waiting for us. Our grandfather told us that this village was entirely populated by our extended family. It was then that we learned that the seven families who had fled because of the *Munsab*'s threats had all settled here. They gave us land to farm to make a living. I would go along with my friends to look after my grandfather's goats.

Mother took on all the household tasks, with help from my two older sisters. My oldest brother fell ill with a fever, and grandfather treated him with herbal remedies from the village. If anyone fell ill, they would rely on herbal medicines. My grandfather gave the same herbs to my brother. Before fifteen days had passed, my brother passed away. And he wasn't the only one – many people in the surrounding villages were dying from fevers. 'The government's neglect is the reason for these deaths. This time, when politicians come asking for votes, we won't let them set foot in our village,' said my uncle to his friends. I didn't fully understand his words, but from his angry tone, I gathered that politicians were no better than the *Munsab*.

It wasn't clear how long uncle was involved with the Party, but it had been a week since he'd last been home, and grand-mother was annoyed with everyone in the house. She asked everyone she knew for his whereabouts, but none could give her any information. After a week, he returned home. He didn't say where he had gone, but that evening he sat alone deep in thought. Father approached him, greeting him casually before asking him directly about what had happened. Uncle confided in him, saying he had spent the past week with people from the

Party that was working for the rights of oppressed people and Adivasis like us. Father didn't take it too seriously.

Uncle continued spending more time with the Party members, attending meetings in various villages and inviting others from our community to join as well.

Grandmother would get angry that uncle not only went to the Party meetings but he was bringing the Party members to our village and holding meetings. Father, however, would support uncle, telling mother, 'He is fighting against the land-lords for the people, so that they can have their rights and land.' Though I used to always tag along with my mother, none of these things made any sense to me. We came to know later that my uncle was also working for an organisation set up by Party members. Uncle introduced father also to the Party, and both of them were now involved in its activities, leaving the housework and fieldwork to mother. She quarrelled about this, feeling overburdened.

My mind wrestled with curiosity about the Party meetings, uncle, and father's involvement in them. I thought about asking my father, but I was too afraid. Mother didn't have any issues with father working for the poor; she only wished he'd also pay some attention to the housework, and she voiced this concern while serving him food. As she hoped, father started helping in the fields while actively participating in Party work. Gradually, mother also began attending the meetings held in the village along with father. Hearing about the Party from both family members and others, I put aside my fear and made up my mind to ask father about it.

Stars were twinkling in the sky. Father lay there, as if counting them, lost in thought. I slowly went over and sat beside him. I asked him questions in quick succession, 'Father, what is the Party? What does it actually do? Why do you and uncle go to them?' Smiling, he pulled me closer and said, 'The Party unites poor people like us against the landlords who took away our lands and troubled us. By forming an association, it fights against the dominance of people like the village head,

Munsab. Under the leadership of the organisation, we poor people take back not only our land but also our rights from the *Munsab*. We want to start a struggle even in our village.' Then, someone came for father, and he left with them.

I don't know what father discussed with the Party members, but he returned home and told mother, 'We are going back to our old village, Peelbari. We leave tomorrow. Pack everything. I have to meet some people tonight, so I'll be late. Be ready.' I don't know when he returned, but by morning, father was with us, all set to leave. Mother sat there wondering why father had suddenly made such a decision. Grandmother and grandfather were upset about our departure, but he consoled them, saying it was inevitable, and then signalled for us to follow him. Holding my younger brother's hand with one hand and a bag in the other, father led the way while we walked behind.

By the next day, we reached our destination. To our surprise, the old village wasn't the same as before. Father told mother it was due to the influence of the Party. Days started passing quickly. Six months went by like that. Gradually, father became very active in the organisation that the Party had set up in the village. Knowing our situation, the Party intervened and confronted the *Munsab* family in front of the people, finally reclaiming our land for us. That night, father told all five of us a long story.

'Many non-Adivasi people who came from different places occupied the lands of our people in Narayanapatna block. Among those who seized the land were Brahmins, Vaisyas, Sundis, and Dombs. Primarily, the Vaisyas and Sundis held the largest share of land and exerted dominance over us. Most of the Dombs were poor, though. They all indulged freely in the liquor trade, enslaving many Adivasi people to alcohol and taking over their lands. Some other non-Adivasis forced our Kuyi people to work for them without pay, in their fields and homes. However, their games didn't last after the Party arrived in the area. Over the past two and a half years, the Party has organised people from all the villages of Narayanapatna block, formed a Chasi Mulya Sangham (Agricultural labour organisation), and initiated a land struggle against the landlords. In this struggle, land was taken especially from non-Adivasi landlords and distributed to the local poor, landless Adivasi people. Several elder chiefs who were against the people were themselves made to hand over their land to the public. In the case of those who refused, the people rose up, and under the leadership of the Party's associations, planted red flags on their lands.

This campaign by the party created fear among the enemies of the people, with some surrendering to the rebellion and handing over their property to the people, while others, unable to cope with the people's awakening, fled. Even today, the people of our block continue this campaign. The Party has decided that everyone should cultivate collectively on the lands where the red flags were planted, sharing the harvest together. Since this decision by the Party was for the welfare of our people, everyone has accepted it, and now, elders and children alike participate in the collective farming fields. We all have responsibilities in collective work. We, too, must participate.

However, the Party reminded us of something else. Though the lands are now under the people's control with the Party's guidance, the enemy is still strong! He could seize the land we think is ours, by killing our people with his police dogs. For this reason, on December 2nd, as part of the PLGA (People's Liberation Guerrilla Army) week celebrations, the Party clarified an important point. They said, 'We have opposed the dominance of the landlords, stopped the deceit of traders, and reclaimed land from the landlords. These are all good achievements. But to protect the lands we have won, we must take up arms and fight against the police.' To do this, we must join the guerrilla militia and the squad. In line with the Party's call, we must send thirty people from our pocket (group).' he said.

'Who from our household?' *naana* (elder sister) asked.

'The whole village has agreed to send people, but names haven't been announced yet. As the association president, I thought to start from our family. We're planning to send Budri from our house. Even if no one at home agrees, she will go,' said the father, looking at mother's face.

'It's already late; have some food. I also need to go to the meeting,' he said, and left with uncle to meet the group of people gathered together.

Before joining the organisation, father never discussed such matters. As a fourteen-year-old, I understood much of what my father shared. Those who previously whispered secretly to us out of fear of the village head now came to our house with courage and openly discussed their issues with my father. The organisations formed by the Party were actively working in the village. Just as a barren tree sprouts new leaves after the first rain, the entire village was bursting with enthusiasm after throwing off the yoke of the landlords. I was eager and curious to be a part of these activities someday.

In the village, meetings were held regularly, accompanied by lively songs. The moment I heard the sound of those songs, I would rush to the meeting place. The first time I saw the cultural troupe, they were dressed in striking red and white clothes, carrying red flags, with anklets jingling on their feet, beating drums, and singing while hundreds of people danced. Their unique attire and the songs they sang made me want to join in and sing with them. That impression left a mark on me, drawing me to them whenever they arrived.

For everyone my age in our village and the surrounding areas, the Party organised programs to teach songs. I would sing those songs at home, or even while I was working. My father heard me sing, and his heart swelled with pride.

One day, my father received word that the Party members had arrived. I ran over at once, eager for the songs. By the time I reached, the meeting had already begun with the singing. A woman from the group came to me and asked, 'Would you like to sing the song we taught last time in the meeting now?' I nodded eagerly. People gathered around, and the meeting was coming alive. She gestured with her hand, inviting me forward, and I sang the song with enthusiasm.

After the meeting, I was on my way home when, without me noticing, she came up behind me, patted my shoulder, and said, '*Lal Salaam*, Comrade Budri. You sang bravely, you know. So, would you like to join our singing group, G.N.S.?' I asked her what that meant. She explained, 'G.N.S. stands for 'Gono Natya Sangh.' It's a group that unites people through songs, and it teaches those who cause hardship to our poor folk a good lesson. Plus, you'll be able to learn more songs, sing them, and enjoy. Think it over until we meet again. See you, Budri,' she said, slinging her rifle over her shoulder, and shook hands with me saying '*Lal Salaam*' once more before she left.

Her words, the warmth with which she spoke, and the new phrase '*Lal Salaam*' kept coming back to me again and again. When she returned about ten days later, the moment I saw her, I told her what was on my mind: 'I want to join the singing group.' From that day on, my happiness doubled. I shared this news with my father. He said, 'Joining is just the beginning; now you must learn well and sing like them.' With a smile, I nodded in agreement.

However, my mother, who was clearing the cow dung in the courtyard, became very upset. With my father already engaged with the organisation's work, one of my uncles being busy with the Party work and not paying much attention to the house, with my sister attending meetings with my father, and another uncle involved in militia duties, my mother was furious at the thought of me joining the G.N.S. She roared like a lioness at my father, 'You're taking my children away from me!' and cried. My father offered no reply to her words or tears.

The rest of us gathered near the vegetable garden behind our house. My father asked me to sing a song. I started singing, and my sisters, father, and little brother joined in as the chorus. My mother, still with dung on her hands, came over and joined the chorus with us. My father signalled with his eyes to us to look at her, and suddenly, our laughter echoed across the entire garden.

After joining the G.N.S. troupe, we started organizing cultural programs not just in our village but throughout all the neighbouring villages in our pocket. The 'Village *Militia*' was particularly active in this area, led by Commander Comrade Poorno. Together with the militia, we held various meetings and organised cultural activities.

One day, after a meeting, Comrade Poorno said, 'Budri, I need to talk to you. Let's sit down after tomorrow's meeting.' As planned, after the meeting in a nearby village, we sat down to talk. He said, 'While working with G.N.S., it would be great if you also took part in militia activities. As part of the revolutionary reforms initiated by the Party in the villages in our pocket, there are activities to level lands reclaimed from landlords, engage in collective farming, and other initiatives where we have to fulfil our role responsibly. Being involved in these activities would provide valuable experience for you. Think about it. This isn't just my suggestion; it's something the Party has directed. We need to walk a long distance to meet with the squad, so let's talk again soon.' With that, he shook hands and left.

This wasn't the first time I'd heard this. Since I joined G.N.S., my father has often encouraged me not just to sing songs but to take an active part in the work initiated by the Party. The very next day, I started going along with the militia comrades. I participated in activities like assisting people with farming tasks, and organizing cleanliness initiatives in the villages. Additionally, around fifty of us from the pocket[1] *militia* joined the land levelling efforts on lands acquired through the land struggles. Alongside us were members from the Chasi Mulya Sangham, the women's organisation activists, and villagers of all ages, totalling nearly two hundred people. The community took it upon themselves to prepare meals for everyone.

One afternoon, after lunch, we sat down to rest, and the president of the women's organisation began explaining the details of the land struggle. She said that under the leadership of the Party, there was a large *"manobal"* (morale-boosting) meeting attended by thousands of people. In that gathering, our leaders called for the seizure of lands. Inspired by this call thousands of people under the leadership of Comrade Singanna swept down upon the lands of outsiders, landlords, oppressors, and anti-people village leaders like a wave. This people's movement drove them away from their lands and homes.

To suppress this land struggle, the government established a "Peace Committee," much like the notorious *Salwa Judum* in the Dandakaranya region. This committee included anti-people political leaders, landlords, oppressors, and violent mobs. The Geno Bahini militia, under Singanna's leadership, bravely faced these anti-people mobs, killing a few of them in self-defense. As the struggle intensified, the government and police directly intervened. During this period, armed police and oppressors attacked the village of Dumbaguda, turning it into a wasteland. The police sexually assaulted a woman from the village, and when villagers tried to intervene, they were beaten and injured.

Realizing that direct confrontation was futile, the villagers sounded the horn, gathering about five hundred people, including Singanna. In protest against the attacks on villages, they marched together under Singanna's leadership to Narayanpatna Police Station. They demanded, 'What is the reason behind these attacks on our villages?' and raised slogans against the police. Terrified by this uprising, the police opened fire without any warning. In this shooting, the courageous people's leader Comrade Singanna was martyred, along with Chasi Mulya Sangham activist Andhru, who also fell to the ground. A total of nineteen people were injured in the incident.

With tears in her eyes, the president said, 'We will never forget the memories of how we fought side by side with Singanna for this land under the leadership of the Party.'

'Comrades, it is two thirty. We need to get to work,' said Poorno. As I went to work, her words kept circling in my mind. I had heard stories about Singanna from the people. They would say that bullets couldn't harm him. I had seen him once or twice, but it was through her that I came to understand him deeply. The Party worked for the people; the leaders of the Party, and many people had sacrificed their lives for these lands. Working in such lands filled me with immense pride.

Party comrades Jairam and Munna *dada* would come often to meet with the militia. They would explain how to carry out the activities of the militia. They decided that the militia should receive military training and in consultation with Commander Poorno, they set a date for this purpose. Our commander informed my father about it, and my father shared it with my sister and me. My sister had already been working in the militia before me. Upon hearing this, my sister said she would definitely go and my father agreed. At that time, I was suffering from malaria. Although I wanted to go, my father did not permit it. Without telling my mother, my sister left, and as a result another argument arose between my parents.

I overheard my father telling someone that all forty people from the area had gone for training. I was close to tears and angry with myself, for having fallen sick. Exactly twelve days later, my sister returned home. I was so upset that I didn't speak to her, so she came to me and began recounting the experiences of the past ten days.

'I really liked the discipline in the party, you know! Wake up at four in the morning, finish the morning routines, put on pants and a shirt, and gather on the ground for roll call at five. There, they divide us into groups of ten for different sections. At roll call, they announce the day's drills. Then, comrades Munna and Jairam begin with exercises. Seeing both of them in uniforms, shoes, caps, and armed, we all longed to wear uniforms and carry weapons ourselves. Alongside physical training, they taught us drills to attack enemies. They explained military techniques such as setting up booby traps and detonating mines to attack armed enemies. Punctuality and discipline were strictly enforced for everyone. Being with the party comrades, going to the grounds... Ten days went by quickly. If we get another chance, let's go together, all right?' With that, she walked over to my angry mother to placate her. I felt a deep regret for missing out.

A month after the military camp, Comrade Munna *dada* came to the outskirts of the village to speak with the militia. About thirty of us gathered. After sharing the program with us, he read out a pamphlet about the Devamali hills. Explaining it, he said, 'The aluminium companies, NALCO (National Aluminium Company) and Hindalco, intend to seize the Mali and Devamali mountain ranges. These mountain ranges stretch across Kotia, Turia, and Kanti panchayats in the Pottangi block of Koraput district, covering a distance of seventeen kilometers. At an elevation of 4,385 feet above sea level, the Devamali mountain range is the highest in Odisha. Scientists estimate that these mountains hold three hundred million tons of bauxite reserves in their depths.

To exploit these resources, the Hindalco Company leased the area for fifteen years. However, there are twenty-two villages in these mountain ranges, home to more than ten thousand people, the majority of whom are indigenous tribes. They rely on these hills for their livelihood. The government of Naveen Patnaik[2] issued notices to the villagers to vacate the area. If mining operations were to begin here, not only would a large number of our people be displaced, but extensive environmental pollution would also affect many surrounding villages. There is a risk that the indigenous culture and traditions would vanish. This has now become a matter of life and death for us. Previously, an Adivasi Rights Organisation held a public meeting with twelve thousand people, calling for a struggle against it. All of our people mobilized in large numbers back then,' he said. He barely finished talking before I asked, 'What is produced by the NALCO Company?'

'The NALCO Company is located sixteen kilometers from Damanjodi town, within the limits of the Mathalput panchayat in the Koraput block. The bauxite mines are here from which bauxite is extracted and transported to the NALCO Company, where it is refined into powder form and exported. The impact of these mines on the local communities is enormous. All right, comrades, it's getting late. We'll discuss this in more detail while looking at the map of the area the next time we meet,' he said, bidding us goodnight that evening.

I knew about the existence of Devamali hills and the Hindalco Company but understood their import only after Munna *dada* explained them. I could comprehend the condition of the people living around those hills, but my mind couldn't fully process the environmental issues and the challenges faced by the people due to it. I decided that the next time *dada* came, I would ask him about these issues. I felt glad within myself, realizing that staying with comrades like Munna *dada* in the party would help me learn more about such exploitative companies, especially the problems poor people face due to them, the changes happening in the outside world and society, and many more things.

A year had passed since I began working in the militia. A call came from the party asking me to join it. Commander Poorno told my father, who informed my mother, and my mother argued with him over it – all of this in a single day. 'I've made up my mind to send Budri to the party. It would be good if you thought the same way. Don't you ever think beyond our family about the Party that works for people like us?' my father replied angrily to my mother.

'I have no issues with the Party. She's working in the militia, isn't she? I think that's enough,' my mother replied calmly. The next day, when I went to visit some relatives, my aunt took me away by force. My family didn't know about it and assumed I was engaged in Party work. After a week, I escaped and returned home. This happened two or three times, after which my father had a serious argument with my aunt's family, warning them of serious consequences if it happened again. At dawn, my father told me there was a meeting in the village. I didn't understand. Commander Poorno had called a meeting of those being recruited from the militia.

By noon, we all gathered there. In front of the people, they asked us to speak. The parents of each comrade also spoke. My mother didn't know about it, so my father spoke on my behalf, saying, 'The Party is the people, and the people are the Party.

Betray anyone, and you will be remembered as a betrayer of the people. If you surrender or run away, punishment will await you in front of the same people. You must stay committed to this decision you have taken for *Jal, Jangal, Jameen, Izzat,* and *Adhikar* (Water, Forest, Land, Self-respect and rights) until your last breath. If you fall into enemy hands, you must protect the secrets of the Party. Even if you have to endure brutal torture, you must not yield to the enemy. Every last drop of your blood should serve these oppressed people,' my father concluded. Oh, the words my father spoke held profound meaning. We all promised there, before the people, never to betray the Party. All the people raised their fists in pride, with tears of joy in their eyes, saying *'Lal Salaam'* to our group of thirty.

It was afternoon. The heavy rain that had poured until then had ceased, leaving a calm silence. The fresh leaves glistened with raindrops from the recent downpour. Flocks of birds soared across the sky. Red flags flew freely on the land we had fought for and reclaimed from the landlords under the Party's leadership. The villagers, who were supposed to leave, halted in their steps. I turned to the side to see my father and told him a final *'Lal Salaam.'* I remembered the vow I made in front of the people to stand on the side of the poor, oppressed masses for as long as I lived, and my father's words echoed in my mind. By then, the squad had come closer, waiting for us, signalling it was time to go. Munna *dada* from the squad gave a knowing glance. Without hesitation, I donned the cap and slung the rifle my father had given me over my shoulder and joined the squad, heading toward the Mali hills.

(Written in Telugu by Vannada Vijayalakshmi as narrated to her in Kuvi by the author Budri, who is an Adivasi belonging to the Kuyi tribe)

Translation of 'Nenu guerrillanendukayyanante'. (Initially published in *Bolshevik*, January–June 2018)

Translated by P. Aravinda

Notes:

1. Pocket: a region comprising a set of villages belonging to a particular area
2. Naveen Patnaik: the chief minister of Odisha state from 5 March 2000 to 12 June 2024

Ramko

Nitya

I t was nearly seven in the morning. Ranitha set off towards the village MakadiChuvva, situated in the Chamorshi Taluka of Gadchiroli district, along with two people from her team. The village was a tiny hamlet of just four houses. Among the four houses, two belonged to the Oraon Adivasis, who had migrated from Rayagada, while the other two were owned by the local residents.

It was the rainy season, and the agricultural activities were in full swing. Farmers were getting ready to head to their fields, with their oxen yoked to the ploughs. The women had finished cooking and packing the rice into containers. They placed these containers into a basket covered with leaves, and were getting ready to head to the fields.

The people recognized Ranitha from a distance, and they started coming out of their homes to greet her with *'Lal Salaam'* (Red Salute). They smiled warmly and shook hands with her. She greeted everyone in return with equal warmth.

Ranitha had a fair complexion, fine features, a smiling face, and a slender frame. She was the President of the *Janatana Sarkar* of the Chadgaon area. She had come to the Pottegav area to establish new Revolutionary People's Committees (RPCs) and strengthen the existing ones.

Pottegav area was at the very edge of the Surjagarh hills, where work was underway to start iron ore mines. Road construction was also progressing rapidly. The village of Makadichuvva was among those affected by the mining operations.

Ranitha stopped in the middle of the bazaar. Children and

women gathered around her. An old woman, struggling with her steps, came up and affectionately touched Ranitha's cheek, saying, 'How long has it been since you came, dear?' Just then, a farmer from the last house came running over and said, 'the police are coming into the village.' Even as he said that, the police entered the village.

Two days earlier, the squad had set fire to the vehicles of contractors involved in the road work. The police, having guessed the squad's route, had surrounded the village early in the morning and waited on the outskirts. Spotting the squad entering the village, a team of police advanced parallel to them.

The police were the first to open fire. Ranitha's team members turned back in the direction they had come from and ran quickly towards the forest. The COBRA[1] forces chased them to the edge of the forest.

Ranitha immediately turned around, and quietly slipped into a sorghum field through an alley, and took cover there. The woman who owned the house near the field, seeing Ranitha entering the yard, approached her and whispered, 'There are no police around; leave quickly, *Didi*.'

Ranitha had firmly decided not to run aimlessly without knowing the exact movements of the police. She camouflaged herself within the tall sorghum field and adapted to the terrain. She quietly loaded her .303 rifle, which was already half-cocked. Keeping her finger on the trigger, she controlled her breathing and waited silently.

After driving out the PLGA members, the COBRA forces gathered in a group in the village. They were speaking in a mix of Hindi and Marathi. Suddenly, a COBRA collapsed on the ground, foam forming around his mouth.

'What happened?'

'Whose gun went off?'

'The bullet hit the heart. Spot death.'

'Was it yours? Was it yours? Someone's gun got fired

accidentally. Whose?' The group of COBRAs was in a panic. They searched around but found no imminent danger. It was clear that it was an accidental fire from one of theirs. The COBRA commander sent a message to the Gadchiroli headquarters via his wireless. 'A helicopter is coming to transport the body. If we move the body to the plains, the pickup will be easier.'

All the scattered COBRA forces gathered to lift the body.

Bang! Bang!

This time, two bullets were fired in succession. One hit a soldier's thigh, and he collapsed on the ground, screaming in pain like a beast stung by bees. Another soldier fell to the ground, unconscious. This time, the direction of the shots was clear.

The COBRAs understood now that there was someone in the sorghum field and panic spread through them. The two bodies and the injured COBRA were evacuated by helicopter. Transporting the bodies on the road was considered unsafe due to the fear of landmines, so air travel was chosen.

Mobile phones and walkie-talkies buzzed with urgent orders. The Gadchiroli Police Superintendent's office was in chaos. C-60[2] commandos were on edge, as if some major disaster was about to strike. Reinforcements were rushing to MakadiChuvva.

Mine-proof vehicles offered some safety to the forces. The COBRA forces surrounded five or six villages around Makadi-Chuvva, and there was palpable tension in the air in all the villages. It was calm before the storm. Even the slightest sound made the battle-hardened COBRAs jumpy.

Wearing a bulletproof jacket and helmet, armed with an AK-47, a COBRA soldier advanced towards the sorghum field, saying, 'Let's see how the Naxalites are.' Just as he was about to reach the field, there was a loud sound of the gun going off, and the

COBRA with bulletproof jacket was flung into the air and fell to the ground. The surroundings became tense. The faces of the COBRA and C-60 forces turned pale.

Outwardly, they displayed a facade of bravery, but inside, their hearts were pounding with fear. Who would be next? Orders from the officers had to be followed.

In the sorghum field, surrounded and trapped in a *Padmavyuha*[3], was Ranitha – alone, resolute, and still. She had to fight until her last breath, making sure not to be captured alive by the enemy. She held her gun firmly, listening intently to the sound of footsteps around the field. She used her gun judiciously.

She checked her watch. It had been more than four hours since the battle began.

The COBRAs were hissing around her. Voices could be heard.

'Drop your gun and come out with your hands up. We won't harm you.'

After a while, they said, 'If you surrender, you'll get money from the government. You can live well.'

By then, they figured out who was in the field.

After a while, one of the COBRAs addressed her by name, 'Ranitha! If you have guts, come out! What kind of a fight is this, sneaking around?' He challenged her in typical police language.

But all of this was from a distance, away from the killing zone. No one had the courage to go closer.

They started launching grenades with K launchers. One, two, twenty, thirty – they threw countless grenades. The lush green sorghum fields were being destroyed.

Gathering courage that she must have died from so many grenades, they approached the field from the backyard. Ranitha's gunshots didn't miss their mark. One bullet hit a fellow's hand, another tore through a hip. After a while, silence fell over the surroundings.

Ranitha's stomach had been empty since morning. If the police hadn't come, she would have asked for some gruel in the village and drank it. She had left her water can in the camp. She wondered if the two comrades who came with her had escaped safely. She hoped her squad was safe. She felt weak, devoid of energy.

The sound of grenades and explosions had caused a block in her ears.

In a semi-conscious state, Ranitha mentally replayed the scene from the morning when the police had confronted them.

She realized that the police hadn't noticed her. If she remained still and didn't move, the police would watch the group in front of her and leave and she could escape safely.

If she fired even a single shot, escaping would be difficult. She had to fire only if she was ready to sacrifice herself. She struggled with this decision for a while.

Even then, her thoughts remained sharp. 'Why am I thinking about saving my life at this moment? What legacy shall I leave for my successors?

I shouldn't waste the opportunity at hand. Ever since I joined the party, every summer, I had trekked in the scorching heat on party work. How could I now leave the opportunity that came my way today? It's better to die than to lose this opportunity.' She made her decision.

She came to her senses and observed her surroundings. There was no sign of the police nearby. She drifted back into a semi-conscious state.

Ranitha understood the situation she was in. In her semi-conscious state, her childhood memories flooded her mind, and she couldn't push them away.

She remembered her journey to Kolkata. She would have died back then but somehow survived. She couldn't recall the exact year, but it might have been the summer of 1998. It was the season when tendu[4] leaves were plucked. She had gone to the Shaheed Minar grounds in Kolkata for the 30th-anniversary celebrations of Naxalbari. After the events concluded, she mistakenly boarded a train heading to Gujarat from Howrah Station, thinking it was heading towards Durg.

As the train started moving, someone alerted her and she tried to jump off the train. Her one foot was on the platform, while the other was still on the train's step. She held tightly to the door jamb. The train dragged her along and her hands and feet got bruised. The railway police saved her. Had she slipped onto the tracks, she would have been crushed under the wheels of the train. With that, her existence would have been erased.

Even after returning home, she couldn't do any work for several days.

'It's the season of leaves, child, it's the crop we wait for all year. Now is the time for us to get some money. I told you not to go, but you didn't listen. You let go of the crop in hand and now you've returned with broken legs and hands. Who will pay for the injections the doctor will give you? Do those meetings fill your stomach?' Her mother rebuked her while she listened with her head bowed.

That was the first time she saw a train in her life and also the last. What if she had died then?

She was called Ramko back then, the name given to her by her parents.

Ramko was the fourth of five children and there was another girl after her. Ramko's family belonged to the Hichami clan. Although their village was the ancestral village of the Potavi clan, there were an equal number of Hichami families too in the village. Like all Adivasi villages, theirs too was governed by the traditional Adivasi headmen.

When the squad first came to the village, Ramko was a ten-year-old. She loved songs and the moment she heard the news of the squad's arrival, she would rush to them. While working in the fields, she would hum the songs she had heard. She was active in household chores, worked hard, ploughed the fields, chopped wood, and built embankments. She carried water from the bore well using a shoulder pole. It was common in the village for girls and women to carry pots on their heads, but Ramko, like the men, carried the water on her shoulders with a shoulder pole. She split bamboo with a knife and made baskets.

'Why can only men do certain things? Why can't a girl?' she used to say.

Axes, knives, sickles, bows and arrows, and *Bharmar* guns were considered men's tools, symbols of male identity. Baskets, brooms, grinding stones, bundles, and sickles were for women.

Ramko started her struggle against customs at home. After joining the squad and becoming a guerrilla, she roamed around with a cap on her head, a gun on her right shoulder, and an axe on her left, becoming a fighter named Ranitha. Her image of that time was etched in the memories of her fellow comrades from those days.

As time passed, Ramko's thoughts matured. She joined the revolutionary Adivasi women's organisation (Krantikari Adivasi Mahila Sanghatan)[5]. Pressure began to mount both at home and outside as the village elders started pressuring her family to get her married. 'Why don't you get the girl married? Shouldn't a girl be married off? Who will marry her when she gets old?' they mocked. But Ramko endured it all. She stood firm with her peers, advocating that marriages should not take place until one is fully aware of everything.

At that time, the authority of the village elders was dominant. The organisations were not yet strong. The elders would insist that young children and those of marriageable age should not go to the squads and that village matters should not be reported to the squad. People were fearful of witchcraft and kept silent. However, none of this could dampen Ramko's enthusiasm.

She exposed the real nature of things in the village to the squad. She won the battle at home and she wanted to reform the village. The women's organisation in the neighbouring village handled all the village matters on their own. Ramko was concerned that her village's organisation was lagging behind. She used to gather the young women of her village and visit the neighbouring village Koyamdudu to speak with the organisation members there. At the end of a year, she had united the girls of her village.

By the end of the year, she became the leader of the Range Committee[6]. She also established the Potavi Jewelli Women's Organisation as a leader in the region.

Her elder cousin Rishi, who worked in the organisation, joined the squad. When he came to the village, she inquired about the squad. She thought, 'I can walk, I can resist if confronted by the police, I can carry weights – so why delay?' She then became a member of the Etapalli Squad.

Since childhood, she had a strong desire to learn to read and write. As a squad member, she stood sentry, went to the villages, made tea as part of the kitchen duty, and performed other duties. Whenever she found time from duties, she practiced her letters using a slate and chalk. She learned to read and write through sheer determination. Apart from this, she joined the party-run Mobile Academic School and Mobile Political School[7].

She wrote songs and shared her comrades' experiences through letters. She documented the experiences of the struggle in her region for the newspapers. She prepared agendas for *Janatana Sarkar* meetings and wrote reviews evaluating the work. Ramko, who used to look at a hundred-rupee note with wonder, now wrote numbers in lakhs without a mistake and without batting an eyelid. People would tease her as being stingy because of her thriftiness.

After working as a squad member in Etapalli for a year, she moved to Tipragarh, where she was given the responsibility of overseeing women's organisations. Later, she became the in-charge of the Chadgaon squad.

Ranitha slowly regained consciousness and tried to pull herself together. But the past was still coming back to her.

She had never once uttered the words, 'I can't do it, I won't be able to do it.' She mingled with people like a fish in water, and she attracted people like a magnet.

While she was in Tipragarh, one day the squad was heading towards Bandur and had stopped midway for a break. Those who needed to relieve themselves went ahead, others smoked *beedis*, and those who chewed tobacco were crushing it in their palms.

The police had tracked them along the same path they had taken and had come upon them. At that time, the squad had little experience with exchange of fire. They scattered in all directions. Ranitha had never directly participated in an encounter before. Once, when she was at home, she had heard the sounds of gunfire when a squad clashed with the police near her village. That day, all of it happened unexpectedly, catching her by surprise. She stood there for a moment, unsure of which direction to go. The police had come very close and one of the policemen charged toward her as if to catch her. Ahead was an open field which wouldn't provide any protection. She saw a large rock and quickly ducked behind it, loaded her gun, and fired at the approaching policeman. He stopped in his tracks. Taking advantage of the situation, she retreated safely. From the next year, when the PLGA forces took up the tactical counter offensive campaigns (TCOC) and chased the police, such incidents did not occur.

In November 2009, during the Chhattisgarh Assembly elections, PLGA forces engaged with the enemy near the border region. They received intelligence that the enemy was about two hours away from their location. Moving swiftly was the only way to catch them. It was about 8 kilometres away. A roll call was conducted, and a team that could move quickly was selected. No women were included in the team. Then three women, who were physically weaker, came forward to join the mission. Among them was Comrade Ranitha. They ran with determination, gathering all their strength, and reached the target. In the encounter that followed, two policemen were killed, and two others were injured, boosting their morale.

Ranitha regained her consciousness. She came back into the world of sound and her memories of the past faded. She heard voices that were shouting at her in frustration to surrender.

Even in that situation, Ranitha couldn't help but laugh at their foolishness. Two paths lay clearly before her. One was to surrender, the other was to fight and die. The brave die fighting.

'My party has instilled in me the self-respect that rejects surrender,' she thought to herself.

She readied herself for what lay ahead, and checked her watch. There was just an hour left before dusk in that rainy season. She could then escape under the cover of darkness.

Even as she considered that possibility, she heard the sound of grass being cut close by. She lifted her head slightly to see what was going on. The farmer who owned that field was cutting the stalks of sorghum with a sickle. She wondered why he would do that at that time. Then she heard someone outside ordering him to cut them to the roots. She realized that the enemy was making him cut the crop to locate her position.

She signalled to the farmer with a hand gesture. Just as she was about to tell him to cover her with the cut sorghum stalks, a harsh voice said, 'Come out of your hiding.'

Ranitha counted the bullets left in her pouch. She had spent 14 bullets since morning. Seventeen were still left. If the battle continued at this pace, she could keep fighting through the night and into the next day. She carefully arranged the bullets back into her pouch.

She moulded her body to fit into a small trench and listened intently to the sounds around her. A helicopter was circling above. The sound of mine-proof vehicles could be heard around noon. Perhaps additional forces had arrived! The noise of people in the village was quite audible, and the dogs kept barking without a pause.

Ranitha didn't notice the policeman who, too scared to shoot from below, had climbed up a nearby Mahua tree (Indian Butter cup tree) to observe the area. He ordered the farmer to cut the crop and identified her location from above. Once he figured out her location, he unleashed a barrage of bullets.

This time, the bullets penetrated her body. She still held onto the gun in her hand. Her open eyes appeared as though she was still watching. Even in that state, the police were too afraid to approach her body.

The villagers carried her dead body out of the yard, and the farmer was also among them. The Superintendent of Police in Gadchiroli was curious to see Ranitha. Was it this frail, young woman who had caused so much trouble since morning? He was astounded by her combat abilities. It took 600 soldiers, helicopters, MPVs, thousands of bullets, hundreds of grenades, the deaths of four policemen, and injuries to three others to bring her down.

Hundreds of police personnel surrounded the area. Despite that, the villagers carried Ranitha's body with respect. The memories of her past that faded away in Ranitha continued in the memories of the farmer who knew her very closely as both Ramko and Ranitha.

Translation of 'Ramko'. First published in *Vasanthamegham* web magazine on 30th April 2022 under the pen name Narmada.

Translated by P. Aravinda

Notes:

1. COBRA: acronym for COmmando Battalion for Resolute Action, is a special operation unit of the Central Reserve Police Force (CRPF) of India proficient in guerrilla tactics and jungle warfare, originally established to counter the Naxalite movement.

2. C-60: The C-60 commandos are a special police unit in Maharashtra, India that fight against Naxalites in the Gadchiroli district.

3. Padmavyuha: also known as the Chakravyuha. This is a military formation in which warriors from one side (e.g. A) become surrounded by the warriors of the other side (e.g B) in multiple layers. In this way, it becomes extremely difficult for the A warriors who are surrounded to find a path to escape out from the many-layered 'wall' formed by the B warriors around them.

4 Tendu: leaves of the Tendu (Indian ivory) tree are used in locally made hand-rolled cigarettes for wrapping the unprocessed tobacco. Plucking the Tendu leaves is a major economic activity for the Adivasis in India. Many struggles were waged under the leadership of Revolutionary mass organisations to increase the wages for Tendu leaf collection.

6. Range Committee: The forest area is divided into several divisions and in turn a division is divided into several ranges by the forest department of India. A Range committee is formed at a Range level.

7. Mobile Academic School and Mobile Political School: mobile classes conducted for the squads to teach them regular academics and political lessons respectively.

Marriage
Tayamma Karuna

'There are five unmarried women in our district committee area. We can ask any of them except Urmila, if they have any intention of getting married,' said Balaram in the Squad Area Committee (SAC) meeting. Balaram was one of the members of the District committee. He said this during a discussion on the topic of Sampath's marriage that came up in the meeting.

If any of the squad members were unable to find someone they would like to get married to, the committee members tried to find someone suitable to them based on their personality. As district committee members, they meet all the squads and are familiar with all the members. If the two parties were happy with the suggestion, they got married.

When Deepa came to know that there was a rule that men could not express their 'interest' in any woman directly, she was very surprised. Rigid 'rules' governing marriage alliances are common in general society. She wondered about the existence of such 'rules' in these circles too!

In the 1990s, there were fewer women in the squads compared to men. What would be the state of mind of a woman if multiple men proposed to her saying that they love her? Whatever said and done, it would disturb her and the whole situation would be embarrassing and might affect her functioning. Deepa understood later that the 'rule' was brought in under these circumstances. It does not mean that this 'rule' was an answer to all problems. However, until women are able to freely express their views and handle such circumstances, this 'rule' may need to be in place. This may help the women comrades to grow in an unfettered manner. This is why the 'rule' is applicable only to men. A woman can express her interest in a man if she likes him but only a year after joining the squad.

If a male comrade liked a woman comrade, he had to tell the squad commander or the district committee member. That is how Sampath conveyed to the District Committee member his love for Sony, who had come from a neighbouring squad for a camp.

It was two years since Sony joined her squad and three years since Sampath joined his squad. Sampath was an active and disciplined youngster. He would never say 'I will not do' or 'I cannot do' for any work assigned to him, even if he was ill. He was ever ready to do any task, however difficult it may be. It was up to the others to perceive that he was not well and not give him work. He was willing to do sentry duty any number of times. Everyone in the squad liked and admired him. He was not only disciplined but was also always eager to educate himself politically. He read a lot of books and wrote down any questions he had and sought answers to them. When he had joined the squad, he had studied until 5th class whereas Sony had not been educated at all. She learnt to read and write after joining the squad. Some of the Adivasi children were educated to an extent because the Ramakrishna mission had started some schools in Abujhmad. Sampath had studied in one such Ramakrishna mission school.

The district committee meetings took place once every 3 or 4 months. Balaram went to the district committee meeting about two months after Sampath had expressed interest in Sony. In the meanwhile, Sony expressed her interest in her commander Prabhakar. Prabhakar also liked her. Since they were in the same squad and worked together, they had a good opportunity to observe each other and get to know each other intimately.

The commander of a squad was responsible for looking after the welfare of his squad members, distribution of duties, looking after them if they were unwell and so on. In the light of this, it was natural that Prabhakar and Sony would interact more with each other. Even though Prabhakar could not openly express his interest in Sony, he showed more concern towards her. Perhaps Sony understood his unexpressed intention. So, she expressed her interest in him.

Balaram thought of conveying Sampath's interest during the district committee meeting. Before he did so, another committee member, Kesanna, told them about the interest expressed by Sony and Prabhakar in marrying each other. So, Balaram did not speak about Sampath's request as it made no sense in talking about it.

Sampath looked forward to hearing from Balaram when he returned from the committee meeting. He was very tense about the result. Balaram found it difficult to tell him about what happened. However, three days after he returned, he called Sampath and told him that Prabhakar and Sony are getting married. Sampath was pained and told Balaram that had he conveyed his interest immediately, it was likely that Sony would have married him. That was quite possible but there was no way to convey the message immediately.

This happened a year ago. After that, Sampath had not talked about marriage at all. However, the committee members felt that they should see if there was any suitable woman who would be willing to marry Sampath. It was in this context that Balaram had made his comment about Urmila.

Many felt that Urmila and Sampath would make a great couple. However, the parties involved should like each other.

Urmila came into the squad after having worked in the women's organisation. It was two and a half years since she came into the squad. She was as disciplined and dedicated as Sampath in her work. She was transferred from South Bastar to North Bastar. Compared to the northern part, South Bastar is more developed. There are differences in the culture between the two areas.

Even from her younger days, Urmila would accompany the squad whenever they visited her village. In time, she became an active member of the women's organisation and was promoted as the range committee President. She would work day and night to accomplish the tasks given by the squad to her and not even go home for days on end, even if her parents objected to it.

There was another reason for her not going home and going around the villages. Her parents were forcing her to get married, but Urmila resisted it. Despite that, her parents might have gone ahead except that the influence of the party was strong. Also, Urmila being a member of the women's organisation, they were worried what the *"dadas"* would say if they forced her. Nevertheless, they went ahead with trying to find matches for Urmila.

With their traditional outlook, Urmila's parents and community saw her as a beautiful woman in the sense that her hands are like iron rods and the calves of both legs are firm. As soon as you saw her, you knew that she was a hard working person. What other beauty do you need? She would certainly 'fetch' a large amount as bride money.

Urmila was aware of these attempts of her parents. Every time she met the squad members, she would ask them how long it would be before she would be taken into the squad. The squad felt that since she was such an active member, having her in the women's organisation was more useful. However, finally they had no choice but to accept her into the squad.

'Why can't we ask Urmila about marriage?' asked the SAC committee members Sunitha and Mangdu. Deepa came out of her thoughts. Commander Bhimal, SAC members Deepa and Subhash also waited for Balaram's answer with interest.

'Oh, that's a long story. I think it is near lunch time. Shall we go?' said Balaram. He loved keeping people in suspense.

'If you don't mind, please tell us. We are not hungry,' said Deepa, looking for confirmation from others.

'Are none of you hungry?' asked Balaram.

Others said 'Let us eat after half an hour.' So Balaram started narrating the story.

'All of you know Mahesh, the comrade from Gadchiroli, I think?'

'Yes,' they said. Mahesh was also a member of the district committee. His wife died in an encounter. After that, he got transferred to north Bastar.

'He told me he would like to marry Urmila,' said Balaram. 'I sat down with Urmila and asked her 'when are you going to get married, Urmila?'. 'Why, *Dada,* have you seen somebody for me?' she asked. I thought she might be interested and told her about Mahesh.' Before Balaram could finish, Deepa asked him about Urmila's response.

There was a reason behind Deepa's curiosity. Deepa was once in the same squad as Urmila. She had witnessed Urmila's reaction personally when Pandru of that squad had proposed to Urmila. Pandru was from north Telangana. He was educated and had a degree. He became a member of the students' union during his Intermediate education. While studying for his degree, he became a full time member of the party. From there he came to Bastar. He was a hard worker. If anyone fell ill, he looked after them with great care. However, he was impetuous.

The squad had marched a long distance that day and finally made camp. Everyone unloaded their kits in their covers and spread their polythene sheets from their kits. It was getting dark. Urmila was drying her hair which was wet with sweat. Pandru approached Urmila and chatted with her for a while. Then, he told her that he would like to marry her. 'Have you joined the squad to get married?' asked Urmila softly but sternly. Pandru was frightened and went away. Deepa, who was nearby, heard the whole conversation but pretended as if she hadn't. She wondered if she should report it to the commander. But, decided not to, thinking that Urmila would do so herself.

Balaram answered Deepa's question saying that he got a tongue lashing from Urmila. Everyone laughed. All of them liked Urmila. Deepa liked her, especially as she was absolutely straightforward and gave straight answers.

Deepa felt surprised by the fact that Mahesh wanted to marry Urmila. Mahesh was at least 35 years old whereas Urmila was at most 20 years old. When thinking of marrying, should not Mahesh have thought of it from the woman's perspective? There were so many youngsters in the squads. She would probably prefer to marry someone closer to her age. Did he think that she would agree because he was a district committee member and came from the plains area? It was true that some of the women were influenced by these factors.

'If she did not want to marry him, she could have said so politely. Why speak so rudely if it were not for arrogance?' said Sunitha. It appeared as though Sunitha had an axe to grind with Urmila.

Hinting that Urmila had her reasons to talk in that fashion, Balaram said that Pandru had also told him that he would like to marry Urmila.

Deepa realised that Pandru had chosen to hide the fact that he had approached Urmila on his own from Balaram and pretended to follow the rule set down by the party. She thought he was 'cunning'. Subhash asked 'Did you convey that to her?'

Balaram said, 'I did. She told me that she did not wish to get married as of then.'

'Oh?' said Deepa, realising that Urmila also had chosen not to reveal the fact that Pandru had proposed to her. She might have decided that she would report it only if Pandru troubled her further. By the time this had happened, Deepa had moved to another squad and so was not aware of any further developments.

'This happened more than a year ago. So, I thought I can bring up Mahesh's proposal', said Balaram. 'And so?' asked the commander thinking that Urmila must have scolded Balaram definitely.

'She said 'Why are you constantly bringing up the question of marriage? Earlier you brought the proposal of Pandru. Now you are asking again.' I told her since you said then that you would not marry immediately, I am asking again now since some time has elapsed', said Balaram.

'What did Urmila say?' Everyone was eager to hear her answer.

'What did she say? She said 'Don't I have a body? Don't I have desires? Wouldn't I think of getting married? Do you have to ask? When I was at home, my parents were after me asking me to get married. I thought I escaped from that. Now, even here, you are pestering me about marriage. If I like somebody, I will go and ask that person myself. I will not tolerate it if the question of my marriage is raised again.' She gave me a good dressing down'.

'Well, she is right', said Deepa. Everyone looked at Deepa. Deepa's admiration for Urmila increased. Deepa was amazed that a girl born and raised in the Adivasi culture was able to articulate her innermost thoughts so boldly. A drowning person would be happy to find even a reed for support, how elated would that person be when she found a boat to support her! That's the elation Deepa felt.

Translation of 'Pelli'. (First published in Kolimi, online magazine, August 2019)

Translated by P. Anupama

Adivasis and Untouchability
Tayamma Karuna

In the past, the squad had bombed Shivaling[1] and the temple. This was the first time they had returned to the village after that incident. Squad Area Committee (SAC) member Kosi, commander Ramdev and squad member Budral went to the village to ask the residents to attend the meeting and also bring some vegetables and rice.

It was almost a year since they had visited the village. It was getting dark when they reached. Ramdev addressed the people as *Dada* and *Didi* and requested them to come to the meeting with rice. Even though the villagers said "okay", he, being an adivasi himself, sensed something different in their response. Normally, a commander does not come into the village. However, considering the situation with respect to this village, Ramdev himself had come to the village. On seeing the response, he decided to cut short the visit to the village and returned to the squad.

The squad, as was the norm, had camped outside the village. As soon as the backpacks were dumped on the ground, there was a roll call (where everyone stands in a line in front of the commander). The commander would decide who would go into the village to invite the villagers to the meeting, the schedule for the day regarding youth and women's organisations' meetings etc. Those identified to go to the village would leave for the village.

Those who were assigned the cooking duty would start collecting wood and preparing things. Except the commander, everyone, male or female, had the cooking duty by rotation.

While the comrade who had been assigned cooking duty made tea, the other comrades would go and wash in the streams nearby. They also wash their footwear. Since there are no thorny plants in Chhattisgarh, they use plastic footwear. North Bastar and Abujhmad regions have lots of streams and brooks all over the place for them to wash.

After having tea, everyone would gather in one place. Whoever was responsible for the evening class would listen to the news on the radio and inform all the others. Not everyone has a radio. It is usually with the commander and those of higher cadre. Sometimes, everyone would listen to the radio together. After listening to the news, they would discuss national, international politics or Marxist theory and so on for about an hour. In the meanwhile, people from the village would start arriving at the campsite. By the time they finished the meeting with the villagers, ate and packed up, it would be midnight or later. They would walk for about half an hour before they spread their polythene sheets and slept. Only one or two people died due to snake or scorpion bites even in that dense forest when resting. When they were on the move, they had never been bitten by snakes or scorpions. As long as there was enough space to curl up, they would fall into a deep sleep. The sheer tiredness of a long day drove them into deep sleep despite the lack of comforts. There is a saying in Telugu that sleep doesn't know comforts and Kosi didn't understand it before coming here.

Kosi came from mainstream society. She had changed her name to an Adivasi name after coming into the forest in order to mingle freely with them. She had studied until her degree. After that, she quit her studies midway and became a full time activist. Four years later, she entered the forest in December 1996.

As soon as the squad lay down to sleep, the sentry duty would start. If people sleep by 11:30 p.m., each sentry duty was for one and a half hours whereas if they slept after midnight, the duty would be of one hour each. The sentry duty would go on till 5 a.m.. Sentry duty is decided by the deputy commander. When their duty was done, the person woke up the next person on duty. Sometimes, if someone was very tired, they would request for a specific sentry duty such as the last duty.

On hearing the whistle blown by the last sentry at 5a.m., everyone gets up. No one could sleep beyond this time even if they had slept late the previous night. Everything had to be done as per the schedule. It is difficult to manage a squad if there is no discipline. They would freshen up in half an hour and pack up their backpacks. As soon as there was a whistle from the commander, they would stand in a formation with their backpacks. Some of the people might skip the daily ablutions and come straight to the formation on the commander's whistle. They cannot do this every time as they would be criticized for it if they did so.

Squad members march in formation. In the front, there are pilot-1 and pilot-2 followed by deputy commander, squad member, commander and then the other squad members. In the rear, there are the two back pilots. The first three members should be ever ready to handle any firing they may encounter. A special mention must be made of the pilot-1. Only those who are totally familiar with the forest and would not be rattled on encountering the police are made pilot-1. They are capable of leading the squad even in pitch darkness. Even if there were no roads / trails or there were dangerous beasts or even the police, they could lead the squad following the commander's cautions. Sometimes, in the dark, the pilot-1 might even fall into a pit. Their main job is to move forward bravely. They are like the head of the formation.

Ramdev, Kosi and Budral came back to the camp in haste. The District committee member, Sukhdev was also with the squad. Ramdev told Sukhdev about the situation in the village. 'Oh, is it? Let us then eat and leave. Do we have provisions?' asked Sukhdev.

'We do,' said Ramdev.

'Okay. Cook them. The villagers may delay bringing rice. We had better leave as early as possible. Do not speak about the sacred thread wearers in the meeting,' said Sukhdev. 'Call

all the squad members and ask them to be alert,' he cautioned Ramdev.

'Situation in the village is not good. They may even attack us. So, everyone had better be alert,' said Ramdev, having gathered the squad together.

'It may be good to inform the sentry,' said Kosi.

'True,' said Sukhdev and added 'Keep another sentry towards the village.'

'If the situation is bad, why don't we leave immediately?' asked Vinod, a squad member.

'We can. However, it is possible that the villagers will think we left because we were frightened. That is dangerous. We need to show them that the squad is not frightened of threats. So, let us eat, conduct the meeting and then go,' said Sukhdev.

'Will they dare to attack the squad?' asked Kosi unbelievingly.

'It depends on the situation,' said Sukhdev.

Mangdu, who was on cooking duty, started making dal and rice. While they were expecting the villagers to come late, they came while it was still light and brought the rice. But they also came armed with bow and arrows, axes etc. and came marching in a line. Not a single woman had come. The squad became alert. Ramdev went forward and wished them *Lal Salaam* (Red salute). They also wished everyone a red salute and sat down with Ramdev.

Ramdev sat down, chatting with them but was constantly observing them. Kosi also chatted with them. However, she still had not got the hang of their dialect since she had come to the Kondagav squad only recently from south Bastar. The Gondi language differs a lot between North and South Bastar. In the meantime, the food was ready. Instead of everyone sitting down to the meal together, they ate in batches.

Ramdev talked about the harassment faced by the Adivasis from the forest officials before the squad came into the area. The villagers seemed ready to attack if any questions were raised about the sacred thread. Since no mention was made of it, they listened to the meeting. Kosi observed them keenly. But she couldn't find any change in their facial expressions. She wasn't sure about the impact that the meeting made on them. After the meeting, the squad shook hands with the villagers, wished them a red salute and left.

Into the dense forest and the adivasi areas, some people had made an entry saying they were *Baba*'s disciples. They had meetings with the adivasis. Normally, the adivasis do not trust outsiders easily. They had not believed the comrades who entered the Dandakaranya in the 1980s. They believed that they perform black magic, kidnap women etc. They wondered how anyone could visit so many places unless they had magic; they thought that they disappear from one village and apparate in another, that they can fly, that they drink the liquor of their *gorga*[2] trees and so on. They would attend the meetings called by the squad, listen and go away never trusting them. The Adivasis faced a major problem with forest guards and officers in those days. These personnel were so authoritarian and arbitrary that they would fine the Adivasis for even plucking a leaf from a tree or for using parts of a tree to construct a new hut. They would molest the Adivasi women who went to the forest to cut and collect the stacks of cut bamboo. Life under the forest guards and officials became hell for the Adivasis. It was in such circumstances that the squad killed a particularly cruel forest official. That was when the Adivasis started to trust the squad and accepted them as one of their own.

The adivasis did not trust the disciples of *Baba* also. However, the disciples succeeded in converting the *Vadde* (the priest) and a few others into their ways. In the village, what the priest said was the law. The priest used to pretend he understood natural phenomena that did not make sense to them and that would frighten them. If someone had a fever, he would tie a thread and recite some *mantras*. He would frighten people by talking about God. He would control the whole village in this manner. He was the only person who did not do physical labor in the adivasi villages. He would also possess more land and better land than the others. However, he was more interested in controlling the village than accumulating more wealth. His permission was necessary for celebrating festivals or to start any important tasks. Typically, an Adivasi woman is kept in isolation during her menstrual cycle and not supposed to be seen by the men, especially the Priest. If the priest encountered such a woman he would impose a fine. After the squad came into the life of the adivasis, the priest lost his control over the village. The priests bowed down as they had no choice.

The disciples took the priest and a few others to the *ashram*[3] of *Baba*. The adivasis who had never gone beyond the small market town near their village, were amazed to see acres of land under cultivation and the large houses. The adivasis were treated with great respect and given a lot of importance in the *ashram*. The disciples gave them a tour of the tilled lands. 'You can also till the land in this fashion. Stay in the *ashram* for a few days. We will teach you how to farm,' they said. They had the adivasis stay for about 10-15 days and then brought them back to their villages. The priest and others shared everything they saw and learned with the villagers. They said that they were treated very well, were given very good food, that the *ashram* people do not eat meat at all, that their farms are large and they are able to grow large quantities of crops and that the Gods there are very different. Everyone listened to them with amazement.

Adivasis are organised into clans and they have clan Gods. Surnames such as Madavi, Naitam are derived from the clans. There are Gods of two clans, three, five and seven clans. They have male Gods such as Budal Penu, Lingo Penu and female Gods like Tallur Muthe. The idols of these Gods are made with wood. Adivasis within the same clan cannot marry each other.

The disciples of the *Baba* returned after 10-15 days. The priest received them with a lot of affection. The disciples took the same set of people who had gone before back to the *ashram*.

There, the adivasis got up early in the morning like the others and had a bath with soap in the bathrooms, did *surya namaskar*[4], meditation and *puja*[5] of the Gods. Then, they would have breakfast, a tour of the farms, lunch and a nap in the afternoon. After that, they would have lectures on agricultural methods and how to increase yield in their own villages. In the evening, there would be tea and snacks followed by *bhajan*[6] and cultural programs. Then, there would be lectures on religion, dinner and then they would retire for the night to their rooms. They found all of this very interesting. They had never known life of this sort, with the tremendous variety of food and activities that were foreign to them. After a few days, they were dropped back in their villages.

The next time, the disciples returned after a week. They held a meeting in the village. They preached that eating meat and drinking alcohol angered the Gods and they should refrain from them. They asked the adivasis to pray to God daily. They urged those who had gone to the *ashram* to not mingle with the adivasis who eat meat or drink alcohol, and that those people were impure and therefore they should not be touched. If they are touched, then these people would also become impure. They extolled the virtues of Rama and the beauty of the *Bhagavad Gita*[8].

Then they asked who would accompany them back to the *ashram*. In addition to the earlier five, another five volunteered and these ten people accompanied them happily. Most of the people had only come to the meeting curious to see those who had gone to the *ashram* and come back.

The disciples came every ten or fifteen days and had meetings with the adivasis. Each time they would recruit some new people, in addition to the old members. They would teach them new methods of farming as well as the Hindu rituals of worship. Thus, they 'purified' them.

The adivasis usually grow rice in the slopes barricaded by ridges where water would accumulate (aka terrace cultivation) or on flat lands. They would not remove the weeds on a regular basis. They would grow foxtail millet in shifting cultivation. They would cut down trees of the forest and set fire to them once they were dry. They would sow foxtail millet as soon as it rained. A lot of weeds would sprout along with the foxtail millet. They would reap the foxtail millet searching for these plants amongst the weeds. They would cultivate the land for 4-5 years until the fertility of the soil goes down. Then, they would cut down the forest in another location and cultivate that land. The forest would regenerate in the old land. They relied only on the rains for their cultivation. They did not know about digging wells.

There are forest fires every year. They know that this is natural and do not panic about it. All the dry leaves that have been shed, burn away in these fires and sometimes some branches burn too. However, the trees later develop new shoots from the burnt parts too when it rains. If there are no fires, it is possible that the leaves rot and lead to a miasma.

The adivasis grow more millets and less rice. Since they do not remove weeds and are entirely dependent on rains, the yield is not abundant. They also raise mustard. When Kosi was new to the forest, she was thrilled to see the carpet of bright yellow flowers on the green mustard plants and that view continued to fill her with wonder every time she saw it.

The lifestyle of the adivasis who had stayed for months in the *ashram* changed altogether. They kept their homes very clean. They started having images of Shiva, Krishna and Rama (Hindu Gods) in their homes. They would pray every day. They would wear beads (*rudraksha*[8]) around their neck and tie saffron threads around their wrist and wear jackets. They changed their cultivation methods. They stopped eating meat and drinking alcohol.

Of two biological brothers, the younger who went to the *ashram* became a sacred thread wearer. In one sense, he became a 'brahmin'. Those who did not go to the *ashram* and ate meat and drank alcohol became 'untouchables'. The 'brahmin' brother did not want his elder brother to visit his home. If the elder brother did, he would clean his house with turmeric water. This would lead to fights among them. It took more than 4-5 years for these changes to take place in the adivasis. The disciples of Baba organised the adivasis with patience.

Slowly, however, the number of those who went to the *ashram* came down. Those who decided that they would continue to live with their own traditions refused to go to the *ashram*. The disciples started attacking the adivasis who would not listen to them. They were aided by the sacred thread wearing adivasis. Together they broke the breweries where mahua liquor was made. They beat up those who tried to stop it. They decreed that nobody should eat meat. The adivasis were distressed by the turn of events.

When the squad went to the village, the villagers told them about the attacks on them. They lamented that their own brothers were not allowing them into their homes, not touching them, not celebrating their own festivals, that they were worshiping different Gods and constructing temples for them. They bemoaned that just when they were happy to be rid of the harassment by the forest officials, the disciples of the Baba took over. Ramdev, who had become a commander recently, discussed this immediately with Squad Area Committee (SAC) members. Based on the resolution passed in the SAC, the squad had demolished the *Shivaling*.

The sacred thread wearers became vengeful due to this incident. They felt more hurt by the destruction of the Shivaling than if they had been thrashed. In addition, the disciples added to the sense of hurt. All this history is what led them to come to the squad armed with weapons.

The squad left for another village. However, everyone was thinking about the villagers coming to meet them with weapons. They started wondering as to how the situation could be returned to normal. Sukhdev was wondering how to eliminate the bitterness created between the villagers by the disciples.

Religion is a very fundamental belief in most people. Kosi felt that the squad should not have destroyed the temple.

Another fifteen days passed. Mahesh, who was a member of the State Committee, came to spend a few days with the squad. It was two months since the SAC meeting had happened. So, they camped for two days to conduct the meeting. In the SAC meeting, Ramdev, Kosi, Mangdu, Nirmala and Subhash participated. They discussed the activities taken up by the squad in these two months. They discussed the problems brought to them by the villagers and also about the mistakes committed by the squad. They also discussed the problems of the squad members and went through the process of criticism and self-criticism. In the process, they discussed this incident too.

'You should educate them that their belief is wrong. You cannot change their belief by blowing up the *Shivaling*, right? If we look at it objectively, those who went to the *ashram* learned some good things such as how to improve their farming techniques and increase the yield. We could not stop them from drinking alcohol but in the name of God, the disciples succeeded in it,' said Mahesh on listening to the entire story.

'Does that mean that the disciples are good?' asked Ramdev sharply.

'Good done by anyone is good, isn't it?' said Kosi.

'They attacked the adivasis. That is why we had to blow up the *Shivaling*,' justified Subhash.

'Do not underestimate the disciples,' said Ramdev implying that Kosi did not know enough of the local conditions. He was annoyed with her and felt that she did not know the reality of the adivasi lives as she had come only recently into the forest. She was simply parroting the principles she has read in the books.

'When a change for the good is brought about, regardless of how it has come about, we should accept it. Of course, we should also analyze the aim behind the change. We should understand their methods. Revolutionaries should be even more sincere in this,' said Mahesh guessing what was going on in Ramdev's mind.

Kosi agreed with Mahesh. Sukhdev sat listening to the discussion.

Mahesh continued 'At the same time, it is wrong to stop them from eating meat. It is important for health, especially for people like adivasis who have to do heavy physical labor. Similarly, drinking alcohol is not good but if somebody attacks others for drinking, that is not to be tolerated. We should educate them that the sacred thread wearers behaving like Brahmins and treating those who do not wear them as untouchables is wrong. We should tell the sacred thread wearers that some of the things they are doing are good and other behavior is bad; that they should not shun those who do not wear the sacred thread; that they should celebrate their own festivals along with the new Gods they have learned to worship such as Shiva, Rama and Krishna.'

'The sacred thread wearers are refusing to participate in adivasi festivals saying that meat is served in the festivals,' said Ramdev.

'We can tell them that each group can cook their own food but celebrate the festival together,' said Kosi. Ramdev glared at Kosi as he felt she did not understand the situation at all.

'I think Kosi is right. Even if they cook separately, they can celebrate the festival together,' said Mahesh.

'We claim there are neither Gods nor Ghosts. Are we now encouraging them to celebrate festivals?' asked Subhash in surprise.

'It is indeed surprising that a party which claims there are no Gods or Ghosts should ask that people celebrate festivals. Since even the smallest criticism of their Gods can lead to rebellion by the sacred thread wearers, there may be no other way to convince them,' thought Kosi.

'Let us not insult their festivals and hurt their sentiments. These festivals are part of their culture. When they do no harm, there is no need to destroy them. There is nothing wrong in making use of their belief in Gods to do them good,' said Mahesh. Then, he continued saying 'Print a pamphlet with all these details. Distribute them in those villages which have seen large scale conversions. Do not forget to print that blowing up the *Shivaling* was a mistake from our side.'

Sukhdev started the meeting by greeting the adivasis in their own language. 'Blowing up the *Shivaling* was a mistake from our side. We should not have done it. Please forgive us,' he said in self-criticism on behalf of the squad.

'Oh, that is okay,' muttered the sacred thread wearers uncomfortably. They were surprised by the fact that the squad was willing to admit its mistake. They had come to the meeting because the comrades had called but they were not really interested. However, due to Sukhdev's opening, they started listening keenly.

'You went to the *ashram* and came back having learned some good things such as how to improve your agricultural methods. You have increased your yield. You should also teach others these methods.' They agreed happily. 'Similarly, the others should learn these methods from them. Otherwise, there will not be enough food for everyone in the future. What do you say?'

'We are okay but these people do not want to touch us. If we go to their homes, they tell us not to visit them. Or, they clean their homes with turmeric water,' said one of the adivasi women. In the meeting, those who had gone to the *ashram* and their families sat on one side while the other adivasis sat on the other side.

'Is it right to shun your own families just because you have started wearing the sacred thread? No God says that you should not touch other human beings. If any God says so, then he is no God! Are the adivasi Gods who treated all of you equally good or Rama and Krishna who are separating you? What do you say?' said Sukhdev.

There was pin drop silence. Earlier, such sentences would have led to resentment in the thread wearers. However, due to the self-criticism of the squad, their anger had subsided. That's why they listened to Sukhdev with open minds and started thinking about what he said.

Sukdev continued after observing them. 'Please remember how closely all of you used to live together earlier. How happy all of you were. Do you see that now when you see your own biological brother you shrink from him? Brothers and sisters, we are all people who live by doing physical labour. They will try to separate us in many ways. Learn good stuff from the disciples. Ignore those which are not good. You should live together as in the past. What do you say?'

'They are not clean,' said one thread wearer.

'Then teach them how to be clean. Keeping them apart is not the solution. Our adivasi brothers and sisters also bathe every day except that they do not use soap. Teach them other ways of being clean that you have learned. What do you say?' Kosi hinted to Sukhdev regarding alcohol since he had not touched upon it.

'Our adivasi brothers should learn from the thread wearers how to stop drinking alcohol. You people say that you are willing to leave your wife but not your *gorga* liquor, right? How come your own brothers have been able to give up on the mahua liquor, *gorga* liquor, and are doing fine?' asked Sukhdev addressing the adivasis. The thread wearers' faces lit up on hearing his words. The adivasis agreed sheepishly. 'Even if you cannot give up altogether at once, try to reduce the consumption slowly. If you drink alcohol, you will feel sleepy and go to sleep. So, you do not spend enough time on farming. Only if you stop drinking alcohol will you be able to do good farming. Learn from the thread wearers good methods of farming.'

'You thread wearers should celebrate the adivasi festivals along with the new festivals. If you only worship the new Gods and not the adivasi Gods who have been worshiped for generations, they also can get angry, right? The adivasi Gods who treat everyone equally are really good. What do you say? Will you celebrate your traditional festivals?'

'What you say is true. We will celebrate the festivals but we do not eat meat, right?'

'You cook your own vegetarian food and they will cook their non-vegetarian food. But, all of you should celebrate together. We should not give up the good in our traditions. What do you say?'

The thread wearers agreed wholeheartedly. When the same was asked of the rest of the villagers, they also agreed happily.

The meeting was over. It was past midnight. The villagers started returning to their village. Those of the squad who had not eaten sat down to eat. Others who were done started packing the back packs. Mahesh observed the villagers keenly through this entire meeting. He thought the *Baba*'s disciples may come again and try to indoctrinate them but he hoped the adivasis would not believe everything they say as they did in the past. In any case, this was also a small victory. Kosi wondered if this was how the caste system might have originated. Ramdev felt relieved on seeing the response of the villagers and happy on having learned something new. He said 'It is very late. Get ready fast'.

Translation of 'Adivaseelu-Antaranithanam'. (First published in Kolimi online Magazine-June 2019)

Translated by P. Anupama

Notes:
1. Shivaling: Stone carved in the shape of phallus as a symbol of the God Shiva
2. Gorga: A tree (FishTail Palm) from which toddy is collected and fermented
3. Ashram: hermitage
4. Surya Namaskar: sun salutation, yoga practice of paying respects to Sun
5. Puja: worship
6. Bhajan: hymn
7. Bhagavad Gita: Hindu scripture, dated to the second or first century BCE which forms part of the epic poem Mahabharata
8. Rudraksha: spiritual beads associated with the Hindu deity Shiva and are commonly worn for protection and for chanting mantras

Famine Raid

Myna

I t was the winter season. Due to the biting cold, people in the village at the foothills didn't venture out. Instead, they sat talking around the fire in their homes. It would warm up only when the Sun was fairly high in the sky. The conversation in all the houses was around the same issue – the produce from the farms this year was very low, how were they going to survive? It was becoming difficult to find even water and fodder for the cattle. At such a time, the village committee president Kosal came shivering to Jogi's house.

'Jogi! hey Jogi! What are you doing?' Kosal called out.

'Here, I am sitting by the fire. It was too cold, so I didn't feel like moving away from the fire. It feels like it is colder than usual today. So tell me, why did you come?' Jogi said and pushed a small piece of wood to Kosal to sit near the fire.

Kosal sat near the fire and asked Jogi's father Maasal to give him some tobacco. He put the tobacco in his mouth and said, 'Let's have a committee meeting today, Jogi. I sent a message to Budral and Gangi yesterday night. I came to know that you went to the Range Committee[1] meeting, so I didn't come here last night. Bring Mangudu with you. I will go to the fields and collect whatever grass is there and then come to the meeting.'

'All right, we will come now. But don't spend too much time in the fields and be late for the meeting,' Jogi said.

'After asking all of you to come, why will I be late? I'll come immediately.' Saying so, Kosal warmed his hands and feet near the fire and left.

The five village committee members met in *ketul*[2]. There were two women and three men among them. Except for the president Kosal who was older than the others, the rest of them were 25 to 28 years old. They were all members of the Party in the village, which is why they reached the meeting place in secrecy. Apart from being a village committee member, Jogi was also the president of the Range committee of KAMS[3].

Kosal spit out the tobacco in his mouth and started the meeting.

'Comrades! What is the situation in our village? Are there any new problems that we need to solve? What are people saying about the famine situation? Let's talk primarily about the famine today. Jogi went to the range committee meeting yesterday. If they had made any decisions about the famine situation in that meeting, let's also discuss them,' he said looking around at each of them.

'Those who have ponds in their fields could get some yield this year, but the rest of them couldn't get anything,' Budral said.

'The small and large ponds in our village are not more than ten. The remaining 50 families are looking at scarcity,' Mangudu said.

'As per my rough estimate, there may be 25 to 30 families among the fifty, who may have a yield that is just about sufficient for seeds for the next planting season' Gangi said.

'It is not just our village but the entire Bastar region is reeling under famine. During the squad's last visit, they told us in detail about the famine situation and how to deal with it. In the reports presented by the RCMs (range committee members) in the range committee meeting, they talked about villages like Nimmalgudem where there isn't a single field which yielded any produce. Our village is in a better condition thanks to some of the ponds we have. Also, thanks to the big lake we built with collective effort, there is no water scarcity for us or our cattle,' Jogi said.

'What Jogi said is true that we don't have a water problem in our village. We also took control of two big ponds belonging to the village head. As we did collective farming this year, we don't have any problem with seeds either. We can provide seeds to people from our village,' Kosal said.

'Ok, we will give seeds but the crop will not be ready for months. We cannot even collect the Mahua flowers for another four months at least. In the meanwhile, what will people live on? We need to think about that,' Budral said.

Mangudu came out of his thoughts and said, 'That's right, we need to think about not only these four months but even after sowing the seeds, the months of July, August and September are typically when we see real famine. We must distribute the famine rations sent by the Party taking into consideration all these things.'

'That's why we met today so that we may discuss all these things,' said Gangi.

'Our Party promised six quintals of rice to our village to tide over the famine. We have to distribute it amongst the poorest families in the village. While sustaining themselves on the famine rations, if those families carry on agricultural activities in their fields, they should be able to make some profits by raising rain fed crops. Let's give 50 kilos of rice for 16 days to a family of five. Apart from this, we all have to manage by gathering forest produce such as mahua flowers, gum etc and by doing daily wage work for Andhra farmers,' said Kosal.

'Kosal, isn't it better to ask them to repair the broken embankments of lakes, lay bunds between the fields and do leveling of the land in preparation for sowing?' asked Budral.

'Well, that's what I meant by the agricultural activities to be carried on by farmers and their families,' said Kosal.

Jogi intervened in their conversation saying 'Currently, we can give famine ration to some families only. From where will the Party get additional food grains to satisfy all? We had a discussion in the range committee meeting that it is good to get food grains by raiding the landlords' houses. Either the landlords give willingly or we take from them forcibly by raiding their granaries. So, the range committee laid out plans for famine raids. Let's discuss this with the people and take their opinion. We thought we should give people the entire amount of grain that they manage to take in the raid.'

'Isn't it theft if we get things belonging to others? In the past, if anyone did this, didn't we conduct people's court and make them return those things to the owners? Similarly, in the past when our people from Bastar used to bring red chillies from Andhra, didn't the range committees stop them from doing that because of the wisdom imparted to us by the Party?' Budral asked doubtfully.

'We also discussed this aspect in the range committee. What I understood after the discussion is this – our people from Bastar used to go to Andhra for wage labour and continue to do so to this day. The landlords there give very low wages to our people and sometimes, they make us do the work but don't pay wages for it. There are many such instances. Many of them became rich by exploiting our labour. So, we concluded that we will conduct famine raids only on such people and not touch the middle and poor peasants. Let's discuss if any of you have any disagreements with this,' Jogi said.

'There is no disagreement with it. We are going to conduct famine raids only on landlords and not on poor peasants. It is not wrong to act from a class perspective. We are only getting back the fruits of our labour, and that is not theft. The real robbers are the landlords, political leaders and the imperialists. We must also participate in the famine raids,' said Kosal.

All of them agreed that famine raids cannot be seen as robbery and they aren't wrong when people are dying of hunger due to famine. On reaching that conclusion, they looked at one another with smiles on their faces.

'Is there anything else to discuss?' Gangi asked Jogi.

'Yes, do you remember the thing I told you earlier about confiscating the money from wood smugglers? That money and the money from the fines came to about 25000 rupees. The committee passed a resolution to use that money also to buy food grains for villages reeling under severe famine. Our village may get two quintals out of those,' said Jogi.

'All right, let's call for a village meeting and tell the people about all the things we discussed now. We'll also explain to them why we should participate in the famine raids. What do you say comrades?' Kosal asked.

'Sure. Let's also conclude about how many families we shall support with famine rations so that they can also start their agricultural activities in parallel,' Mangudu said.

'Let's start with thirteen families. When we get additional grains, we can give them to other families. Do you agree, comrades?' Kosal asked. All of them agreed.

'So comrade Kosal, you call for a village meeting and explain all the things we discussed to the people in the village. Our squad sent a message yesterday that they will send the food grains with the organisation from our neighbouring village. So, we can start the distribution as soon as we get them. I have to go to the RCMs (range committee member) meeting this evening. I will take two young women along with me. When I come back, I will present a report on the meeting. If there are any other things to discuss, you go ahead. I shall leave now, otherwise I will be late,' Jogi said and took permission to leave.

'All right, you go ahead. We'll discuss a couple of more things and conduct the village meeting in the night,' said Kosal.

A four-member team of Jogi, Lacchu, Budral and Rame went on a recce for the famine raid. They split into two teams – two of them became agricultural labourers harvesting rice for the landlord, in order to understand his routine; while the other two surveyed the incoming and outgoing routes for the raid and where to place the sentries etc. Both teams completed their recce in 2 to 3 days and returned to provide a report to the RCMs. The RCMs discussed all the points they heard, and decided that they would inform people the next day and conduct the famine raid the day after. They assigned the job of informing different villages to different people and split up.

Hundreds of people joined the famine raid. One person was

made responsible for each batch of 30 people. They decided to place three sentries holding *bharmars* and bombs to the right of the landlord's house. Jogi had the primary responsibility for the entire raid. Then the march of the people for the raid began – like ants marching in lines to get to their food, overpowering even a mighty snake in the process.

The sentries were at the front of the march followed by Jogi and behind Jogi were batch after batch of people totalling around 250. Jogi's heart beat faster as she anxiously wondered if she could control so many people and if she could successfully conduct her first such raid without unnecessary violence. She looked back to check if everyone was coming in an orderly fashion.

As soon as they reached the road, the sentries left to take up their position. Jogi increased her pace towards the landlord's house and the people followed suit. As soon as they approached the landlord's house, Jogi raised her voice and ordered the landlord to open the doors. As soon as the doors were opened, people rushed into the house and started filling sacks with the mounds of grains in the house.

A team of people coordinating the entire operation herded the landlord's family into a room and told them firmly, 'we aren't going to harm you. We are all victims of famine, that's why we are taking the grains. We came on a famine raid only to satisfy our hunger, not to kill you or steal any of your things.'

The landlord's family stayed silent after that. The people filled up 100 sacks with food grains and left the landlord's house one after the other. They waited near the road until Jogi and her batch came and asked them to start moving. All of them crossed the road and started walking towards the forest at a rapid pace. Jogi gave caution to the sentries to join them. But around the same time, a tractor came on the road with a load of rice and the sentries were busy trying to divert the route of the tractor into the forest. When the sentries didn't respond, Jogi was worried if the Police had come. She asked two members from her batch to run and see what's happening. They went running and came back and reported the matter to her.

In the meanwhile, the police who were doing night patrolling realized that something was going on. They got frightened and started firing. The sentries returned the fire using their *bharmars* and started retreating. In the process, the sentry in-charge's *bharmar* got stuck in the fence near the road. As the firing continued, he went down into a crawling position and retreated leaving behind his weapon.

Jogi went into shock momentarily as soon as she heard the sound of firing. She couldn't breathe for a second and then her heart started beating rapidly. 'What happened? The sentries were quite alert, then where did the police come from and how did the sentries not see them?' she wondered. She called Budral from her team and said, 'Go there and bring a sentry, I will wait for you near that tamarind tree.' Budral moved swiftly towards the position of the sentries using the houses as covers but he couldn't find anyone there. He went cautiously towards the road looking to his left and right. There he saw a figure of one of the sentries and called out 'who is it?' 'It is me, Lacchal,' said that figure and came towards Budral.

'Oh, it is you Lacchu *dada*! Where are the others?' asked Budral looking around for the others.

'They left already. As the police were firing, we went down into a crawling position and retreated, so we got late. Let's go,' Lacchu said.

Both of them went to the tree where Jogi was waiting. As soon as they reached her, she literally rained questions on them out of anxiety 'did all our people return? Nothing happened to anyone, right? I hope our sentries came back safely! Is anyone left behind?'

Lacchu understood Jogi's anxiety and told her reassuringly 'Nothing happened to anyone, we are all fine. We are all here, so let's go.'

'Then where is your weapon?' Jogi asked. Lacchu was embarrassed. 'I will tell you later. People are waiting for us. If we are late, it will become daylight,' he said and started walking towards the waiting people.

Jogi and Budral followed him. After walking some distance, they reached the people waiting for them. Then all the batches of people headed to the place previously identified as the meeting point. The people put down the heavy sacks of grains from their heads, gave the sentries' quota of grains to them and then put the sacks back on their heads.

The dawn was breaking in the East and Jogi addressed the people along with other RCMs.

'Comrades! We completed the famine raid successfully. The patrolling police fired on the sentries. When our sentries returned the fire, the police ran away. One of the policemen fired three times but none of our people got hurt and all of us came back safely. If the police come raiding on our villages tomorrow, let us resist them together! The in-charges of each village take the people back to their respective villages' Jogi said. Lacchu couldn't lift his head with embarrassment at having left his weapon.

Budral started giving slogans:

'Let's continue the famine raids!

Let's defeat the police repression!

Let's win the new democratic revolution!'

People responded to the slogans by giving chorus with raised fists as they marched forward to their villages with sacks of grains on their heads.

(On the basis of a report regarding a famine raid in south Bastar .... Dedicated to the people carrying out such famine raids due to sheer hunger ....)

Translation of 'Karuvu Dadi'. (First published in *Porumahila*, November 2002 – March 2003)

Translated by P. Aravinda

Notes:

1. Range Committee: The forest area is divided into several divisions and in turn a division is divided into several ranges by the forest department of India. A Range committee is formed at a Range level.
2. Ketul: field

People are the Bulwark
Chada Vijayalakshmi

B hagya lived in a small village. There was a big village nearby that was a stronghold of the Party that she worked for, where she used to go to buy various things including medicines. People from another ten villages also go there regularly for their day to day needs.

One day comrade Bhagya fell sick with diarrhoea. She always kept medicines for such common ailments. She even gave tablets to people in emergencies. She already took a tablet for it two times and she didn't have any more of those. Initially the medicine seemed to have worked but now the loose motions started again. She became weak, her energy fast depleting. She was in a dilemma whether to send someone to the doctor and get medicines or go herself. What if she didn't get better with the medicines given by the doctor, what if her situation deteriorates further...! Wouldn't it be better to go personally so that the doctor could give her saline if needed? She finally gathered some energy and decided to go.

The only way to go to that village was on foot. She got up and slowly started her journey. In between, she stopped to attend to nature calls and took rest when she felt too tired to walk; she finally managed to reach the doctor's house (which was also his clinic). The doors of the house were closed. By then, she was totally exhausted, unable to take another step. She collapsed on the bench in the front veranda and immediately dozed off. When she woke up after around 15 minutes, she heard someone groaning in pain. She got up slowly and knocked on the door very carefully so as not to disturb everyone. Immediately the groaning stopped, but no one came to open the door.

Actually there was an emergency inside, unknown to her. A comrade accidently got wounded by a gunshot in the thigh leading to a serious injury. The village in which the doctor lived was close to the forest. Since it was a Party stronghold, the squad brought him there. Hearing the knock on the door they suspected it might be the police and became tense.

'Comrades... take the patient inside the room. I will see who it is,' Doctor Satyam told them. As soon as they took the patient inside, he bolted the door of that room from outside. Though he tried to stay calm he was a little scared. He slowly went to the main door and opened it. He saw Bhagya lying on a bench in the veranda. Hearing the sound she slowly turned her face towards the door.

The doctor was relieved to see her instead of the police. 'Oh...is it you, Bhagya? I thought the police had come. That is why I didn't open the door immediately. No one else is there, right?' He checked carefully and closed the door as soon as she stepped in. Pointing to a chair he told her to sit and pulled another chair for himself.

'Why are you looking so weak Bhagya? Is something wrong?' the doctor asked her. Bhagya told him about her problem.

The squad members who were listening to the conversation also breathed a sigh of relief upon knowing that it was not the police but some outpatient who came to see the doctor. Doctor at least is not exposed for now, they thought.

'Doctor... a few minutes back I heard someone groaning in pain. Who is that patient? What happened to that person?' Bhagya asked the doctor.

'Our squad members are here,' the doctor said in a low voice and explained about the injury.

'You lie down on this sofa and take a rest. I will go inside and tell them about your arrival.' He went inside.

'Who is it, Doctor?' asked Commander Radhakka. The doctor told her about Bhagya.

Another comrade Jyothakka, who was also there, said immediately 'Oh...Bhagyakka! What happened to her? Why did she come?' Even before the doctor explained why Bhagya had come, many worrying thoughts passed through her head. The Doctor's explanation put her at ease.

Radhakka came out and took Bhagya inside. Bhagya felt she got half her strength back upon seeing familiar faces. They greeted one another with *Lal Salaam*. Bhagya was not a full time Party worker at that time. But she used to go often to meet her partner, who is a whole-timer. So she was familiar with all of them.

'Who is injured, Radhakka?' Bhagya asked.

'It is Suresh,' Radhakka said.

'Suresh! How did it happen?' Bhagya asked in anguish.

Just then someone knocked on the door. The entire squad once again went back into the room silently.

The doctor was clearly aghast. Slowly he went and opened the door. In front of him was a villager very familiar to him.

'Ramaswamy... how come you are here?' Before the doctor could finish the sentence the visitor said 'police have come to the village, Doctor. Mallesh told me to alert you. Where are the squad members?' Mallesh was the leader of the *Sangam* and the *Sangam* knew about the squad's presence in the village because they were the ones who stood sentry for them.

Hearing this, Radhakka came out and asked anxiously 'What is happening?'

'All of you should immediately get away from here. The entire village is surrounded by policemen. Looks like all of you are exposed,' he said.

Radhakka wondered how they could escape safely from the village.

Ramaswamy read her thoughts and said 'Child... I will give you some advice. Listen and do as I say. Only then can all of you escape safely.' Radhakka agreed and passed on the information to other members. They too agreed, but wondered how to go out in uniform in these circumstances.

Ramaswamy gave them a plan. 'My brother and I have some cattle and goats. You people immediately change into civil dress and take the herd out posing as its herders.' After this he hurriedly left the place.

'But what about the guns and the wounded Suresh?' thought Radhakka. She told Bhagya to hide the guns somewhere and entrusted the responsibility of Suresh to the doctor. Squad members did exactly as Ramaswamy told them and left the place without anyone suspecting them.

'Bhagya... What shall we do now? Have you thought about something?' Satyam, the Doctor, asked.

'First, let's put these guns in a bundle and hide them. Then shift *Anna* into the delivery patient's room. If the police come, we will tell them that there is a delivery patient inside. They may not go in.'

She quickly went to see the pregnant patient. It was Lakshmi. She and Bhagya were from the same village.

'Bhagya... What brought you here?' Lakshmi asked in surprise.

'Lakshmi... I have something important to tell you. I need your help badly. It is very urgent.'

Tell me.'

'The Police have come to the village. Our comrade is injured. He is here right now. He is in no situation to walk. Only you can save him. You are our saviour now. There is only one way to keep him alive. If we can hide him in this room till the police go away, we can save him. It looks like his presence here is exposed. Chances are that the police would come here. Hopefully they might not come into this room if they know there is a delivery patient inside. So shall I bring him here, Lakshmi?' Bhagya asked.

'What are you saying Bhagya? You are also a woman. How can you ask me to keep a man in my room when I am undergoing labour pains?' said Lakshmi.

'Please, Lakshmi... I beg you to help him. We should somehow save our *anna*. I will fall at your feet" pleaded Bhagya. She held Lakshmi's hand tightly and kept on pleading. "*Anna* will not look at you. He will turn the other side and sleep. When the police come, please make noises pretending you are having labour pains,' Bhagya tried her best to convince her.

When Lakshmi finally agreed, Bhagya immediately took Suresh inside and made him lie down. She breathed a sigh of relief and went to the Doctor to discuss hiding the guns.

'What happened, Doctor? You are looking very dejected,' asked Bhagya.

'I am feeling very scared and unable to think of anything,' said the Doctor.

'When I went to the lavatory, I saw a trench. I think it is meant for a septic tank but it's yet to be finished. Let's store the guns in that,' said Bhagya.

'Okay, let's do as you say. I will be on guard; you do the rest,' said the doctor. Bhagya quickly tied the guns into a bundle and put it inside the septic tank.

Just when she finished covering it with a lid she heard Sub Inspector (S.I)'s voice from behind enquiring what she was doing there.

'Nothing sir... I have come to use the lavatory.' Without further conversation, she quickly went inside.

The Sub Inspector (S.I.) called the doctor and asked about the number of patients inside.

'Only one, a delivery case,' the Doctor replied.

'Can I go inside and see?' asked the S.I.

'A woman is having labour pains. How can you go inside, Sir' said the Doctor.

'Sir, if you agree I will go and see.' Bhagya offered to help the S.I.

'If you don't tell me the truth, you will face the consequences,' threatened the S.I.

Bhagya went inside to check.

'Lakshmi... please pretend to have labour pains. Make loud

noises. The S.I. has come. He is watching,' Bhagya fell on Lakshmi's feet again and begged her.

Soon after, Lakshmi's cries could be heard.

'Okay... okay...' said the S.I. and went out.

As soon as the S.I. left, Bhagya once again went inside and gave both of them water to drink. She told Lakshmi not to worry; she would definitely have a safe delivery.

Meanwhile the S.I. came back to find out how much more time there was for the delivery.

'It may take another one or two hours, Sir,' said the Doctor.

Along with the S.I. a few more policemen came inside; they increased the fan speed and sat down. The rest of the police were outside keeping a watch. Bhagya hoped for an interruption in the power supply. That is exactly what happened, the power went off.[1]

Bhagya felt very happy and reassured.

The S.I. was fat and looked like a hefty buffalo. He couldn't tolerate the heat there without a fan, so he got up to leave but stopped again. He seemed to be in a dilemma whether to go in and check the patient or leave.

Suddenly loud cries came from the room. Lakshmi delivered the baby. The child was crying at the top of his voice.

Muttering 'Yes, yes' the S.I. went out.

Afterwards Bhagya went inside and told Lakshmi, 'I am hugely indebted to you. Along with the baby, you gave life to *anna* too. I cannot repay your kindness. You are very kind-hearted.'

Later, she shifted Suresh to another room and made him eat a little rice. He asked her also to eat a few bites.

'*Akka...* hope the guns are safe.' Suresh was anxious about them.

'Yes. They are safely hidden,' Bhagya said.

'Where did you get such courage? If you were not there, I wouldn't have been able to do anything. They might have caught me,' the Doctor told Bhagya.

'Why, Doctor; if we stay courageous and think anything is

possible. Now, I will take your leave and go home doctor,' said Bhagya.

'Wait, Bhagya, I will give you some medicine. Someone will drop you on a vehicle. I will arrange it,' the doctor said.

'There is no need, Doctor, I will go on foot. Now my health is better. Until our people come back, please keep the guns safe.'

All the way back home, Bhagya felt a great happiness in her heart.

That night, the comrades came to her place and wished her Lal salaam and left.

Just like fish in the water, so is the Party among the people. People are the invisible bulwark for the Party.

(This story is based on a real incident which took place in Medak district, South Telangana.)

Translation of 'Prajale ukku kota'. (First published in *Viplavi*, October 2006)

Translated by Prabhatha Rigobertha

Notes:
1. In India power-cuts are a routine feature of life for most people.

Security Ring

Sujatha

In the Eastern hills, dawn broke through the darkness, embarking on its journey. Spreading its tender rays across the land, it infused it with a new vitality. The radiant light shining through the crevices of the hills seemed to pave the way for a brighter future.

As the eastern glow of dawn appeared, the darkness retreated fearfully into the hills. The farmer, awakened by the rooster's crow, slung his plough over his shoulder and headed to the fields. Women, lighting fires in their hearths, immersed themselves in cooking to prepare meals for the day. It is the harvest season. The green fields swayed gently in the cool breeze. The grass, sprouted as if a green velvet carpet had been laid on the earth, cushioned the feet of passers-by. Japanese Quails (mid-sized birds) crowed melodiously from the branches, their songs merging with the rustling of leaves to create a harmonious symphony of nature.

'Madam, here's the milk,' called a voice. Rajitha, who was deeply engrossed in reading the newspaper, looked up. 'Oh, isn't the senior madam around?' asked Enkamma.

'Who is it?' an elderly lady stepped out from inside the house.

'It's me, madam! I've brought the milk,' said Enkamma. 'Keep the milk there and leave,' replied the elderly woman. Rajitha resumed her reading. After Enkamma left, Rajitha asked, '*Avva*, who was that?' 'She's our farm servant's wife. She brings milk every day. Since their buffalo went dry, they milk the buffalo that was loaned to them and sell its milk,' the elderly woman explained.

The previous night, a squad had arrived at this house. It was one of the few large houses in the village, sufficient to accommodate the entire squad. The house belonged to a rich peasant who maintained cordial relations with the party. As per the commander, he wasn't a problematic individual, so the squad decided to stay there. The house was like a mansion, but it was empty. When the elderly woman saw the squad entering, her frightened voice wavered as she asked, 'Who are you?'

'We're members of the revolutionary squad,' replied one of the comrades. Everyone spread out in the hall, placing their kits on the floor. The commander approached the old woman and said, 'We'll stay here.'

'All right son but there is no one at home. My son Venkata Reddy and his wife have gone to a wedding in the neighbouring village,' she replied.

The squad settled in the large room behind the kitchen. That morning, Rajitha was assigned sentry duty at the house because Rajitha has a quality of blending seamlessly with any family, so that any onlooker would assume her to be a relative of the family.

Rajitha was tall, with a sturdy, proportionate build and black complexion. She was the deputy commander of the squad.

In the kitchen, food was being prepared for the squad. A plate slipped from the hands of a comrade on kitchen duty and fell to the floor with a loud clang. Hearing the noise, Rajitha remarked, 'Be more careful, comrades. Avoid making too much noise.'

Rajitha was reading a newspaper while keenly observing every sound and movement outside. The elderly woman came and sat on the cot near her and asked, 'what's your name, child?'

'Rajitha,' she replied.

'Do you have parents?' the elderly woman asked again.

'Yes, they are there,' Rajitha answered.

'What is your educational qualification?' the woman asked, glancing at the English newspaper lying nearby. Rajitha brushed off the question, without answering it. The elderly woman laughed and said, 'You people won't tell, huh?' Rajitha smiled faintly and remained silent. As Rajitha remained silent, the elderly woman went inside the house after a few minutes.

Just then, a middle-aged man entered the house and called out, 'Is Pedda Ramamma here?'

'Yes, she's there,' Rajitha said as she went inside to inform Ramamma. 'Someone's here to see you,' she called out.

The visitor mentioned Pedda Ramamma's name but was looking around, seemingly trying to figure out who else was inside the house. The elderly woman wiped her hands with her sari and stepped out, saying, 'Oh, Kishtha Reddy, is it you? How is it that you are here?'

'Nothing specific, has Venkata Reddy arrived yet?' he asked.

'Maybe he'll come tomorrow,' she replied. After some casual conversation, Kishtha Reddy left.

'Who is he?' Rajitha asked.

'He's from my village, a relative of ours,' the elderly woman replied.

'Is he trustworthy, or does he have a shady side?' Rajitha inquired.

'Oh, he's not that kind of person. He even said that he knows about you people,' the woman added.

'Did he recognize me?' Rajitha asked.

'Doesn't look like it,' the elderly woman said.

Rajitha went inside and informed the commander, 'Some man claiming to be a relative came and left. Something about him felt suspicious.'

'It's good to stay cautious,' the commander agreed.

As darkness began to fall, the squad finished their tasks and prepared for dinner. In the dim light, street lamps flickered faintly here and there. Outside, in the dusky surroundings, police had encircled the house. A sentry noticed movement and said, 'It looks like shadows are moving. I suspect it's the police.'

Rajitha observed from the window for a few minutes and confirmed, 'Yes, the police have surrounded the house. We can escape through the cattle shed behind the house, but the enemy has taken cover behind the houses in front of the shed.' 'If the pilot team advances first, the rest of the squad can follow,' suggested the commander.

Rajitha's team began moving out through the goat shed behind the house. Even though it was still dark outside, the faint glow of streetlights nearby created visibility. 'In the light, we'll become easy targets for the enemy. Let's stick to the shadowed side near the trees,' Rajitha instructed her comrades.

As planned, the pilot team stepped out from the goat shed, only to be met by a sudden hail of bullets from the enemy. In the first volley, comrade Deepa fell with blood gushing from a wound, collapsing instantly. A bullet struck Rajitha in the stomach, causing her to lose consciousness and fall.

The rear team kept firing back, crawling out while dodging enemy bullets. Amid the chaos, they had to leave the unconscious Rajitha behind as they moved forward under relentless enemy fire.

Within five minutes, an eerie silence enveloped the surroundings. When Rajitha regained consciousness, she found herself in total darkness, lying near the gobar gas setup[1] behind the house. As she looked around, she thought, 'I'm not dead, I'm alive.'

Reaching for the rifle lying beside her, she tried to load it, but the cocking mechanism was jammed. Blood was oozing from her abdomen, soaking her pants and shirt. 'I need to get out of here somehow,' she resolved. 'The enemy might assume everyone has fled. There could be police ahead.'

As she mulled over her options, a policeman appeared from behind, shining a three-cell torch and muttering something in code: 'Bombay... Bombay...' Rajitha knew her chances of survival were slim. 'If I must die, I'll take him down with me,' she thought. She forcefully pulled the bolt of her unloaded rifle to create the impression it was ready. Then, shouting loudly, she bellowed, 'Hey, you scoundrel! Beware!'

Startled, the policeman retreated slightly and began firing his automatic weapon. All the bullets struck the lifeless body of Deepa, lying on the ground. Realizing what had happened,

Rajitha thought, 'Ah, he didn't see me. He assumed it was Deepa who was shouting after loading her rifle. Now is my chance to escape. He won't move forward immediately.'

Gripping her rifle tightly, she crawled slowly between the houses until she reached the main road leading to a nearby village. 'My tongue is parched and I feel dizzy,' she thought as she staggered towards a nearby house. Inside, the homeowner and his wife looked alarmed upon seeing her. Rajitha requested, 'Please, can I have some water?'

The homeowner nervously replied, 'The police are nearby. If you stay here, we'll get into trouble. There's a bore-well in front of the house. Please leave.'

Hearing police voices in the distance, Rajitha stumbled to the bore-well, took out tablets to control bleeding from her pocket, and swallowed them with water. She could hear faint whispers from a distance. 'It seems like the dogs (police) are heading this way,' she thought and began walking carefully. By the time she reached a thicket beside the road, her vision blurred, and she collapsed near a tree.

When she regained consciousness, her mouth was parched. 'I'm so thirsty,' she thought. The croaking of frogs in the distance caught her attention. 'There might be water nearby,' she reasoned and crawled towards the sound. However, all she found was mud. There was no water. Exhausted, she fainted again.

She had no idea how long she had been unconscious. When she opened her eyes, a faint light was breaking and the silence was broken by the chirping of birds. Two farmers from a village neighbouring the one where the firing had occurred were walking towards her. The villages were close to each other. Summoning all her strength, Rajitha called out feebly, *'Anna!'*

The farmers approached and saw her – clothes soaked in blood, face and hair caked with mud. Tears welled up in their eyes. She pleaded, 'Take me to Narkundi village.'

The two men supported her from either side and carried her to a secluded spot among the bushes, where they helped her sit down. 'I'm thirsty. Please bring me some water. And ask someone from the house near the well for a saree,' she requested.

They ran back and returned with a black saree and a small jug of water. Rajitha drank the water eagerly, removed her blood-soaked clothes, and draped the saree around herself. To stop the bleeding, she tore a cloth into strips and tightly bound it around her abdomen. Then, she washed the mud off her face.

The two farmers arranged for two bicycles and brought along two young men. They instructed the young men, 'You both take a bicycle and go ahead. We will follow behind, holding the other bicycle with our *Akka* seated on it. If you notice any police ahead, rush back and inform us immediately. In that case, we will hide her in the nearby fields among bushes.' The two young men agreed, took their bicycles, and started moving ahead. The farmers then made Rajitha sit on the other bicycle and said, 'Just sit on the bike and hold on,' as they began pushing it – one from the front and the other from behind.

By then, it was daylight, and the sun was shining brightly. Villagers who saw Rajitha began gathering around her. Seeing the growing crowd, she said, 'Please leave. If anyone sees this, there could be trouble.' Left with no choice, the villagers dispersed and went back to their homes. By this time, the news of the encounter had spread across the area. The district SP had issued an order that all medical shops in the mandal center[2] should remain closed, and no one was to open them. Newspapers published the news prominently that "Rajitha escaped with injuries."

The farmers took Rajitha safely to a house and laid her down on a bed. They explained the situation to the house owner, who immediately went to bring a doctor. The doctor arrived, examined Rajitha, and rushed to a medical shop in the village. However, the shop was closed. Knowing that the shop owner's family lived in the rooms behind the shop, he approached from the back and called out to the owner. In a low voice, he explained, 'There's a delivery case. Glucose must be administered immediately; otherwise, the girl's life is at risk.' Hearing this urgent plea from the doctor, the shop owner handed over six bottles of glucose, some injections, and tablets.

The doctor returned quickly, cleaned and dressed Rajitha's wounds, and administered the glucose. The two farmers sat nearby, keeping watch, while the young men observed the surroundings from outside.

Rajitha was well-acquainted with the household where she was being sheltered, and the doctor was sympathetic to their cause. The housewife asked the doctor, 'Shall I offer her some milk?' The doctor replied, 'She can't drink anything yet.' By evening, as darkness fell, the six bottles of glucose were exhausted. Rajitha began to regain some strength. The doctor asked, 'How are you feeling, comrade?' Rajitha replied, 'I'm okay, doctor.' The doctor noted, 'An operation might still be necessary.'

Meanwhile, the farmers from the neighbouring village, who had been waiting anxiously, felt relieved as they heard Rajitha speaking. They bid her farewell with handshakes and left.

Outside, the sound of a van approaching was heard in the darkness. Everyone froze, straining their ears to listen. The van came to a stop. The sounds of dogs barking and boots clattering reached them. The doctor began to sweat. The police could check each and every house.

Rajitha called the house owner and said, 'Take me quietly on the scooter to a house in the mandal center, using this darkness as a cover.' She mentioned about the house to which she was to be taken. The house owner took the scooter to the outskirts of the village. The two young men seated Rajitha on a bicycle and took her through a side path to the outskirts of the village. There, they put her on the scooter and the house owner rode forward in the darkness.

As soon as Rajitha stepped inside the house in the mandal center, she was met by two journalists. It was as if she stumbled upon the very thing she was looking for. These journalists were already acquainted with Rajitha. They had come to the village to gather details about an encounter. Seeing Rajitha, their faces lit up. They helped her onto a bed, visibly happy to see her. It was around 10 p.m. then.

'How are you, Rajitha?' they asked.

'My stomach is burning terribly. I was hit in the abdomen by a bullet. It would be best if you arrange for an operation immediately,' Rajitha replied.

Due to excessive blood loss, Rajitha struggled to keep her eyes open. She spoke with great effort, forcing her voice.

'You just rest; you'll be fine. We'll take care of everything,' they assured her.

The two journalists were young, energetic, and were very sympathetic to the 'Party'. They quickly devised a plan to get Rajitha to the hospital.

'I'll take Rajitha on the scooter,' one of them said. 'You ride ahead, find a car, and bring it to us. On the way, there's a small house by the road. We'll wait for you there. Make sure to return quickly.'

'All right,' the second journalist agreed.

By then, dawn was breaking. In the dim light, the second journalist sped off on his bike.

The house by the roadside was small, with a little tea shop in front of it. The first journalist parked the scooter outside the shop.

'We'll wait here for a while. My sister is unwell, and we're taking her to the hospital. She has severe abdominal pain and can't sit properly on the vehicle,' he explained.

'Oh, poor girl! So much trouble for her. Please, come inside and sit,' the shopkeeper said sympathetically.

As planned, the car arrived soon. They seated Rajitha carefully in the car and sped off, leaving the village behind and heading towards the town.

At the hospital, an X-ray revealed that bullet fragments in Rajitha's abdomen had damaged her intestines in two places. The doctor immediately began preparations for an operation. Special surgeons were called in. Meanwhile, a nurse came running to inform the doctor, 'Doctor, you have a phone call.'

'I'll be right there,' the doctor replied, stepping out to answer the call.

On the line was District SP Prabhakar Rao.

'You need to come to the station,' the SP instructed.

After hanging up, the doctor turned to his junior and said, 'Doctor, make sure the patient receives a blood transfusion first. I'll return before the operation,' and then he left.

Dr. Venkatesh was about 40 years old. He was familiar with left-wing politics and was a kind and democratic man. The day after the encounter, the SP had issued notices to all nursing homes in the town. When Dr. Venkatesh arrived at the SP's office, he greeted the SP with a smile.

'What's the matter, Sir? Why did you call me?' he asked.

'Look, doctor, we've been receiving complaints that you've been treating Naxalites,' the SP said.

'Oh, there's nothing like that. We're just doing our business as usual,' Venkatesh replied.

'We're just warning you for your own good,' the SP said, in a stern tone.

'All right, understood,' the doctor said.

By the time he returned, the operation theatre was ready.

'Where did you go, doctor?' Rajitha asked.

'I just came back from meeting the SP,' he said with a smile.

Seeing the doctor's calm and resolute face, Rajitha felt a deep sense of admiration for him.

After the surgery, Rajitha was brought to her bed and laid down gently. As soon as the doctor emerged from the operation theatre and settled into a chair, police officers entered the room. One of them said, 'Sir, we need to check the patients in the nursing home. It's an order from the SP.'

'Go ahead,' the doctor replied.

The officers began visiting each patient, asking for their name, address, and case details. When they reached Rajitha's bed, one of them asked, 'What's her case?'

Unable to speak, Rajitha pointed towards the case sheet beside her. The nurse quickly intervened and said, 'She was just brought out of the operation theatre. She can't talk yet.' 'Then you tell me, what's her case?' the officer demanded.

The nurse replied curtly, 'Her ovary was damaged and had to be removed.'

While noting down the details, the officer raised his voice, saying, 'Speak clearly.' His tone irritated the nurse, and though she kept her composure, she couldn't help but think – 'These police officers lack even the basic courtesy to speak softly in a hospital setting.'

After the operation, Rajitha's condition began to stabilize. One day, the doctor's mother visited the hospital, bringing some fruit juice for Rajitha. As she handed it to her, she said, 'The day the police came, my son sat in a chair and didn't leave until they were gone.'

'Only those who truly value humanity and the worth of people act like that,' Rajitha replied, addressing the doctor's mother. 'We are fighting for the oppressed people of the world. What your son is doing to save lives like mine is also a part of the liberation struggle of the downtrodden.'

The elderly woman proudly reminiscing about the past said, 'Just like his father! During the Telangana armed struggle, so many injured people came to our house, and we treated and sent them back.'

As they spoke, the doctor arrived. 'Hello, Rajitha! How are you?' he asked warmly.

'I'm doing well, doctor,' Rajitha replied with a smile.

'We'll discharge you tomorrow,' he informed her.

As she listened, Rajitha's thoughts wandered. She recalled people like the doctor, the two farmers and journalists and the young activists who stood by her, and helped her cross police checkpoints at every turn, preparing her to re-join the struggle. In her mind, she offered revolutionary salutations to all of them. They had formed a strong security ring around her amidst the serious police cordon and search and enabled her to recover and re-join the movement. Feeling rejuvenated and determined, Rajitha embraced the warmth of the forest mother's lap, ready to continue her fight.

Translation of 'Rakshana Valayam'. (First published in the anthology *'Samaanyula Sahasam'* [Courage of the Ordinary], January 2015)

Translated by N. Ravi

Notes:
1. Gobar gas unit: A bio-gas generation unit using cow-dung
2. Mandal: Administrative sub-unit of a district

Little Red Guards

Shaheeda

The winter sun was cuddled up inside his warm quilt and unwilling to get up. Just like the *ashram*[1] children who were sleeping in two separate rows of girls and boys, he tossed and turned and by the time he slowly and finally got out of his quilt it was already six a.m.

Twelve year old Maini hurriedly folded the bed sheets that she used to spread on the *jhilli* and to cover herself, placed them neatly in their regular places and ran to the washing place to wash her face. It was a Saturday and it had had its effect, as she got up ten minutes later than others.

She came across fourteen year old Maasal who had already brushed his teeth, washed his face and was even combing his hair. Maini felt a bit ashamed that 'she was late'.

Wiggling his eyebrows Maasal said, 'You do remember what we thought of doing today, don't you? We must finish our chores early today.'

Maini replied, *'Ingo dada,'* and ran to the wash area.

The roll call was at 6.30 a.m. as it was winter. Lakke, the *Chhatra Nayak*[2], was about fourteen years old. As soon as Lakke blew the whistle the children came running.

In accordance with the discipline of roll call, the children hurriedly pulled off the mufflers and kerchiefs they had draped around their ears, threw them over the hut where they kept their rations and stood in rows according to their classes, in ascending order of heights and the three ashram *gurujis*[3] also stood in the lines behind the children. They did not consider themselves as being above the children or separate from them.

Lakke said, *'Ginti'* (Roll Call) and everybody shouted their number. Lakke confirmed that all the children were present.

'Today is Saturday. So we will have one period of drawing and one period of singing. Later, as we do on every Saturday, we must bring clay to pave the floors of our entire ashram on Sunday. Then we can go to bathe,' Lakke breathed deeply after explaining the day's chores. Then she added, 'So, did anybody throw stones or flash lights during yesterday's sentry?'

The children replied in chorus, 'No.'

'Is there anything else anybody wants to say?' asked Lakke.

'After bathing, let's go into the villages and look at the status of our chicken and our vegetable plots; it's been many days now,' said Maasal.

Lakke looked at Raamal *guruji.* He nodded.

'Ok, let's do so. We will come back by 5.30 p.m. Otherwise it will be late for dinner and sentry duty. Anything else?' questioned Lakke.

The children were silent. After half a minute, Lakke said 'Disperse'.

Maasal and Maini smiled at each other and ran towards the kitchen.

Every year, the *Krantikari Janatana Sarkar*[4] gave one set of stitched uniforms each to the ashram students. When the ashram students wash their uniforms, they wear the clothes they had brought from their homes. Almost everybody washed their uniforms that day. After bathing, as was the routine since their childhood, they poured a few drops of mustard oil into their palms and rubbed it over their faces, hands and feet. They applied oil to their hair too and got ready to tour the village. The *Sarkar* supplies them with soap and oil too.

The children walked in batches, flocking together according to their ages and Raamal walked behind them. Lakke walked with the younger children. Raamal always thought fondly of *'Chhatra Nayak'* Lakke who displayed a responsible attitude in whatever she did. He always thought that she would develop into a good comrade if she joined the PLGA in future. 'What a nice idea she came up with during the meeting they held after the police attack!' Raamal could visualize that meeting vividly even now.

During the two times the *looti sarkar*[4] *jawans* attacked their school, one thing they did without fail was to rob the chicken and ducks the ashram children were rearing and destroy their vegetable plots. After the second attack, the *gurujis* and the children had held a meeting to discuss how to protect themselves from such attacks in the future.

'Their next attack may take place much sooner than the time between the first attack and the second one. So it may not even be possible to run the school in the same place in future. At least, till our PLGA and our party gain an upper hand. So I feel we may not be able to continue rearing our ducks and chicken or even continue growing our vegetables,' said Raamal, introducing the topic even while keenly observing the faces of the children.

'Why are they so angry with our schools? What harm are we causing them? Most of our fathers, mothers, elder brothers and sisters hadn't studied in schools. Why does the *looti sarkar* want to keep us uneducated forever?' Lakke's voice filled with surprise and agony rendered Raamal speechless.

'I believed that the *looti sarkar* was our enemy and the enemy would behave in no other manner and so I joined the fight. Will that be a good enough answer to this little one's question? Indeed, why is the State so angry with our schools?' Raamal wondered. He had identified himself so much with the ashram school that Lakke's question left him shaken for some moments.

'The government doesn't consider us the future citizens of India. If it does, why would it attack us? Though no children or *gurujis* have died in attacks on schools, children have died in attacks on villages and in massacres, *gurujis* have been caught and killed in fake encounters or in real encounters. Some were arrested, tortured and they stopped some from attending schools. In *looti sarkar*'s view, you may not be future Indian citizens but you are future revolutionaries. They are afraid that the education you get here would make you realise the truth and transform you into revolutionaries,' Sunita *guruji* replied, noticing Raamal's silence.

'Did everybody who studied in *looti sarkar*'s schools turn looters? Did not *dadas* and *didis* who had studied in those schools join our party in Dandakaranya, Andhra, Telangana, Bengal, Bihar, Jharkhand and other regions? So, not everyone who studies in our schools may turn into a revolutionary, right?' Everybody laughed at Maasal's logic. The somber mood in the atmosphere lightened a bit.

'That is *looti sarkar* education. There are falsities and deceit in it. So those who understand it may turn into revolutionaries like our *dadas* and *didis*. But our education does not contain falsities or deceit in it. So it is easier to turn into revolutionaries. The students would understand what is useful to society and what is not. So even if they do not become full time revolutionaries, the *looti sarkar* knows that the majority of the students would support the revolution,' Raamal spoke, weighing every word of his as if he was analyzing himself.

'Okay, let us get back to our problem. What is to be done?' questioned Sunita.

'If in future, we are to run our schools in mobile mode, then maybe it would be better to stop rearing ducks and chicken,' said Rambatti, anger and impatience ringing in her voice.

The children were looking at one another. It was true that the majority of things they needed were supplied by their *sarkar*. However, whatever they and their *gurujis* were rearing also helped them. They had experienced happiness and self-respect in eating whatever they had reared or grown with their own labor and now they were reluctant to lose that.

Lakke's eyebrows were drawn together and she was thinking seriously, looking at nothing in particular. She started when she heard her name being called. She understood that Raamal was asking her opinion in the end as she was the *'Chhatra Nayak'*.

'*Dada*, if we give our domestic animals to the village people, two or three heads per household, then the villagers would rear them along with their own animals. Then the police would not know that they belong to the school. So why don't we have a talk with the villagers?' Lakke said in a low voice as if she was thinking aloud.

The children became enthusiastic at once. Everybody started talking at the same time. 'Yes', 'Let's do so', 'Oh, it would be so good', 'The animals aren't branded saying these belong to the school, isn't it?' Everybody had something to comment.

'So our animals would join the animals of the villagers and get themselves camouflaged,' Raamal added laughing. The students laughed merrily.

'And likewise, let us mix up our plants with those of the villagers. And then our vegetables would become camouflaged too!' added Somey.

'*Ingo, Ingo,*' the children cried gleefully.

The *gurujis* were proud of the fact that the children they had taught had excelled them in cleverness.

Raamal even remembered how he fondly referred to the children as 'Our Little Red Guards' when he spoke with his fellow *gurujis* on that day.

Since then, the animals and plants of the students were reared along with those of the villagers. Sometimes it was the villagers who reminded them, 'Your chickens have grown up, take them' or that 'Your vegetables are going to go stale, don't forget to collect them.' Not just that, whenever they harvested new crops or whenever they killed a bull for meat, they never forgot to send 'the share of the students' to them. Whenever they visited the village, the students too repaired fences, chicken coops and pig sties, watered the plants and weeded the plots belonging to them and the villagers.

'As long as there were no cracks in the unity of the villagers, all this went on smoothly. But now some changes are occurring. When the villagers go to work as labourers in Telangana, the SIB[5] there is trying to turn them against the movement by bribing them with money. Nowadays anti-people elements are throwing stones on the schools or flashing big torch lights on the schools and running away. Our Sarkar could not catch the culprits yet. We came to know that recently an informer had entered the No.2 ashram school with the intention of killing the *guruji*, but due to the alertness of the sentry, the danger was averted. We are getting information from other places that each ashram school is taking up some measures according to their conditions to survive. But as we all know, Operation Green Hunt Phase 3 is going to be more severe than ever. We do not know how long such measures would help us survive.'

Though Raamal was walking along slowly, his brain was working on overdrive.

It was afternoon and Jogal was basking in the winter sun. It's hard to guess his age. His wife Seethi was older than him. Their lean, sun-baked bodies steeled with hard physical labor were now covered in wrinkles. But they never behaved like 'old people'. They would do all their work themselves with enthusiasm and were very active. However, a few days back, their fully grown son Rinku had died due to a snake bite and old age mercilessly pounced on them at once. Their backs became bent with grief.

The Krantikari *Janatana Sarkar* had given them support and through the villagers extended the necessary help to them in agricultural and other works. However much help may be extended, there are always some daily chores which cannot be avoided. But Seethi was not able to carry them out as before. Anybody who took a look at their home could easily gather that much.

Hearing the merry laughter of the ashram students, Seethi looked happily into the street and said, 'Looks like the students are visiting the village today.'

But Jogal did not stir, nor did he say anything.

'Why are you so annoyed with the ashram children?' The question was at the tip of her tongue but she did not say it aloud. Since her son's death, she stopped arguing with her old man as she used to. She knew very well how much suffering he was going through.

Seethi crossed the bamboo threshold and stepped outside. The children were weeding the vegetable plot in her neighbour Kosi's yard and were merrily chatting with her. Seethi watched them fondly.

And then she found two children coming towards her hut. Theirs was the last hut in the street. So, she questioned them with surprise, 'Where are you going?'

'To your home, *kako (grandma)*,' replied Maini with a smile.

'Is grandpa not at home?' Maasal crossed the bamboo threshold and entered the yard displaying familiarity.

'We do not have any chicken belonging to the school children,' she said, following the children into the yard.

'Do you think we come only if you have our animals with you?' answered Maini while taking the broom into her hands.

Jogal did not even say a 'hello' to them and went outside. Seethi sighed.

Maasal took hold of metal pots and went away saying, 'I shall bring water.'

The two children finished doing all the household chores while chatting with Seethi and had even chopped some firewood.

'*Kako*, tomorrow after we finish paving our school floors, we will come and pave the floors here,' informed Maini while taking leave of Seethi.

Jogal came home after it turned dark, after roaming about here and there.

'The children said they would come tomorrow to pave the floors, get some tender corn cobs for them,' Seethi said to him.

Though he could discern the works done by the children at their home, Jogal kept mum. He washed his feet and began building up a fire at the hearth in the yard.

'Where did you disappear? It is almost five o'clock, go, go,' Lakke tried to hurry Maini and Masaal who came running panting.

'We went to Seethi *Kako*'s home and did the entire house work,' replied Maasal.

'*Didi*, we also promised that we would pave their floors with clay tomorrow,' Maini said enthusiastically, holding Lakke's hand and walking beside her.

'Good. Poor old Seethi *Kako* is unable to do her chores. Okay then, tomorrow you need not participate in school paving work. You come directly here, I will send two more children with you,' said Lakke.

The children of this No.1 ashram school had decided long back that they would help the families of martyrs, elderly or sick people as much as they could and had been following it since then. They had a Chinese story titled 'Little Red Guard' in their syllabus and the schoolgirl who similarly helped elderly people in her village was one of their favourite characters. After reading the story, they decided that they would also help the elderly people of the village. Lakke naturally thought that Maini and Maasal were just continuing that practice. Only Maini and Maasal knew why they went to the elderly peoples' home. Nobody knew what happened 'that night'.

'That night,' Maasal took over sentry duty at 12 o'clock. Sentry meant just a watch, without any weapon. Though they were at a guerilla base and though the militia sentry was also on watch in and around the village, it came naturally to the ashram children to have their own sentry. It was unimaginable even for such little children to be without sentry while residing amidst a 'battlefield'. Though there was no menace of wild animals, nobody knew what may happen and when. So sentry was necessary on those grounds too. How could they afford not to be alert?

In all these years, they had faced no problems. However, for the past two months they had been facing a new problem. At night, somebody was throwing stones at the school and it had already happened twice. They unsuccessfully tried to catch the culprits. Sometimes the culprits focussed bright torch lights on the school and ran away.

Who was against the school? No amount of analyzing and several days of keeping a watch on the suspects by the *Sarkar* had yielded any results. So, the children carried on their sentry duties with much more alertness and determination.

'Let them come today, I'll show them,' thought Maasal on that new moon day, while trying to pierce the darkness with his eyes in all directions. Exactly at one o' clock, two stones landed in front of him. Immediately, Maasal switched on his torch and began running, guessing the direction from which they were thrown. He saw somebody running and Maasal ran at top speed after the figure. But the figure was running faster than him. He could reach the figure at the end of the street near the tamarind tree. 'I caught you, you thief, I will not leave you,' thought Maasal and extended his hand to catch the figure. But then he stopped short. Utilizing that opportunity the figure merged into the darkness and escaped.

'What happened *dada*?' Maasal started when he heard Maini's voice.

'A few more seconds and you would have caught the thief, what happened?' questioned a disappointed Maini.

Maasal turned back and began walking towards the school with her. He was in serious thought.

'I woke up to attend nature's call and saw you running, so I also ran,' said Maini waiting for his answer.

Maasal stopped walking and said, 'Maini, the thief is none other than our Jogal grandpa.'

Maini also stopped and cried out in surprise, 'Really? Is it true?'

Maasal nodded. Maini could not say anything for a few moments. All the children loved Rinku who had been active in the militia. Everybody cried when he died. Maini could not at all believe that Rinku's father had done this.

'Did you see properly? Are you sure?' Maasal nodded.

'Hmm. What can we do? We will inform the *gurujis* and the Sarkar and then they will ask him why he did so,' said Maini feeling dejected.

'No, don't tell anybody.'

Maini was doubly surprised. 'Even to Lakke?' She had not known even one instance where they did not inform the *Chhatra Nayak*.

'Hm, we will inform her later. The old couple is already in distress after Rinku's death. If the villagers come to know that Jogal grandpa had thrown the stones, they will become more depressed. And Seethi *Kako* may not even know that he is behaving like this.'

'So what do we do?' questioned a puzzled Maini.

'We will think later. Go and sleep,' said Maasal assuming his sentry post again. He was finding it difficult to erase Jogal grandpa's figure out of his vision.

'What happened to you? Why are you behaving as if you cannot bear the presence of ashram children?' Seethi questioned Jogal as she followed him out of the hut quickly. Jogal had just then started going out as soon as he saw four children coming towards his hut carrying clay. But Jogal walked so fast that he had already reached the end of the street and Seethi turned back. By then, the children had reached the hut and immediately began their work.

Though Jogal walked out of his home hurriedly, he now walked slowly as if he did not know where to go. He was in an agitated state and many thoughts crossed his mind.

'If the student sentry had caught me on that night, what would have happened to my honour in the village? Somehow I ran fast and escaped. Rinku was to become the militia commander within a few days; he had won everyone's love.

Everybody in the village respects us a lot as Rinku's parents. And now if this becomes known what would they think. Let alone others, firstly Seethi herself would not approve of my conduct.

I don't know what is happening to me. Since Rinku's death, my courage has left me. I became a coward. True, the Sarkar, the Army and the Party have stood in our support, but somehow that is not giving me enough courage. How terrible the recent police attack was! We did not think we would survive. Every one of us knew that the attack was so vengeful because the village sheltered the school. The police shouted threats before leaving that they would destroy the village if we allowed the school to continue. And my house is near the school. If they come once again to attack, I don't think it would even be possible for me to build the hut again. What should I do?

When I said, "Why don't they shift the school to some other place? Why should we be subjected to attacks again and again because of that?" Seethi countered by saying, "We have to follow the path the villagers follow; we can't live in isolation. We have the Sarkar, we have the *Bhumkal*[6], and everybody will collectively take the decision, why are you bothered?" The villagers are no better. They say, "It is not just that the children have a school to go to. Because of the presence of the school, the *gurujis* are present to examine the sick and give them medicine. They are also running a night school for us. The children are helping the sick and the pregnant women as if they are their own children. How can we let the school go? Let us protect it, let it not go anywhere."

Do I not know all this? Am I a person who does not want the children to get educated? Did I open my mouth all these days? Since my house is nearby, how many times had I not helped with several small things required by the school along with Rinku? There was never a day when we had eaten something without first giving the children a share. But the conditions have changed. And nobody seems to understand this except me. They had even threatened that they would carry out another massacre like *Basaguda*[7]. Is that threat not enough? Why doesn't anybody understand?

Mallesh told me that if I throw stones at the school, they would get frightened and close down the school. That hasn't happened and instead now the children started coming to my own home! Their sentry has become more foolproof. Oh, I hoped for something but something else is happening. I must be careful and see to it that my secret doesn't get exposed.

What a shame! What kind of a situation am I facing after Rinku's death? I lived with my head held high my entire life and now what is this clandestine way of living? I never kept anything secret from Seethi till now. Should I tell her? No, no, she would be utterly devastated....'

Jogal was filled with self-pity and anger towards himself. He recoiled from his own shadow.

After paving the floors of the hut with clay, the children took the pots to the stream for another round of water filling. Maasal did not go with them and started chatting with Seethi.

'*Kako*, since Rinku's death, grandpa has changed a lot, he is not talking to us as he used to.'

'True. I have given birth to Rinku, am I not grieved? But what can we do? I am seeing Rinku in all of you and am surviving. Recently this Mallesh started meeting your grandpa and began clinging to him like a leech. I don't know how he had worked in the squads even for a few days. He never does any work, lazy-bones. I think that is why he abandoned his life in the squads. Now he has turned into a *vadde*[8] and is gobbling up the goats, pigs and cattle of the villagers. I don't know when our *Sarkar* will tackle this corrupt fellow; meanwhile he is brainwashing my old man. He is going on and on about how the police are targeting our village because of the presence of the school. It became so intolerable for me that I warned Mallesh not to come to our house anymore. Did those bastards not destroy the villages that did not have a school? My old man is crazy enough to believe it.' Seethi poured her heart out to the small boy. She had not been able to share her complaints with anybody all these days.

Since he got the information he wanted even without asking for it, Masaal expressed some words of sympathy for *Kako* and kept chatting with her. As soon as the children returned with the water, Seethi gave them some tender corn cobs. They wrapped them in a towel. Seethi knew that within a few days, the corn would be fit to eat and the children would be given special holidays to go home and eat them.

So she said, 'Before you go home for the holidays, do come. By then the corn would be fit to eat and you can eat your share.'

The children replied, '*Ingo,*' and ran towards the stream with muddied clothes to have a bath.

Maasal let the other two children run and stopped Maini and told her about the real issue. 'Maini! This is the doing of Mallesh *Vadde*; he tricked our grandpa into doing this.'

'Oh, is that so. The *Sarkar* would teach him a nice lesson someday. But you told me not to tell anybody. So what do we do?' Maini had trust in him.

'That's the question. What do we do?' counter questioned Maasal. Both walked slowly, deep in thought.

'Let's continue coming every week and help the old couple in their chores. Maybe that would change grandpa's heart. Let us not tell anybody about what grandpa did. But we will tell everybody what *kako* told you about Mallesh. Do you agree?' Finally it was Maini who untied the knot.

'Yes, that is what we will do,' said Maasal looking admiringly at Maini.

Looking at the more than half a dozen letters that the Area *Janatana Sarkar* President Ungal was handing over to her, Area Committee Secretary Sushila said 'Oh my, I haven't yet read the letters you had given me yesterday *dada*. By the time the Division Committee was concluded it was noon. I got up very early to talk and send each of them on their way.' She looked tired. There were black circles under her eyes and her eyelids were drooping.

'That is the nature of our work, isn't it, *didi*?' said Ungal. As they had been working together for ten years, they knew each other's work. There was a lot of respect and understanding between them.

'Let's have some tea first, that would give the energy to look at the letters,' said Sushila yawning.

'No, you drink. Vikas *guruji* sent word that he would come to meet me. So I must go. You can read the other letters later, but first read this. Neither you nor me or anybody else for that matter, would have seen such a letter till now,' Ungal smilingly took out a letter from his shirt pocket and gave it to her.

'Oh, is that so? And whose is this special letter?' asked Sushila curiously.

'See for yourself. In the meantime, I'll meet doctor Kosi and give her the herbal medicine roots she asked for.' Ungal left.

Sushila asked Raje to prepare tea, sat on a stone near the fireplace and opened the letter.

Dear Area Krantikari *Janatana Sarkar* President Comrade Ungal *dada*,

Lal Salaam.

We are students of the No.2 ashram school run by our Krantikari *Janatana Sarkar*. Recently an informer had come into our school with the intention of killing our Vikas *guruji*. Since our sentry Somey was alert, she shrieked loudly, ran and fell over the sleeping *guruji* to protect him. The informer got scared and ran away. We all got up and ran with the intention of catching him but he escaped. None of us know who that informer was till date. You are aware of these happenings. So under these circumstances if we are to protect our *gurujis* we need guns. The informers know that our sentries are just watches without guns and that is why they are coming to attack us with such audacity. If they knew that we have guns, they would not dare. So please consider our request and give us some guns. If we have guns we would do sentry duty more boldly.

Our *gurujis* are teaching us very well and working very hard for our development. And we think it is our duty to protect such *gurujis*. Our *gurujis* do not know that we are writing this letter. We know that if they knew they would not allow it. So we haven't informed them. We thought it over among ourselves and are writing to you in consultation with our *Chhatra Nayak Bhimal*.

Please excuse us if there are any mistakes in spelling and try to understand by correcting them mentally while reading.

With Revolutionary Greetings,
Students of No.2 ashram school

By the time Ungal came back, Sushila still held the letter in her hand and was looking at the fire as if lost somewhere. The mug of tea on the ground beside her had gone cold.

'Did you read it? Isn't it true that none of us had read a letter like this till date?' asked Ungal. When Sushila lifted her head, he could discern a layer of tears in her eyes and was moved.

'Just look at the amount of love our *gurujis* had earned from the children!' It was obvious that she was moved.

'It is not just the children, *didi*; even the *gurujis* behave as if they cannot live without them. You know, the demand of the children in both the No.1 and No.2 ashrams is that we should extend the school to include sixth and seventh standards. They do not want to go to schools outside the *Sarkar* areas after they complete their fifth standard here.'

'Is that so? Why?' asked Sushila curiously.

'If I tell you, you will be even more moved. They say – if we go to outside schools we will learn bad habits like *gutka*[9], tobacco etc, we have seen children who had gone and joined outside schools and they are even forgetting our own mother tongue Koya. Here our *gurujis* teach us all good things, they look after us with a lot of love, we live a disciplined life, even *gurujis* from outside schools are surprised after seeing how clever and knowledgeable our students are. Those who have studied fourth standard here are being admitted in sixth or seventh standards there. So they demand that we start the higher standard classes here.'

Sushila could not control her laughter. 'What! They themselves are saying that they may learn bad habits?' She laughed out loud. Ungal said, '*Ingo,*' and he also laughed.

'So what do the *gurujis* say in response to that?' She was still chuckling and the earlier tiredness in her face just vanished.

'They also echo the same. If the Sarkar starts higher classes, then they are ready to teach even if it means harder work for them. Not just that, in the No.1 ashram they had already built extra classrooms in advance!'

'Oh, what a lovely combination our students and their *gurujis* make,' said Sushila fondly. After a second, 'If we are able to resist the State better, then why not, we will definitely be able to increase the classes. Let us do it; after all, our entire fight is for the sake of our children,' she said deep in thought.

'That's what even I told them,' said Ungal and extended his hand for the letter. Sushila made it as if to give him but then withdrew. Saying, '*Dada,* leave this letter with me; you had already read it,' Sushila secured the letter in a plastic cover and put it in her bag, cherishing it as something precious.

'Vikas *guruji* had asked to meet me to talk on these same security related matters, so what do I tell him?' Ungal asked her softly.

'We have to tell all of you the resolutions passed by the Division Committee. We had discussed in the Committee about the proposals you sent and we discussed the schools too. In order to protect all our activities inside the guerilla base, including the schools, our higher committee has decided to conduct another round of military training camps to the *militia* and the people on a vast scale. They are also sending the Instructor Team to us for this purpose. We should discuss the plans for the same,' said Sushila pouring her cold tea into the kettle to heat it again.

✳

Nearly 150 women, men, old persons and children came towards the military ground from their camping places under the trees to attend the flag hoisting inaugural program of the military camp. Instructor Mahender was engrossed in looking at the stream of people pouring towards him and there was a look of wonder in his eyes.

It had been nearly ten years since Mahender was transferred to Dandakaranya (DK) as a military instructor. Before the transfer, he had worked in *Nallamala*[10] as a Local Guerilla Squad Commander. During those ten years, he had given military training to scores of PLGA fighters. Even so, every instance where he was to give military training to the militia remained an exciting prospect to him. These instances gave him a feeling of talking directly to the earth. It wouldn't be an exaggeration to say that Mahender, who spent most of his time conducting military camps, eagerly awaited opportunities where he could gauge the pulse of the daughters and sons of the soil.

The Party's review which pointed out that one of the main reasons for the Nallamala movement taking a back step was their failure in achieving such progress in *militia* building as in DK was something that he never forgot. For that reason too, the militia that is visible in every village of DK with bows and arrows, *bharmars* and sometimes with big guns was a source of constant inspiration for him. There were hundreds and thousands of examples in all guerilla zones about how the people were ready to sacrifice everything in the real People's War and *Nallamala* was no exception. However, it was the DK movement which showed him the extensive participation of militia in a People's War.

He keenly observed the stream of people approaching him. Children above the age of twelve, young women and men, some married persons, some middle-aged ones and even some whose hairs had turned grey could be seen in the crowd. Women who wore saris and had knives secured in their hair buns, young men with bows, some wearing skirts and some shorts...all of them laughing and hopping merrily and moving forward with such enthusiasm...

His heart was filled with happiness to the brim. It was a People's War where there were no hurdles or restrictions of height, weight, body mass indices, age or physical fitness to join up as soldiers, unlike in the bourgeois army.

It was a war for the people, by the people, where all kinds of people could participate.

A war waged by the people under the leadership of their own Party and Army to protect themselves, their crops, their children, their lives, their land, their forest, their culture, their wealth, their heritage, their history, their villages, their schools, their future and also their country.

As it was in the case of Vietnam and China, now in DK and Bihar-Jharkhand ...

Mahender walked towards a group of children.

'Did you come to learn how to lay booby traps and unarmed combat or did you come to sing the flag song?' Mahender deliberately taunted them, curious to see how they would respond.

'We would sing the song and also take training,' pat came the reply from Maasal. All the children flocked around him in support of what he said.

'You very well know that you cannot join the PLGA unless you are sixteen years old, so why do you want to learn to fight from now? You know very well that your duty is to go to school and get an education,' Mahender upped the taunting attack a notch more.

'Of course, we know. But if we have to study, first of all we need our school. If we have to protect and preserve our school we need to learn about booby traps. Our school had already been attacked twice,' said Lakke, explaining the relation between cause and effect.

'Are the police sparing us from their attacks because we are children? We will decide whether to join PLGA or not when we grow up, but for that firstly we and our school have to survive, you know,' argued Rambatti.

'See *dada*, if the informers come to catch us or our *gurujis*, won't it be better to be trained in unarmed combat so that we can free ourselves from their clutches?' countered Somey.

'*Dada*, isn't it true that last year during the 2013 Chhattisgarh assembly elections, after our Bastar people had dug thousands of pits and laid booby traps, the police commented that now they were more afraid of these than the big guns of PLGA?' Sannu displayed the results for everybody to see.

'*Dada*, is it true that the Militia Company Deputy Vijay was able to beat the three informers who had planned to grab him and arrest them, because he learned unarmed combat from you people? You know *dada*, our sentry duties are still performed without any guns. If we learn unarmed combat, even we would grab the informers just like Vijay *dada*,' Mairi expressed confidence.

Mahender crossed his chest with his hands in mock fear and said, 'My, my! Nobody can argue with you *Janatana Sarkar* school children.' The children burst out laughing.

'Okay, learn well then,' Mahender waved his hand in a goodbye and walked towards an elderly man who was looking like the oldest among the lot.

'Oh *Pepi!* (uncle) All this training is for the rough and tough, for those who can run around and the young. Why did you come? Did you come to see how they are learning?' asked Mahender.

'I still have a lot of strength left in me. If I do not perform every exercise they are doing, you can question me then; let me see how many of these can compete with me,' said the old man, whose two front teeth were long gone, laughing and filling the people around him with mirth. Everybody burst out laughing.

After the laughs and the friendly banter about the elderly man had subsided, Mahender said, 'It is not just about learning, *nayana*; if you know that the police had arrived, irrespective of whether it was midday or mid-night, you would have to run hither thither, dig, lay traps, saw the logs, carry them... how will you be able to do all that? Even if you learn unarmed combat, how would you be able to fight with informers and the policemen who look like fattened bulls?' Mahender asked sympathetically.

The elderly man was silent for a few moments. Mahender felt sorry for asking him that question. After seeing his wrinkled body, he could not help asking it. All those who had been laughing till then were looking at him with interest to know his answer.

'If I had children, I would have sent them for this training. But the only son I had died of snake bite. So I came. If I have the training, I will do the running hither and thither as much as I can. And when I cannot, at least I can teach a bunch of children how to go about it, don't you agree?'

Mahender moved forward to pat the elderly man's shoulder affectionately and two children who had followed him came into the old man's vision.

Looking sideways at the children, the elderly man said in a serious manner 'The ashram school is still in our village as yet. Even if they change their location in future, how far can it go? It is our school, so it will be in our Panchayat and in our Area. So if we have to protect and preserve the school, our village and our children, it is always good for all of us to have the training, comrade.'

Everybody nodded in agreement. The whistle for flag hoisting sounded and everybody moved. Mahender respectfully followed the elderly man.

Maini and Maasal who had listened to Jogal grandpa with rapt attention without batting their eyelids looked at each other happily and ran, skipping and hopping to stand in the children's line.

Translation of 'Chinni red guardulu'. (First published in *Arunatara*, June 2015)

Translated by the author

Notes:
1. *Ashram*: School cum hostel
2. *Chhatra Nayak*: Student Monitor
3. *Guruji*: Teacher
4. In Dandakaranya, the Krantikari *Janatana Sarkar* (Revolutionary People's Government) is referred to as the *Sarkar*. To distinguish, the Indian government is referred to as *'looti sarkar'* (exploitative government).

5. SIB: Special Intelligence Bureau
6. *Bhumkal*: The literal meaning of this Gondi word is struggle. The militia is also named as *Bhumkal*.
7. Basaguda massacre: on 28-06-2012, 17 innocent unarmed villagers including children at Basaguda, and two more at Simlipenta were murdered in cold blood by the Indian State.
8. *Vadde*: akin to a priest
9. Gutka is a mixture of tobacco, areca nut, slaked lime, and various other ingredients like spices and flavorings, all in a powdered or granular form. It is a type of smokeless tobacco widely used in South Asian countries, including India and Pakistan, where it is placed in the mouth to be chewed like chewing tobacco. The consumption of gutka is a significant public health concern due to its strong addictive nature and its link to oral cancer and other severe health problems.
10. Nallamala: Forest area spread in some districts of Andhra Pradesh and Telangana, reference to the AP movement that suffered a setback

Defiance
G. Renuka

'**R**un! The Police are coming! Run!'
The entire village was in a state of havoc with the news of police coming to their village yet again. Police raids were nothing new to the people of Dandakaranya. Still, every time the police enter any village, the villagers, including the babies, are in dread of their arrival and the baggage of humiliation, abuse, and harassment that came with them.

The moment the people heard these words, all those who were capable of running began running frantically.

The women, men, and children had just reached their homes from the farm work. They had just started preparing dinner. Most of them were hungry after a hard day's work and would have shortly started gulping down the food. But this wasn't one of those days. The daily routine in the village would be disturbed today. Not just today, but for years and not just in this village but in all the neighboring several villages, the daily routine was frequently disturbed by the police forces.

Mangli immediately ran to the cradle in her tiny hut's veranda. She did not know what to do. She thought that maybe her husband ran from the brook where he had gone to take a shower. She was fearful and confused about how to run with a three-month old baby. On top of that, the baby had a fever from the day before. Meanwhile, she saw her mother-in-law, Sanki, approaching the house with a pot of water on her head.

With the heavy water pot still on her head, Sanki asked apprehensively, 'Did Lalu come back home?'

'No, he did not. He must have run from the brook itself.'

Before she could feel relaxed that maybe her son escaped the wrath of the police, Sanki started to worry about her daughter-in-law. 'How will you manage then?' she asked with concern.

'I don't know. Where do I run with a sick, three-month old now?' helplessness reflected in her voice.

Not knowing what to say and do, Sanki looked around to find some solution. The fear of police abusing her young daughter-in-law if she remained at home made her feel restless. If she went to the forest with the fever-ridden baby, what if both were stuck in some thunderstorm and that worsened the baby's fever?

The sounds of police scolding, beating around, and shouting reached their ears. There's no chance of taking a considered decision now. Sanki grabbed her granddaughter and placed her in the arms of her daughter-in-law and signaled that she should sit silently when the police arrived at their doorstep.

Her intention was to make it obvious to the police that her daughter-in-law was really the mother of an infant. Sanki sat right next to her daughter-in-law who was holding the baby. They could see the police outside the door. Then the police entered their house.

The mother-in-law and daughter-in-law began panicking.

Adivasis do not think of the police as humans. They are used to confronting and living with wild animals in the forest. But for them, especially for women, the police are worse than those animals. There is only a threat to life with any wild animal. But with the police, there is a threat of rape and sexual assault.

'Oi, where did the men of your house go?' the police asked in their natural threatening, arrogant voice.

'Men? There are no men. I just have one son. He went to see his sister,' replied Sanki while trying hard to put on a brave face. Sanki's husband died only three years ago. The police did not ask for her husband's details and she did not mention it either.

'Who is this? Your younger daughter?' asked another voice, but in the same threatening, arrogant fashion.

'My daughter-in-law'

'Daughter-in-law? Why are you lying that this unmarried woman is your daughter-in-law?'

'Why would I lie? What do you mean 'unmarried woman'? When she's the mother of this child…' said Sanki humbly.

'What? She's a mother?' asked the police not because he distrusted it but with a deliberate intent to trouble her.

'Yes, don't you see the child in her arms?' she said, hoping they would believe the truth and leave her daughter-in-law alone.

'Are you fooling us by claiming that this child is hers? Did you people borrow someone else's child?'

The panic of the mother-in-law and daughter-in-law intensified hearing this.

Sanki said in a wretched voice, 'Why would we get somebody else's child? It is her child.'

'Do you think we cannot figure out if she's married or not merely by looking at her face? If you're going to such lengths to stage such a drama, perhaps this girl belongs to a naxalite squad. Come on, come outside,' said the police. While one police forcefully snatched away the baby from Mangli's hands, the other pulled her up by her shoulder.

As the police harshly handled the baby, the baby shrieked. Sanki immediately rose and took the baby from the police. She then got all riled up with the police for mishandling the baby and spoke angrily with them. 'How terrible! You don't care that you are dealing with an infant and an infant's mother.'

'How dare you speak to us this way?' The police forcefully pushed her away. Another one grabbed Mangli and pushed her out of her home into the street.

Mangli struggled to free herself from their clutches and pleaded with them, 'My child is unwell. Please leave me.'

Sanki walked behind the police officers dragging Mangli and continued pleading with them. 'Please see the face of the small baby and show some mercy. My daughter-in-law is innocent.'

The police threw Mangli into their jeep and took her away. Crying, Sanki continued to walk behind the police jeep.

Meanwhile, an old lady living in the neighbouring house offered to take care of the crying, sick baby. The old woman could not run anywhere because of her age. She sat stubbornly in her house even though everyone else was escaping the police. She heard the mother-in-law and daughter-in-law pleading with the police. Unable to get up and intervene, she remained seated and began cursing the police until she saw Sanki following the police helplessly with the baby still in her arms.

Sanki handed over the baby to this old lady and followed the police tracks to reach her daughter-in-law.

The policemen who went in large groups to every corner of the village, converged at the centre of the village after finishing their raids. There were a total of seventy to eighty policemen with almost ten captives. Out of the ten, three were women including Mangli. All their faces reflected anxiety and fear. Ten to fifteen middle-aged women like Sanki followed the police and reached the center of the village.

Some of the middle-aged women were pleading with the police to leave the captives. Others were questioning angrily, 'Why do you always come and disturb the peace in our village? Why are you holding our people?'

Hitting them with hands and batons and pushing them away, the police tried to move the captives forward. 'What injustice is this? Why are you taking a small baby's mother to the station? What will happen to that baby?' Sanki questioned loudly. All of the women's attention was drawn to Mangli. Everyone was moved thinking of the small baby's fate.

'How can you take away a child's mother? What injustice is this?' All the women started to question the police again and again. It seemed like their primary collective duty now was to free Mangli. Seeing how everyone was so concerned about Mangli, a police officer came up with a cruel idea. If the police think of doing something, what could stop them from doing it? The state itself empowers them to torture and harass the people anyway.

'If she is really the mother of the child, we will leave her right now, right away,' said the officer.

Mangli and others thought that the police would really release her.

'She really is the mother of the child,' everyone replied.

'How can we trust this?' said the officer slyly as if planning something heinous. The women did not understand his intentions. They responded, 'We're telling you, right?'

'Maybe all of you are lying to let this woman free.'

'You have seen the baby with your own eyes. What else is there to prove?' pleaded Sanki.

'Yes, we've seen the baby, sure. But how can you prove that that baby is hers?'

'You said you will leave her if she is the mother. Now, you do not believe us. How do we prove it to you?' Sanki asked helplessly.

'We will believe you if she does what we ask her.'

'Tell us what!'

All the women including Mangli were shell shocked and disgusted at what the officer said.

The entire group of policemen laughed derisively.

'What are you saying? Don't you have any shame speaking like this?'

'How dare you humiliate a mother? Aren't you born to a mother?'

The women angrily questioned the police.

The policeman did not back out of the plan. 'You claim that she's a mother, and we claim that she is not. As promised, we will leave her right now if she proves herself to be a child's mother. Otherwise, we will put her in jail. It is up to you now,' he said calmly. The police started pushing the captives forward. They used the lathi mercilessly on the middle-aged women following them.

Mangli thought of her child. If she was put into jail, what would happen to the child? Would it even survive? The mere thought sent tremors to her heart.

Would the police lock her up or would they send out all the other women and assault her at the station? Hadn't they already ruined so many women's lives? The mere thought made her shiver.

She recalled the words of the police officer. To prove herself as he suggested was not an option; it was disgusting.

Helpless, her grief overflowed.

Sanki's thoughts at this time were almost the same. She intended to get her daughter-in-law freed from their abusive clutches. If not, her fate would be deplorable. Besides, she was concerned about the well-being of the child too! Her heart trembled with grief!

Slowly gathering herself together, she said to her daughter-in-law in a strong voice.

'Dear, do as they say. Nothing will happen to you. This sin is upon them. Think of your child, she cannot live without you. Do it for your child.'

Mangli cried her heart out on hearing her mother-in-law's words. She finally readied herself to do the most humiliating thing that the police had asked her to do to prove that she is an infant's mother. The policemen's gaze felt like a thousand caterpillars crawling on her skin. For the first time, she detested being born a female.

Humiliated, she milked her breasts in front of the police and everyone else to prove herself. That was not milk but the anguished tears of a mother.

'Run! The Police are coming! Run!' These screams alerted the entire village.

All those capable of running began running frantically.

Somaari, who was cooking at the time, immediately left all her work to grab her child lying in the cradle. Unfortunately, there was no one else home. It was harvest time, so her in-laws were all at the field. Her husband left for the neighbouring village to attend the meeting of the village organisation.

Somaari, who ran some distance with her baby, was caught by the police coming in that direction.

They pounced on her and dragged her out of the village. In a short while, the police forces which went around the village gathered outside the village. They brought along captives from the fields, and homes. The wives and mothers of these captives followed them to the end of the village. The atmosphere was tense with the policemen's abuses, their brandishing the batons, the captives' wails, the children's cries, and the relatives' pleadings.

'Move! Move!' ordered a policeman.

Somaari shouted at the police pushing her by her shoulder. 'Where are you taking me? What did I do?'

Sarcastically, the police replied, 'Sure, all of you are innocent. Now who exploded the booby trap the other day? Isn't it your militia?'

'If it is the militia, arrest them! Why are you arresting me?' Somaari asked loudly without backing down.

'Hey! Enough of this! Is militia some abstract thing? All of you young people make up the militia!'

'How will I work in the militia with a small baby? Can't you see this baby in my arms?'

'Oh we can see the baby all right. Are you trying to escape us by holding somebody else's baby?'

'What are you saying? Why should I hold somebody else's baby?' shouted Somaari.

There were many such arguments going on between the captives and the police.

But when Somaari shouted loudly, all the other arguments halted for a bit. Everyone's attention was drawn to Somaari. Some of the women joined Somaari to continue arguing with the police on their unjust behavior.

'Where will you take the mother of a small baby?'

'You do not care for mothers. You do not care for old women. Why do you all harass us so much?'

'Who gave you the authority to enter our villages and disturb our lives and harass us at will?' The women took turns to question the police.

The police yelled, threatened, and beat them all. Yet, the women did not back down.

'It seems I am working in the militia. And according to them, this child is not mine. They claim I am holding this baby only to escape the police,' Somaari added fuel to the fire by giving them the details of the absurd charge that the police made against her to arrest her.

'How can you say this? How can you call her boy as someone else's? ...'

Before even the woman standing next to Somaari finished her sentence, a policeman interrupted, 'yes, maybe it is not her child. Who knows? Is it written on the child's face that he is your son?'

Somaari was furious. She handed over her child to the woman standing next to her. Her hands moved swiftly. Before anybody realized what was happening, she sprayed her breast milk on the face of the policeman who said that to her and he felt as if she spit on his face with disgust.

Everyone was stunned. But Somaari did not flinch. There was no hesitation or shame or fear on her face.

There was only one emotion in her eyes, in her face, in her posture, and in every inch of her body: Defiance!

Translation of 'Dhikkaram'. (First published in *Arunatara*, January 2019)
Translated by Vipanchika S Bhagyanagar

Punishment
G.Renuka

Sannu was walking, taking each step with a broad smile. He had just started to learn how to walk. Maybe because he slept all day and woke up after drinking milk to his heart's content from his mother, his face looked even more peaceful and happier than ever. In the evening sunlight, his dusky body was glowing. He extended one hand forward as if trying to hold onto something, taking each step with determination. To him, every step felt like a great victory. His eyes were shining with the pride of that victory. Looking at him, could anyone not feel a surge of affection?

Boklu, sitting on the cot in their yard, extended his hands upon seeing Sannu coming towards him. Seeing Boklu extend his hands, Sannu started walking faster, with a bubbly laughter. Boklu couldn't remain seated until Sannu reached him. He kept his hands extended and got up from the cot, took two steps out of the yard. In another moment, he would have lifted that little one with both hands, kissed his cheeks, and hugged him tightly! But just then, Sannu's mother, Gulari, rushed in and lifted Sannu, and turned towards Boklu angrily saying, 'Never touch him with your filthy hands,' and hurried back to their house with quick steps.

Perhaps because his freedom was snatched away and he was forcibly picked up, Sannu started crying. Boklu was aghast and his face darkened. Boklu's wife, Kanni, who had just come to the porch from their house beside the yard, and Boklu's mother, Adime, who was sitting on another cot in the yard, saw this scene.

'This Gulari is always like this. Just seeing him makes her eyes burn with anger,' said Kanni angrily.

'Shh! be quiet. If that woman hears, there will be more fights,' said Adime.

'How long should we stay silent out of fear of fights? Should we tolerate everything she does?' Kanni's voice was a mix of anger and sorrow.

'We should stay silent. We must suffer the consequences of our wrongdoings. We should be grateful that they at least let us stay in the village like this,' said Adime.

Kanni's anger started to subside. 'He admitted his mistake. In such a big People's Court, they decided to forgive him and accept him as one of them again. Even the party people are treating him well,' she said.

'It is true that they said everybody has to accept him... but can everyone forget everything and accept as soon as it's said? Poor child, how much she had suffered.'

Boklu again laid back on the cot and closed his eyes. The words of his wife and mother were reaching his ears. Seeing him like that, the hearts of both women ached with sorrow.

'Don't feel bad, my son. We have to endure all this for a few days. As time passes, everyone will forget,' his mother consoled him.

Kanni moved from there and got involved in the household chores. The harsh words Gulari spoke at the People's Court a month ago still echoed in her ears.

'What!! Should we allow these people to live? It is they who brought the (Salwa) Judum goons with them here. Without them, the Judum people couldn't have caused so much harm to our village,' Pozzal seethed with anger.

'It's true, but now they are admitting their mistake...,' Adamaal, the president of the Janatana Sarkar, started to say something more.

Gulari interrupted him before he could finish his words.

'What do you mean? After doing all that, is admitting their mistake now enough? Should we let them live? It is not a sin even if we tear them to pieces...' her face turned red with rage.

'Yes, they shouldn't be allowed to live, they must be killed,' Kamli said.

'Yes, they must be killed!' echoed the voices of many people. Everybody was seething with anger.

This is Pottem village in the Bhairamgad region of Danda-karanya. There are about 150 houses in that village. Along with the villagers of that village, around five to six hundred people from four other villages under the *Janatana Sarkar* had gathered near the mango trees on the right side of the village. It was the first week of August, so the sky was overcast. Everyone had come to the people's court after finishing their lunch in the afternoon.

Jaini, who was the in-charge of the judicial department of the *Janatana Sarkar*, was conducting the People's Court.

The people were sitting in a semicircle. Some were sitting on small stones or wooden logs. Others had placed their shoes on the ground and sat on them. Some were standing. Boklu and Mangal were sitting in front of them with their heads bowed. To their right were Adamaal and some other members of the *Janatana Sarkar*, along with members of the guerrilla squad. To the left were Boklu and Mangal's family members. Jaini was standing.

'It's true that they have committed grave mistakes. But they didn't commit these mistakes on their own. The government brought the *Judum* as part of a scheme. The *Judum* leaders and police officers made them commit these mistakes,' Adamaal began to explain further when Somal interrupted angrily, 'What happened to their sense then? Why did they join the *Judum* in the first place? They went against our word then, how dare they show their faces to us now?'

'Many joined the *Judum* out of ignorance or fear. Now they realize their mistake and are coming back. We should forgive those who realize their mistake,' said another *Janatana Sarkar* member, Jugru.

'What ignorance? Didn't all of you from the committee tell them in a meeting back then?' retorted Gulari.

'Even though we told them, what was the situation like then? The enemy also indulged in large-scale propaganda. Many believed that propaganda,' explained Jugru.

'They did not just join the *Judum* but they chose to become SPOs (Special Police Officers). How many times did they raid our village? How many houses did they burn? How many crops did they destroy? How many did they kill? How many women did they rape?' Somvari's anger was relentless.

'They took the lives of five people from our village. They raped five women,' Idime added.

As Idime said those words, a mix of anger and sorrow overcame Gulari, Kamli, and Aithe. All three of them were victims of rape. Two other young women had left the village and were staying with relatives in remote villages to escape the nightmare.

'The *Salwa Judum* attacks caused a lot of damage to our village. But we know that these two did not personally kill or rape anyone,' said Adamaal.

'They may not have done it personally. But it was the mob they brought that did all that,' Somvari said.

Jaini moved back and forth listening to the people's arguments and observing their expressions. She too felt strongly that the guilty should not be let go. She wanted to join those who were arguing and express her own opinions. But as the one responsible for the judicial department, she knew this was not the platform for her personal arguments, so she forcibly restrained herself.

Since the people were not agreeing despite the committee members' efforts, the commander of the squad, Mangtu, stood up. He began to speak in a convincing manner.

'Comrades! Listen to what I have to say and think it over. When *Salwa Judum* began, there was extreme fear and anxiety among the people. The propaganda they carried out claiming that they would completely wipe out the Naxalites here, and if not today, then tomorrow, everyone would have to join the camps increased this fear. Despite this propaganda, many people stood courageously. They believed there was no life for them if they left this land. So, they decided to stay here, come what may. But some were scared. Some were confused. They thought they would die unnecessarily if they stayed here. They believed the party would either be wiped out or retreat from here. So, they joined the *Judum*.

Once they joined the *Judum*, they had no freedom. If they were told to join the SPOs, they had to join the SPOs. If they were told to join the goons, they had to join the goons. Some might have joined willingly, but some were forced to join. But the party did not get wiped out as they feared. Our resistance grew. Moreover, we called for those who joined the *Judum* to come back to their villages. Additionally, they couldn't bear the atrocities in the camps. They became disgusted with the rotten life there. So, many began to think correctly and wanted to come back and live here under the protection of the PLGA. This is a good development. Even though they made a mistake initially, they are ready to make amends for it. This is an indication of the growing trust among the people in our party and our struggle. Should we then embrace such people or push them away? Would it not harm the movement if we push away those who want to join us? Would it not strengthen the *Judum*?

However, we are not saying we should forgive those who joined the *Judum* and committed rampant murders and rapes or behaved cruelly. Boklu and Mangal joined the SPOs. It's true! They worked for three months. They brought the *Judum* mob into our villages. During those times, the *Judum* mob committed murders and atrocities here. However, they did not commit these acts themselves. Even in the camps, they beat people but did not behave with extreme cruelty, nor did they commit murders or rapes as far as our reports indicate. They responded to our call and returned. Moreover, though they joined the *Judum*, their families remained here with us. Even when they had worked in mass organisations, their behaviour was good. No one holds any grudges against them. They acknowledge their mistakes. Therefore, both the party and the *Janatana Sarkar* believe it is good to forgive and release them. Consider this: if we kill those who responced to our call and came back, would anyone else be willing to leave the camps? Think carefully keeping our opinion in mind and let us know your decision.'

Mangtu concluded by carefully observir_g everyone.

Mangtu's words made sense to some, replacing their anger with thoughtfulness. However, others could not agree, including Gulari.

'Mangtu *Dada*, of course, you will speak like this. They did nothing to you. It is us that they beat, killed, and assaulted,' she said, her voice a mix of bitterness, anger, and sorrow.

Mangtu looked at her as if wounded and he couldn't say anything in response to her.

'Don't speak so unfairly, Gulari. Isn't our pain also the party's pain? Why else does the party exist if not for us?' said Adamaal.

Gulari regretted her harsh words immediately, realizing how much her words would hurt Mangtu *Dada*. However, her determination to see Boklu and Mangal punished remained unchanged. How could she forget that two months ago the *Judum* mob brought by Boklu and Mangal had snatched her infant from her arms and assaulted her? The memory of her baby's helpless cries and her own struggle was still a fresh wound.

'Even if they joined as SPOs, it would have been fine if they had behaved normally. But they were close to that cruel and wicked Karre Ungal. If they were so friendly with him, who knows how many evil deeds they have done?' said Gangal.

The mention of Karre Ungal's name was like salt on a wound for Gulari and many others. His bestial behaviour and the way he incited others to do the same filled Gula_i with disgust once more.

Karre Ungal was a cruel landlord. But the movement weakened him considerably. A ruthless man, he had been waiting for an opportunity to strike back. Now, he had risen again with the *Judum*, living in the Relief camp in Jangla, four kilometres from Pottam. He actively participated in village raids and had earned a reputation as a notorious *Salwa Judum* leader.

'No matter what you say, Mangtu *Dada*, we're not letting them stay,' Gulari's voice was firm, and several others echoed her sentiments.

Jaini, who had feared that everyone might be swayed by Mangtu's words, and would suggest letting them go unpunished, felt relieved hearing the others. She couldn't hide her happiness.

'Comrades, I understand your anger. It's natural to feel this way after the suffering you've endured. But we mustn't take this personally. We need to consider the party's stance and take it forward. The party's position is to kill *Judum* leaders and forgive common people who return from *Judum* camps, and also forgive SPOs who didn't behave cruelly if they surrender voluntarily. Integrating them into our ranks and helping them grow politically is our party's strategy. These people also worked as guides, set houses on fire, and beat people, but they didn't kill or rape anyone. They were close to Karre Ungal, but they admitted that they only did it out of fear of being killed by him. If we kill them now, we would be acting against our party's policy,' Mangtu explained.

'Who knows if they are truly changed or if Karre Ungal sent them here as part of some plan,' Kamli said sceptically.

'Maybe they are just pretending to surrender,' added Aithe.

'If they have any deceitful intentions, we can keep an eye on them. The committee, the militia, and the people will be observing their every move. We won't give them complete freedom. We'll set some conditions, like not leaving the village or talking to outsiders,' Mangtu continued.

"Yes, setting conditions is a good idea," one person agreed, and others echoed, 'Yes, yes.'

'Fine, they didn't kill anyone, but they did beat people and set houses on fire. Shouldn't there be some punishment for that?' one person asked, with others agreeing, 'Yes, we can't just let them go.'

Soon, the place became noisy and chaotic. Voices over-lapped, making it hard to understand what anyone was saying.

Jaini remembered her responsibility. 'Comrades, don't make noise. Speak one at a time,' she shouted two or three times, and the chaos slowly subsided.

'If we don't kill them, there should be some punishment,' one person said, and many others echoed, 'Yes, there should be.'

Jaini noticed that Mangtu *Dada*'s words had a significant impact on the crowd. Those who were previously adamant about killing now seemed to be considering alternatives. Feeling a bit disheartened, she asked, 'What punishment should we give them?'

'Let's beat them and then let them go.'

'Yes, let's beat them and let them go.'

But Gulari and her supporters insisted, 'No, we must kill them.'

Jaini's weariness disappeared, and the environment became chaotic again. She shouted a few times to restore order. Then she decided to move the People's Court forward. She stepped aside, called the other committee members, and consulted with them. Returning to face the crowd, she addressed them.

Boklu and Mangal sat with their heads bowed since the beginning of the People's Court, enveloped in a kind of apathy. Their family members looked pitiable, as if pleading silently for mercy. Boklu and Mangal themselves seemed resigned to their fate.

'All right, comrades. Everyone has clearly understood the matter. You have heard all the arguments. Now, let's take action based on the majority decision. Some say they should be killed, while others say they should be beaten and let go. So, those in favour of killing them, raise your hands,' Jaini said, looking around at the people.

Boklu and Mangal showed no emotion on their faces.

Despite knowing that the raised hands would determine their life or death, they remained indifferent, as if resigned to their fate. Their family members, however, clearly showed fear on their faces, holding their breath in anticipation.

Numerous hands shot up in the air. Jaini began counting them. Boklu and Mangal still didn't lift their heads, but their family members slowly looked up, their faces filled with anxiety, gazing at the raised hands. To them, these weren't just hands; they looked like daggers poised to strike Boklu and Mangal's necks.

After finishing the count, Jaini said, 'Now, those who think they should be beaten and let go, raise your hands.' She felt uneasy, realizing that there were fewer hands for the death penalty.

All remaining hands were raised. Seeing more hands than before, the families of the accused breathed a sigh of relief. Reluctantly, Jaini counted these hands too.

'Now, those who think they shouldn't be beaten or killed raise your hands,' she said, feeling that no one was left to vote for this option.

No hands were raised.

Mechanically, Jaini walked towards her committee members. Mangtu, Adamaal, Jugru, and others joined them. They deliberated for a while. Then, on Jaini's instructions, the militia members fetched two bamboo sticks and began beating Boklu and Mangal.

Jaini had delegated the task to the militia because Mangtu warned that allowing the people to beat them might result in their death. Mangtu had also instructed the militia members not to beat them excessively. He didn't like the idea of beating them at all, believing it could foster resentment among them. However, he bowed to the people's court decision, viewing it as a victory that the majority accepted the party's stance of not killing them.

As the militia began beating them, some in the crowd couldn't contain their anger. They rushed forward, grabbed the sticks, and started beating Boklu and Mangal themselves. Others brought more sticks and joined in, while some used their fists and others kicked them. A mob formed around the two men. Some of their family members circled the mob, pleading, 'Please stop, they'll die.' Others sat in resignation, accepting that this punishment was inevitable.

Jaini stood watching, forgetting Mangtu's warnings. Adamaal, prompted by Mangtu, stepped in and stopped the beating.

With a heavy heart, Kanni finished cooking. As darkness fell, everyone ate their meals in the glow of the hearth.

Feeling dejected, Boklu, who was wiping his washed hands on a cloth draped over his shoulder, saw Mangal coming towards him as he walked into the front yard of the house.

'Why did you come after sunset?' he asked, sitting down on a cot.

Sitting down beside him, Mangal replied, 'I came for no particular reason... If I want to come while there is light, I have to walk through the village from one end to the other. Along the way, I will run into many people. No one greets me... They turn their faces away... Or they look at me with disdain... Some even start cursing... So, I'm afraid to come out in the streets during the day... I just go from my home to the fields. That's all...'

'What can we do, the whole village looks at us like we're outcasts. This is how our lives have turned out...' Boklu's words were heavy with sorrow.

'Don't worry unnecessarily, my boys. Bear it for a few more days, everything will settle down...' Adime said consolingly, lying down on a nearby cot after spreading an old cloth.

'Few more days! It's already been a month since the village trial took place. Still, nothing has changed. .' Boklu responded.

Three children, oblivious to the adult conversations, came and lay down on the cot, falling asleep quickly.

'That damned Ungal's sweet words led us to join the *Judum*. Otherwise, we would have stayed in the village, enduring whatever came our way, good or bad, with everyone else...' Mangal said, his voice filled with regret.

'What's the use of repenting now? I told you not to believe him when I found out he met you. I said we should stay with the villagers, whether it was life or death. Did you listen? You thought you could have a better life. And now look what happened...' Kanni said with frustration as she covered the children with a blanket.

For a moment, both remained silent, acknowledging her words.

'We foolishly listened to him. We didn't plan to stay in the *Judum* forever. If we had, we would have asked you to come too. But once we surrendered and registered at the camp, Ungal assured us that *Judum* would not harm us even if we returned home. But after registering our names there, he kept us there, saying that if we returned, the Naxalites would kill us... After that, we followed his orders like puppets...' Mangal explained slowly.

These were not new things for Kanni. Her husband had told her these things many times. She stood silently for a while, and then walked into the house, carrying the small child who had fallen asleep on her shoulder. Soon, everyone had fallen asleep. Only Boklu and Mangal continued talking.

'Sometimes I feel it would have been better to stay there, good or bad. I can't bear this outcast life anymore,' said Boklu.

'Come on, we made one mistake. Does that mean we have to stay on the wrong path forever?' Mangal replied.

'But how is everyone looking at us? Worse than worms...'

'That's true...'

Even though it was past midnight, the two continued talking, giving vent to their pain and suffering.

✳

'If we had killed them then and there, it would have been better. Did you listen to us, no matter how much we pleaded?' Gulari's face showed a mix of anger, frustration, and helplessness as she addressed Adamaal.

Adamaal, sitting on the cot, didn't respond or even lift his head.

'They lied saying they had changed, and these people believed them naively...' Kumli said.

'They must have come with some plan, but we didn't completely trust them, right? We kept an eye on them. That's why they fled, realizing there was no point in staying...' Somal added.

'Who knows what atrocities they'll commit now ...'

'We opposed them strongly. We even argued vehemently that they should be killed... They might hold a grudge against us...' Kumli continued.

"We had let them go, when they had fallen into our hands. Will we get another chance like that?' Gulari said.

'I also felt it would have been better if we had killed them then. But what can we do? We listened to everyone and let them go...' Jaini said, unable to hold back.

About a hundred people gathered in front of that house, each voicing their opinions. Jugru arrived amidst this commotion, having learned of the situation while returning from work in the neighbouring village. Upon hearing that everyone was at Boklu's house, he headed straight there. As he arrived, he collapsed onto the cot next to Adamaal, wiping the midday sweat with a towel, and asked, 'When did they escape?' Though he already knew most of the details, he wanted to confirm everything.

'Ask them,' Adamaal replied, pointing towards Kanni and Adime, who were huddled under a tree in front of the house, shaking with fear.

'Didn't you have any suspicion, Kanni?' Jugru asked, looking intently at her face.

She slowly lifted her head and glanced at Jugru for a moment before lowering it again. She was in no condition to speak, her heart weighed down by betrayal. She didn't even want to show her face to anyone. Yet, she had to speak.

'After dinner last night, Mangal came. They both sat here on this cot, talking. My mother-in-law slept on that cot. The two children slept on this cot. I slept inside with the little one. After midnight, I woke up to attend to nature's call and saw the cot outside was empty. I didn't suspect anything...'

She started crying, tears flowing freely. The pain of broken trust was evident on her face. Wiping her eyes and face with her saree, she regained her composure and continued, 'I thought he might have gone to attend to nature's call... I went back to sleep. In the morning, when I woke up, he was still not there. I asked my mother-in-law. She said she didn't know. We wondered where he had gone. We thought he might come back, so we waited. When he didn't return by the time we had gruel, I told my mother-in-law to go and tell Adamaal...'

She couldn't continue, overwhelmed by emotions.

'I woke up a few times during the night and could hear them talking. But then, at some point, I didn't hear any more voices. I thought he had gone inside to sleep... I didn't think he would do something like this...' Adime's words trailed off as grief overcame her.

The six and seven-year-old boys sitting beside their mother seemed to understand little of why so many people were gathered in front of their house, why their mother and grandmother were distressed. The little one, about a year and a half old, kept crying unsettled by the noisy atmosphere. Every time the baby cried, the grandmother would take her into her lap and try to soothe her. Until a few months ago, everyone used to dote on the little one, but now no one even touched her.

'Didn't you notice anything? Were there any changes in him over the past few days?' Jugru asked.

'No, we didn't notice anything unusual. He seemed fine,' Kanni replied.

'What were they talking about when Mangal came? Did you hear anything?' Jugru asked again.

'I heard them talking about how nobody in the village trusted them, but I didn't hear the rest. Until yesterday, he didn't seem to have any such thoughts,' Kanni said, lowering her head again.

Adime felt Mangal must have instigated her son. A faint trust in her son flickered in Adime's heart.

'They must have realized nobody believed them and thought there was no point in staying here anymore,' Somvari added.

'If you know anything, don't hide it. Tell us the truth,' Somal insisted.

A few others echoed, 'Yes, tell us. How can you not know anything?'

'We don't know any more than this. Please believe us,' Kanni cried. The sorrow she had been holding burst forth. Adime started crying loudly as well. Seeing their mother and grandmother cry, the children clung to their mother and began to cry too.

'Calm down, sister. We believe you. Please calm down,' Gulari said, quickly putting down the child she was holding and sitting next to Kanni, pulling her close to comfort her. Gulari felt a pang of sympathy looking at Kanni's distressed state. 'What bad luck to be so ashamed in front of everyone for marrying him,' she thought. Kanni and Gulari had been good friends, but since Boklu joined the *Judum*, Gulari kept her distance from Kanni. After the People's Court, they hadn't spoken to each other. Seeing Gulari comforting Kanni, a few others joined in, offering words of solace. Some tried to comfort the children.

However, some people still looked at them with distrust, thinking, 'Do they really not know anything? How can that be?'

Gulari compared her pain with Kanni's sorrow. Gulari had been a victim of assault, but her husband accepted her back into their home, and the villagers stood by her. She never had to bow her head in shame. But Kanni's situation was different. Her husband, who was supposed to be her companion through thick and thin, had abandoned her, leaving her to bear the brunt of his actions. She had to bow her head for the crime he committed. Most difficult of all, some people still harboured distrust towards her. Gulari once thought she was the most unfortunate person when she faced that bitter incident, but compared to Kanni, she felt fortunate. Gulari wondered if Mangal's wife was also crying like Kanni.

'Seriously, Uncle! Do you think we would lie to you?' Boklu said, addressing Karre Ungal, who was sitting on the bench in front of him. 'We were just fed up with staying here and thought we'd visit the village once. We missed seeing our kids. We didn't intend to stay there, Uncle. If we had wanted to stay, why would we come back?' he added.

'Don't you know everything about us, Uncle? Would we lie to you?' Mangal said.

For the past half hour, the three of them had been talking. By then, Ungal began to believe Boklu and Mangal's words.

'Then you should have told me this before,' Ungal said.

'If we had told you, you wouldn't have let us go. That's why we left without saying anything,' Boklu replied.

'All right, I believe you, but the police officer may not. You need to explain everything to him in detail – what you did there, who you met, everything,' Ungal said.

Both Boklu and Mangal nodded in agreement.

'And you won't run away like this again, will you?'

'Uncle, even if we leave, no one in the village will believe us. It's great that we were left alive in the village rather than being killed. We can live peacefully here instead of being afraid and begging everyone over there to spare our lives,' Mangal said.

'Then why didn't you bring the children this time?' Ungal asked.

'The women wouldn't listen, Uncle. They are afraid the Naxalites will kill them,' Mangal explained.

'We said we would marry someone here if they didn't come, but they still didn't listen, Uncle. Now we have to look after our own path,' Boklu added.

'I've told you to remarry here, but you fellows insisted that your wives would join you,' Ungal replied.

'We thought they would,' Boklu said.

'All right, let's go to the police station and talk to the officer. However, they might not immediately reinstate you as SPOs. Please don't be upset. Stay in the camp here with everyone,' Ungal said, and got up after taking his muzzle loader.

'Here you go, Uncle, meat... try it out,' Mangal said, handing a small bundle of roasted meat wrapped in leaves to Ungal, who was sitting on a bench in front of the house. Boklu was also present behind Mangal, holding arrows and a bow, while Mangal had an axe and a sling.

They hunt birds and animals with bows and arrows. However, different arrows are used for birds. They use slings also to hit birds. When squirrels hide in tree holes, they even cut down the trees to catch them, so they also have axes with them while going hunting.

'What kind of meat is this?' Ungal asked curiously.

'Bird meat,' Mangal replied.

Without waiting for a response, Ungal eagerly opened the bundle, took a piece of meat, and put it in his mouth. He chewed quickly and said, 'It's good,' taking another piece.

Adivasis generally are meat lovers, but Ungal's obsession with it was extreme. To satisfy this craving, he used to spend much of his time hunting while he was in his village. After coming to the camp, however, he was too busy hunting humans, and could not find any time for hunting birds or animals. Even if he wanted to, venturing deep into the jungle alone was risky. The camp road was quite close, and many in the camp tried their luck at hunting near the road. They rarely found anything. Since Ungal arrived at the camp, he had been regularly bringing back goats, pigs, chickens, ducks, etc., from raids on villages. Generally, not a day passed without him tasting meat. But the taste of fish or bird meat wrapped in leaves, and roasted over fire is unique. Ungal has been relishing that taste after a long time. After eating a couple of pieces, he took the remaining ones and went inside, eager to savour them along with liquor.

Boklu and Mangal departed.

From that day onwards, it became routine for Boklu and Mangal to bring Ungal meat, fish or bird meat wrapped and roasted in leaves. Ungal enjoyed these more than the meat cooked at home.

One day, receiving a bundle of leaves from Boklu, Ungal remarked, 'You're doing a great job hunting!'

'What's left for us? How can we just sit idly without work? That's why we keep roaming around,' Boklu replied.

'Yet you haven't made us SPOs...' Mangal said in a complaining tone.

'Don't worry. I'll get you reinstated as SPOs by next month. No one here dares to go against my word,' Ungal assured, munching on a piece of meat.

Boklu and Mangal's faces brightened. 'We know, Uncle. No police officer here would dare defy your word. Our complaint is that you are lacking compassion for us,' they said. With a proud smile, Ungal took the remaining meat and went inside.

The next evening, Boklu and Mangal headed towards the canal. It had been nearly two months since they joined the camp.

'Where are you heading?' Ungal, who encountered them, asked.

'We're going to catch some crabs,' Boklu and Mangal told Ungal.

'They're easier to find at night,' Ungal remarked.

'It's okay even now,' replied Boklu.

After a moment's thought, Ungal said, 'All right, I'll come along today.'

'Why, Uncle, are you in the mood to catch crabs?' Boklu asked with a laugh.

'Of course! It's been days since I went after them...' Ungal replied.

'Okay, let's go then. We'll find plenty today. Tell your wife to make some good stew,' Mangal added.

The three of them laughed and set off towards the canal.

As they approached the canal, Mangal and Boklu set their bows, arrows, and an axe against a large tree and started lifting rocks to catch crabs. Ungal, having come along for fun, was only watching them catch crabs. He himself didn't participate in the hunting.

Meanwhile, Mangal lifted a large rock slightly, bent down on his knees, and reached underneath to find crabs. After a few seconds, he called out, 'Hey Boklu, lift this rock a bit more... there's a big crab underneath!' The joy of finding a large crab was evident on his face. Boklu tried to lift the rock with both hands but couldn't get a good grip.

'Lift it a bit more. My hands need to get underneath,' Mangal instructed.

'This rock is too big, and I can't get a good grip. Uncle, come here and help out,' Boklu shouted.

Ungal slid his muzzle loader against a rock and, bending down, placed both hands under the rock.

'Hold it lower, Uncle; I'll hold it from the top,' Boklu directed.

Ungal bent his head slightly and let his hands go under the rock.

Boklu slowly released his grip on the rock.

The villagers, except for the children and the elderly, had almost all gathered near the mango trees on the right side of the village early in the morning. The sun had risen not long ago. Since it was November, it was still quite cold. But no one there was bothered by the cold. They were chatting and laughing. Everyone was there to harvest the collective's crops. Amidst the devastation of *Judum*, they had risked their lives to protect their fields and were now looking at them with satisfaction. Bheemaal and others from the Development Committee were dividing the gathered people into groups. Soon, everyone would step into the nearby crop fields.

In the meantime, someone said, 'The militia is coming...'

'It looks like they are bringing someone...' said another.

'Hey, it's Boklu and Mangal...'

For a few moments, no one could speak. Then a small commotion began.

'They caught the thieves!' shouted Somaal.

'They can't escape now!' said Bheemaal.

Adamaal stepped forward from the group. The militia brought Boklu and Mangal in front of Adamaal.

'Where did you catch them?' asked Adamaal.

'We caught them coming into the village...'

For a moment, Adamaal didn't know what to say. Many thoughts were swirling in his mind. Anger surged within him. He remembered how, on that day in the People's Court, everyone wanted to kill them, but he had convinced everyone to let them go, which later made them bow their heads in shame in front of the people.

Before Adamaal could speak, everyone there started talking at once.

Kanni was also in the group. Her legs trembled when she saw her husband. Her heart pounded. Unable to stand, she moved a little to the side and collapsed.

Mangal's wife should have been there too, but she had gone to the neighbouring village the day before.

The anger in the crowd was escalating with each passing moment. No matter how many words were said, it didn't satisfy them. They were ready to act with their hands.

A couple of blows had already landed on their bodies.

'Wait, wait... let me talk a bit first...' Adamaal intervened.

'What's there to talk about? Just kill them and be done with it!' said Kumli.

'Yes! Just kill them, what's the use of talking?' many shouted in unison.

'Hey! Will you calm down for a moment?' Jugru shouted loudly.

'Calm down? You'll talk to them, they'll tell some stories, and you'll believe them...' said Gulari, her voice trembling with anger, contempt, and sarcasm.

'Exactly! If you talk to them, what else will they do but tell stories?' Aithe's face turned red with anger.

Kanni's mind was in turmoil. Will they kill them? Will they kill them right in front of her eyes? How can she beg them not to kill him? Her whole body was trembling.

Some people were looking at Kanni curiously. Gulari glanced at Kanni and quickly turned her face away. She couldn't bear to see her in such a miserable state. In the past two months, the friendship between Gulari and Kanni had strengthened more than ever. Gulari had supported Kanni in every possible way. After the first People's Court, Kanni used to feel angry with Gulari sometimes, as she realised that Gulari was loathing her husband when he was at home for one month. But recently, Kanni had come to understand Gulari's friendly heart even more deeply.

'Everyone is listening to what the people are saying, right? Tell us what should be done with you...' said Adamaal.

'Please listen to what we have to say, and then do whatever you want...' pleaded Boklu.

'Look, now they'll start telling stories...' Kumli said to Gulari.

Gulari nodded in agreement, but her eyes remained fixed on the two men.

'We did go, but we didn't work as SPOs...' Boklu started to say hesitantly.

'If they didn't work as SPOs, then does that mean they didn't want to? They just weren't given the SPO job!' Somaal said loudly.

'If they didn't become SPOs, so what? Do they think we don't know they roamed around closely with that Ungal?'

'Go on then,' said Adamaal, signalling everyone to be silent.

"We were unnecessarily afraid and listened to Karre Ungal. We made a big mistake. But, realizing that mistake, we ran away from there. Though we were spared, no one believed us. We were ostracized. So, we thought about what to do to make you all trust us...' Boklu paused.

'To make everyone believe you, you should run away again...' Kumli's sarcasm made a few people laugh.

'Not just run away, but roam around with Karre Ungal, cooking meat for him...' added Aithe.

After saying those words, Boklu looked at Mangal. Mangal, interpreting his gaze, took the bag from his shoulder with his left hand and reached inside it with his right hand, pulling something out.

That was it! Everyone who was about to speak or curse became dumbstruck. Their eyes widened. Everyone forgot to breathe.

Mangal held a head! A human head!!

He placed it on a nearby rock.

'Karre Ungal's head...' someone said.

'Yes, yes' many shouted, unable to contain their joy.

'This is the man who distanced us from all of you... He's the one who brought ruin to our village... That's why we killed him. Believe us now...'

'How, how did you kill him...' Adamaal asked, patting both their shoulders with both hands at the same time. He was unable to contain his happiness. The PLGA had made many attempts to kill that man but had failed.

'He came with us to hunt. We had been waiting for the opportunity for two months. We told him to hold a stone, and as soon as he did, we took an axe and struck his head off with one blow...'

Hearing the news, the elderly, men, women, and children from the village came rushing and shouting loudly.

Everyone started speaking loudly at once. Jaini said, 'Everyone, sit down and speak one at a time.' After repeating it firmly four or five times, the crowd gradually settled down. As they recalled the atrocities inflicted upon them by Karre Ungal, their hearts burned with anger. At the same time, there was satisfaction too that he was eventually eliminated.

An old woman stepped forward and said, 'He stole my two goats.'

Another young woman added, 'He took away my four hens.'

And so, the people started airing their complaints one after another:

'He burned down our house...'

'He set fire to the crops on our four-acre field just as they were ready to be harvested ...'

'He beat my son until he bled...'

'He kidnapped my son, took him to the camp, and killed him...'

'He killed my husband...'

'He destroyed my child's life...'

'He stripped my daughter and paraded her naked...'

Their deep-seated pain found expression in their words, their tears and rage and everybody started talking at once again.

'Stop it now,' Adamaal said loudly two or three times, and the crowd fell silent.

After some debate on what to do with the head, Jaini suggested, 'It should be thrown onto the road.'

A week later, Adamaal, Jaini, and Jugru met with Commander Mangtu, who was stationed in a neighboring village, and told him how Boklu and Mangal had killed Karre Ungal.

Mangtu noticed the excitement, rage, and anger in their voices. Everyone expected Mangtu to be happy and praise them for their good work.

However, Mangtu looked somewhat saddened. He lifted his head and looked at everyone's faces.

'So, what did you do with the head?' he asked sadly.

'Our people took it and threw it on the road. The police took it away,' said Jaini.

'That has become a big problem. Our enemies are using it to portray our mass organisations, *Janatana Sarkar*, and the party as monsters in every way possible,' Mangtu said.

'Didn't he commit numerous atrocities? He wreaked havoc in our village, didn't he? Moreover, our militia had decided to kill him!' Jaini replied.

At that moment, tea for the four of them arrived from the kitchen.

'Comrades! Our *Janatana Sarkar* was formed to create a world without violence. It works for higher values. The old method of 'an eye for an eye' is outdated. We are people who understand history and dialectical methods. We are communists. Did we take care of Boklu and Mangal after punishing them? The villagers ostracized them. What should our *Janatana Sarkar* do? After punishment, we should have given them an opportunity to reform through our work. What work did we give them? To remove the hostility among the people, we should have included them in our collective farming and militia, monitored their behaviour, and helped them correct themselves. Did we do anything for that?' Mangtu paused and finished his tea.

'No, *Dada*, we didn't think that way,' Adamaal admitted.

'They became isolated...and had no choice but to go to Karre Ungal. Isn't that so? They decided to prove their honesty by killing Ungal... What if Ungal had killed them? *Janatana Sarkar* needs to include more people, strengthen itself. Instead of individual decisions, we have an organisational structure. Any task should be discussed, decided, and executed through the initiative of the *Sarkar*. We need to improve our working methods, focusing on collective decisions rather than individual impulses,' said Mangtu.

'The burden of that tyrant has been lifted, hasn't it?' Jaini interjected.

'Yes but Boklu and Mangal should have done this along with the people's militia, and it should have been a collective decision. Displaying heads is not our method... We don't act out of anger or rage. We act to stop the violence inflicted on us, and that too, only when necessary and with minimal risk. Violence is not our nature. We are as pure as the forest. We are building a new world with *Janatana Sarkar*. Displaying heads is not our way. We need to explain this difference to the people and our members. I urge all our *Janatana Sarkar*s to discuss crime and punishment more comprehensively with their respective authorities and to act more responsibly in the future,' Mangtu concluded.

The three of them took their leave and started their journey back to their village.

They had expected Mangtu to praise them. 'Talking like this' didn't make sense to them initially. They discussed it all the way back.

Jaini thought to herself, 'We should request a meeting of all the persons in the justice department of the division to discuss such matters.'

Adamaal wondered, 'What tasks should we assign to Boklu and Mangal?'

Jugru seemed lost in thought, not fully comprehending all that was discussed.

Translation of 'Siksha'. (First published in *Arunatara*, January–February 2012)

Translated by N Ravi.

Red Flag

V.R.Chaitanya

The rain had stopped and the sky had cleared up. The landscape lay awash in the moonlight. A squad moved swiftly along the narrow pathway between the fields in the moon's soft glow. Not used to walking on these narrow paths, Padma stepped carefully, with her head down and focusing all her attention on her steps. She was anxious, fearing she might slip, and silently chided herself for still not overcoming this fear so long after she had come here. Somehow, she crossed the fields. Phew! A soft sigh escaped her lips as if she had just overcome a major obstacle, and her pace hastened to catch up with the comrades waiting for her. The squad continued swiftly along the narrow trail. Padma walked with a swift rhythm, matching the frantic pace of her thoughts. She recalled the *Sangam*'s meeting that morning, brooding over the decisions made, and thought about her tasks for the next day to ensure the success of the program scheduled for the day after. She was planning whom to meet and the duties she needed to delegate.

'Comrade, should we head to our den or the village?' asked the front pilot, pausing. Padma realised she had lost track of time in her thoughts. Glancing at her watch, she noted it was nearly ten o'clock.

'Let's not go to the village now; let's go to Birsu *dada*'s hut instead,' she replied, and the squad moved in that direction. In about ten minutes, they reached the hut. The noise stirred a dog barking from inside the hut. Cocooned in a shawl, Birsu *dada* came out, curious to see who it might be. Sunno, his wife, followed him. *'Lal Salaam... Lal Salaam...'* Both sides greeted one another with handshakes. All the squad members unloaded their rucksacks.

'*Dada*, is everything all right here?' asked Padma.

'For now, things are fine. I'll go into the village to fetch some rice for your meals,' he replied, preparing to leave.

'No need now *dada*, we had food,' she said. *Dada* sat down and lit a cigar. Padma blew the roll-call whistle, and the entire squad gathered in a formation. 'Attention... Stand at ease,' she cautioned, adding, 'Comrades, we will stay here for the next couple of days, finish our tasks, and then move on. Raju, Srinu, and Latha need to go into the village. The rest of you, look for your covers[1] and set up sentries in the direction we came from,' she instructed, and everyone moved to take their positions.

'*Dada*, you can go to sleep; we'll talk in the morning,' she said. Birsu *dada* and Sunno went back inside the hut. The squad members settled down with their polythene sheets in their covers and prepared to sleep. The comrades going to the village also identified their cover points and then came over to Padma.

'Comrades, when you reach the village, inform the militia about our location and tell them to perform the sentry duties with alertness. Also, bring Sukku *dada*, the leader of the peasants' association, and Kindo *naana*[2], the leader of the women's association along with you,' she instructed, and they nodded in agreement before heading out.

Everyone soon slipped into sleep, tired from the day's exertions. Although Padma's body felt weary, the cool and soothing moonlight refreshed her spirit. She sat for a while, enjoying the moonlight, and then went inside the hut to dry her sweat-dampened clothes.

Inside, a small fire was burning. Birsu *dada* lay beside the fire on a jute cloth spread on the floor, with a dog curled up next to him and Sunno sleeping on the other side. The hut had neither a door nor a lock – there was little to fear from thieves, as there was hardly any property to steal. The only things in the hut were a small stove in one corner, beside it was a vessel to store water, three earthen pots, a few tin plates and a box in another corner. On a woven bamboo shelf hanging above the stove were some salt, dried chillies, and two onions, all darkened by smoke. In another corner, piles of ears of corn and finger millets were stacked. All that remained for Birsu *dada* now was this small hut. Until a month ago, he had a home in the village. He had built it with great effort, working as a daily labourer alongside his wife. They had raised two children in that house, both born and brought up there. After the *Sangam* was formed, many meetings took place in that house. Just a month ago, however, the police raided and burned it to ashes.

Padma sat by the fire, stoking the flames. As she looked at Birsu *dada*'s face in the light, she recalled what he told her about the incident on that day.

At dawn that day, about 200 policemen, along with hooligans from the peace committee[3], stormed the village like a pack of wolves. They surrounded the village, leaving no scope for anyone to escape. The men in Khaki uniforms attacked the villagers indiscriminately – women, children, and the elderly alike – with sticks and rifle butts. Everyone was forced to sit together near the village centre. Some policemen stood guard around them, threatening to shoot anyone who moved.

Other policemen broke into their houses, stealing whatever little amounts of money and gold they could find. They spilled the stored food grains and other provisions onto the ground and mixed them with pesticide. They chewed tobacco and spat into pots of rice and gruel that had been cooked. Whenever they found anything red – flags, loincloths, shirts, saris, jackets – they stomped on them in frenzy and piled them up in the middle of the village, setting them on fire. Twelve young men were arrested, including Birsu's son, Dasu. Upon realizing that he was the militia commander, the police bound his hands behind his back, stripped and beat him until he bled. The Sub Inspector (S.I.) ordered, 'Burn his house; that's the only way these people will learn!' The police immediately set Birsu's house ablaze. Like the flames burning Birsu's house, the hearts of the people standing there were burning with anger and hatred. They felt helpless, unable to do anything.

Birsu *dada* was overcome with sorrow as he watched his bloodied son and his house burnt down to ashes and tears rolled down his face unstoppably. The S.I. viciously kicked Dasu in the stomach with his boots, saying, 'Get him up... he's overacting!' In pain, Dasu screamed in agony, *'Amma...'* He curled into a tight ball, overwhelmed by the pain. His mother, Sunno, ran towards him, weeping bitterly, but the police shoved her aside and hauled Dasu up. The S.I. turned to the women huddling together and warned, 'All of you, listen carefully! From now on, if you talk about *Sangam*, land struggles, rallies, *dharnas*, or meetings and go to Narayanapatna with your red flags, we will shoot you. Tomorrow, all the men of this village must come to the station and surrender. Otherwise, we will burn your entire village.' As if their task was done, he moved forward, calling out to his personnel, 'Let's go.' The other policemen followed, taking the twelve young men with them.

As the police surrounding them left, all the women burst into tears, wailing and cursing, clutching their children and running after the police. Against two hundred armed men, the twenty-five women were helpless. Once again, the rifle butts of the police struck the women and children mercilessly, leaving them bleeding and wounded. With bleeding bodies and wounded hearts, the women returned to their homes.

As soon as they came to know about this incident, the squad came to the village. The entire village was silent as a tomb, with only the wind left to mourn. There was no fire in any hearth. Meet anyone – tears were the only response. Birsu and Sunno were sitting listlessly under a tree in front of their burned-down home, having cried themselves to exhaustion. They had not even touched the gruel, flies swarming over the pot. The scene was heart breaking for Padma. The squad doctor, Lata, was treating those injured in the village. How many villages were ravaged? How many families were devastated? And how much suffering were they enduring? Can we fathom the gravity of the villagers' suffering? These thoughts weighed heavily on Padma's heart.

Hearing some commotion outside, Padma went out of the hut into the courtyard, leaving her thoughts about the past behind. Those who had gone to the village had returned with Sukku *dada* and Kindo *naana*, who shook hands with the squad saying, '*Lal Salaam, Lal Salaam.*'

Padma told Raju and others to go and rest, and then said to Sukku and Kindo, 'Sit down,' as she checked the time. It was already midnight. 'So, tell me, how is the situation in the village? Have you heard about any programs?' she asked.

Sukku replied, 'The situation in the village is fine. The police haven't come back since that day. The militia is keeping guard on all sides. We're not even sleeping in our homes. Just this evening, the *Panchayat* president told us there is a program to occupy the lands in Narayanapatna the day after tomorrow. So, we decided to hold a meeting of the *Sangam* executive committee, but in the meanwhile we got your message. So, here we are.'

'All right, we've come here for the same purpose. Tomorrow, let's set a clear plan in the executive committee meeting. Ensure the sentries are posted well around the village, and bring all the committee members. Also, assign two people to gather information from the neighbouring villages. Tomorrow night, people from distant villages will start arriving, so arrange *ambali* for everyone who comes along with food for all of us,' she said. They agreed, shook hands, and left.

By 8 o'clock, Sukku and Kindo returned with the committee members. They brought *ambali* for the squad and chilli and salt paste to eat with the gruel. Everyone shook hands, wiped the sweat off their faces, and sat down. When a whistle was blown, the comrades came and had the *ambali*. In the yard, Birsu *dada* and Sunno were drying out ears of corn they had brought out from the hut. After drinking *ambali*, Raju and Srinu joined in to help them.

The meeting began at 9 o'clock. 'Since there's the same agenda, it would be good for the committees from both *sangams* to sit together. What do you all say?' Padma asked, looking around. Seeing everyone nod in agreement, she looked at Sukku as a signal to start. Sukku stood up, put his hands behind his back, and began speaking.

'Comrades, we are fighting for this land, for our rights over the forest. Many have already lost their lives in this struggle. Hundreds have been arrested and are in jail. Recently, the police attacked our village and arrested 12 people. They burned down Birsu *dada*'s house. They're asking us to abandon the *Sangam*, to give up our lands, to surrender. But what wrong have we done? Why should we surrender? Is it a crime to demand back the land deceitfully taken from us? When we ask for justice, the police and landlords attack us together. Can we just watch all this and do nothing? If we remain silent, will they let us live? What should we do? Should we abandon the *Sangam*, abandon the fight, and surrender the land? Or should we keep fighting for our land even if it costs us our lives? What should we do?' Sukku paused momentarily, his eyes scanning everyone's faces for a response. Padma looked around, too, seeing what everyone would say. For a moment, there was complete silence.

'If we give up the *Sangam*, if we give up the fight, then we'll have to go back to working under those landlords and money-lenders again. We'll have to live like slaves under their feet, endure their insults and beatings. Better to die fighting than to live such a life. At least our names will be remembered, and our children might live better because of us,' said Kindo *naana*, stirring up agreement among the group. 'Yes, we won't abandon the *Sangam*, we won't give up the land, we won't give up the fight. Have we committed theft? Have we looted anyone? Have we murdered anyone? Why should we surrender? We'll never let go of this red flag as long as we live. Even if our blood spills on this land, we won't give up our land,' they said passionately. Seeing their spirit, determination, and their anger despite the heavy repression, the police attacks, killings, rapes, and arrests, Padma's heart was filled with admiration.

'All right comrades, our *Sangam* area committee has decided that we will enter the Narayanapatna lands tomorrow. People will bring ploughs and hoes from all the villages. Those who don't have hoes will bring spades. People from distant villages will arrive by tonight and stay in nearby villages. By dawn, we should all enter the land. Everyone must hold the red flags as they go,' said Padma. 'Then we should go at once! We need to gather everyone in the village, hold a meeting, collect rice, and prepare for many tasks,' Sukku said eagerly, ready to leave.

'Everything sounds good, but didn't the police burn all the red flags and red clothes when they attacked our village recently? What will we do now if people don't have them?' Kindo asked with a worried face.

'Yes, that's true...what shall we do?' Padma thought to herself. But Sukku quickly responded, 'Let's hold a meeting in the village and ask everyone to see who has any remaining red clothes or sarees. We can cut them into pieces and share them even if we find one or two. Otherwise, we'll find some solution.'

'All right,' everyone said as they stood up, shook hands with Padma and the squad comrades, and set off.

It was nearing 1 o'clock in the afternoon. All the comrades were working with Birsu *dada* and Sunno in the yard, piling up dried stalks of finger millets and threshing them with sticks. They had wrapped cloth around their heads to protect themselves from the dust, but their clothes were still covered in dust. Padma greeted them, asking, 'Have you all eaten?' 'Yes, we've finished. We kept some food in the hut for you,' they replied. She washed her hands and went into the hut. Having finished all her tasks, Padma ate the food and lied down to get some rest. She fell asleep almost immediately, as she had gone to bed late the previous night.

Suddenly, she woke up to a commotion. The comrades were carrying sacks of beaten finger millets from the threshing yard to the house and lifting the unbeaten ones into baskets, and piling them up in the corner of the hut. 'What's going on, *dada*?'

Padma asked in confusion. 'It looks like it's going to rain. These rains are destroying all our crops. It hasn't given us a break even for a day this year; how are we supposed to survive?' said Birsu as he dumped a basket of finger millet stalks into the hut and ran outside with the empty basket. Padma walked outside and looked up at the sky. Dark clouds had gathered thickly, and it seemed like rain had already started somewhere. The wind had also picked up. The comrades were busy setting up tents. By the time it grew dark, the thunder and lightning had intensified, and large raindrops began to fall, turning into a heavy downpour in no time.

Padma's thoughts were focused on the next day's plan. 'Ugh! This rain seems to be ruining everything. If only it would stop for just one day tomorrow. Everything has been arranged, and we've received news that people are coming from distant villages with ploughs and hoes. Poor folks, I wonder how they're travelling...' she thought to herself as she watched the rainwater streaming off the roof with concern. What should she do now? She couldn't stop the rain, after all! Que sera, sera, she thought, lying down again.

She woke up to the sounds of movement and saw a lamp burning in the hut. She turned and noticed Birsu *dada* and Sunno sitting in the light, working on something. 'Is it dawn already? Why did they get up so early?' she thought as she checked the clock. It was only three in the morning. 'What are they doing at this hour?' she wondered as she sat up to observe them. Sunno pulled a neatly folded polythene cover from under some clothes in a box, unfolded it, and took out pieces of red cloth. 'This one's for you, this one's for me, one each to tie around our heads, one for the plough, one each for the oxen, and one for my axe,' she said as she handed each piece to Birsu *dada*. He opened and checked each one carefully before folding it back. They were small red flags marked with a sickle and hammer, and they appeared even redder in the lamp's glow. At that sight, Padma snapped out of her drowsiness, and the discussion about the flags from the afternoon came to her mind. 'The police burned down your house...where did these come from?' she asked.

'As soon as we heard that the police were attacking villages, we brought them here and hid them carefully,' said Birsu. Padma looked outside, feeling a deep sense of affection, admiration, and respect for how they had preserved these flags with more care than their own lives. Although the rain hadn't stopped completely, it had decreased to a drizzle. Sunno arranged the rice balls she had made the night before in a basket, poured *ambali* into a bottle, and securely tied the polythene cover with the red flags to herself. She placed her axe on her shoulder and was ready. Birsu went outside, untied the oxen in the shed, took hold of the plough, and with an umbrella in hand, they both set off. As they left, Birsu said with a hint of regret in his voice, 'we're leaving you here; don't feel bad...you cook and eat by yourselves'. 'We'll be fine. You both go safely. We'll be waiting here until you return,' Padma said, sending them off.

The morning was upon them, and it was still drizzling. Two comrades, Lachhu and Krishna, arrived from the village, fully drenched, carrying *ambali*. After shaking hands with everyone, they sat near the fire, drying their clothes. Seeing them, Padma thought, 'Ah! They've come; that's good,' and asked, 'Lachhu, did you bring the phone?' 'Yes, it's here,' he replied. 'All right then, call Sukku *dada*. Do not talk to him about anything here, just find out about the situation and what's happening there, and let us know,' she instructed. Lachhu got to work on it immediately. Meanwhile, the comrades drank the warm *ambali*, eagerly waiting for news from Lachhu.

'Even in the rain, people have entered the lands of Narayanapatna'; 'They've tied red flags to their ploughs and hoes, entered the fields from all directions, and started tilling'; 'The whole area is packed with around 15,000 people'; 'From a distance, the fields covered with red flags look as if painted in red'; 'The landlords and shop owners have locked themselves inside their houses, shut down their shops, and vehicles have been stopped on the roads'; 'The police are watching from

the station and the streets but aren't approaching the people';
'Reporters have come to take photos' – Lachhu was giving a
running commentary of the updates, and the comrades were
cheering in excitement. Padma's heart was filled with joy too.
She had been tense, wondering if the program would happen,
but now all her worries faded as she eagerly awaited Birsu *dada*
and the others to return.

By four in the evening, Birsu *dada* and Sunno returned,
drenched in the rain, with their clothes soaked and red cloth
tied around their heads. Their faces were beaming with joy. As
they stepped into the courtyard, the comrades gathered around
them. 'Wait, wait...let them change their clothes first. Clear the
space close to the fire,' Padma said, and everyone moved aside.
After changing and drying their heads with a dry cloth, they
came to the fire and lit their cigars. Someone brought them
tea. 'Now, tell us how it all happened!' Padma asked, and the
comrades gathered around, eager to listen.

Sunno began excitedly, waving her hands as she spoke.
'Our *sangam* people went behind the police station and blew
the Kommu[4] to signal to everyone to enter the fields simul-
taneously. The police sitting nearby were so startled, thinking
something big was happening, that they panicked and ran
straight back into the station, shivering in their bones...' As she
narrated, everyone burst into laughter.

'So, the police didn't come out, *dada*?' asked Srinu.

'Police? They're just cowards! When they hear even a fire-
cracker, they run for cover. In the villages, they intimidate and
harass innocent people, but today, seeing thousands of people
approaching with drums, horns, and red flags, their hearts
sank. They just watched from the station rooftop, not daring to
take a single step forward. We would've dragged them through
the mud in those fields if they'd come out. They're scared of
the red flag...but for us, it's a source of strength.' As Birsu said
this, while carefully drying the wet red flags by the fire, his eyes
glowed with triumph in the firelight and in the glimmer of the
red flags. Padma thought, 'The unity and collective strength of

the people give them so much courage and assurance… nothing is impossible when people are determined!'

Happy with the outcome of the program, Padma stood up and said 'Comrades! It's getting dark, let's move'. Everyone picked up their backpacks and shook hands warmly with Birsu *dada* and Sunno, saying, 'We'll meet again.' The squad marched forward.

Translation of 'Erra Jenda' (First published in *Toorpu Kanuma*, April 2011)

Translated by Vimal

Notes:
1. Covers: When the squad halts at a place, each one of the squad members is allotted a place according to the formation of the squad, to take cover in case of any gunfire. These places are chosen by the commander as soon as they reach the halting place. Usually they would be behind a rock, or a tree or in a pit to cover them from gunfire.
2. *Naana*: Kuvi word for sister; Kuvi is the language spoken by the kuyi (aka Kondh) Adivasis in Odisha.
3. Peace committees: To suppress land struggles, the government established "Peace Committees," in North Andhra and Odisha area much like the notorious *Salwa Judum* in the Dandakaranya region. These committees include anti-people political leaders, landlords, oppressors, and violent mobs.
4. *Kommu*: a musical instrument made from a buffalo's horn

Priceless

Shaheeda

The Division Committee[1] (DVC) meeting was over and everybody was making preparations to go back to their areas. Like every other DVC member, Pusu was terribly busy too.

Pusu was planning appointments (APTs) with the couriers. He checked if things to be taken and given had been exchanged properly or if anything was missing. He wrote some important letters that had to be written. He tried to spend at least some amount of time with the comrades who had come to perform 'protection' duties for the camp from different areas and with whom he was quite familiar.

'Who knows which of them I will be able to meet again and who may be martyred?!'

He planned his journey with the comrades who were accompanying him and tried to make it faultless. This time, comrade Raimati of the higher committee was also accompanying him. So he tried to make the team understand the significance of this and the need for taking more precautions than usual. With all kinds of such tangible and intangible work he did not even have time to breathe.

Maybe the most difficult thing in the world was to understand how the human brain functions. Because even amidst all this, Pusu's brain was grappling with something else! It was wrestling with only one question since it was confirmed that he would be meeting Somaru *dada* within two or three days.

'How do I face him?'

Somaru *dada*'s village was on the way and they definitely

had to stop there for a day to complete their planned work. And if they stopped, they were bound to meet Somaru *dada*. It was not only inevitable, but Pusu necessarily had something to talk with him about. He had been waiting for six months for this opportunity. But even so, it was disturbing to Pusu.

No comrade who had ever worked in the area or is working at present would believe it if they were told that Pusu was disturbed about meeting Somaru *dada*. Because meeting *dada* was always a happy occasion for everybody. He loved the Party so much and is deeply affectionate towards the comrades.

Long back, Pusu had an encounter with the police and he was injured in his hand. After the injury healed, it became a habit for Pusu while sitting, standing or walking to keep touching the badly scarred skin just beneath his elbow where the injury had been. He did it so unconsciously that he was not even aware of it. His mind was similarly sub-consciously occupied with the matter related to Somaru *dada*. But if someone had asked him, he would have countered, 'Who said I was thinking of him?' And it would not be a lie.

'Pusu *dada*, that is the *Lal Salaam* whistle,' reminded his guard Sukku. Pusu hurriedly packed the letter he had just completed writing and wrote 'To Comrade Neela' on the pack and handed it over to Sukku saying, 'Hand it over to Birsa *dada*.' Sukku said, *'Ingo,'* and put it inside his pocket.

'Huh, even this time I wrote the letter hurriedly, sorry Neela,' Pusu tried to apologise to Neela in his mind, got up, folded his small *jhilli*, took his weapon and kit and looked around to see if he had by mistake dropped anything like pieces of paper. He could see none. Thus satisfied, he walked behind Sukku.

After everybody shook hands and said, *'Lal Salaam'* to each other in farewell, the Division Committee Secretary Sukiyari walked towards Pusu.

'Be careful where you have to cross the road...the Green Hunt operations...and with Raimati *didi*...'

'Don't worry we'll take all precautions...'

'It is not just that, her ill health...'

He did not let her finish the sentence. He just took her right hand into his and smiled.

Sukiyari looked at him as if to say, 'Why do we speak of such unnecessary things' and she too smiled. But both of them knew why. It was due to the anxiety that accompanies the moments of parting.

That is why even after the official *Lal Salaams* are over, some comrades shake hands once again in the last moments. With that small gesture, several things that cannot be expressed in words are conveyed to one another.

Sukiyari did not withdraw her tiny palm which nestled comfortably in his large, firm palms. 'When you meet Somaru *dada*, Raimati *didi* would also be there,' she said as if to give him some comfort.

Pusu never thought that it would be good to have somebody with him when he met Somaru *dada*. He didn't even think that talking with *dada* was a big deal. He just hurt inside. If at all he wanted anybody with him at that meeting, it would be Sukiyari. They had been working together for the past ten years. In the past two years since he was elected into the Division Committee, she understood him better. Somaru *dada* also knew her very well. Raimati had just recently taken over the responsibility of their Division. She came to their area for the first time.

Pusu did not say anything. He just shook her hands firmly. She looked at him fixedly for a few moments and turned back after conveying a 'goodbye' with her eyes.

Pusu looked at her retreating back till she disappeared as if to capture the image in his eyes forever and thought, 'Our Secretary reads me like an open book.'

After walking continuously for two days taking breaks just for breakfast, lunch and sleep, Pusu, Raimati and the team with them stopped for one day in a village. They had to finish some 'dump[2]' jobs there and then walk for another four days to reach their destination. Pusu and the comrades who accompanied him had left early in the morning after drinking some gruel for the 'dump' job. They were at it the entire day. They brought some lunch in their boxes and ate it in the afternoon. Though Raimati was in the *dera*[3], she was busy too – taking a bath, washing clothes, reading some necessary documents, writing some reports – and wasn't free even for a moment. After she completed all her tasks, she started translating a China Long March story into Koya for the PLGA comrades. She had been planning to translate it for many days. Now she found the time.

Raimati and others ate by 6.30 in the evening and changed the *dera*. The commander decided where their 'covers[3]' were to be and everyone spread their *jhillis* accordingly. By that time, Pusu and Co had arrived too. The team commander showed them where their 'covers' were and left. Pusu and all the comrades with him ate the meals kept aside for them in utensils and left for their respective resting places. The militia sentries were guarding the village and the area was also a relatively safer one. So all the comrades turned on their solar lights and started reading.

Pusu was dog tired and wanted to rest. But he had to meet Raimati first.

Raimati who was writing in the light of the solar lamp smiled at him and made room for him to sit by pushing aside the translation papers and the lamp.

Pusu recognised the story book and asked happily, 'Are you translating *didi*?'

'Yes. Ever since I told them the story, Siyabatti and others have been after me. They want the translated version.'

'Don't know how *didi* manages to do even such work despite having so much work burden!' thought Pusu admiring her effort. He informed her about the tasks that were completed that day.

'That means we can start tomorrow as previously planned, right?'

Pusu nodded 'Let's get up early and start at 4 a.m.. Our dump jobs should be completed by tomorrow evening there. If we complete that and walk without stopping for the night, it would be easier on the next day. We will send a small team ahead of us in the morning and cross the road by night.' Pusu repeated the plan they already made just to confirm to her that there has been no change in it.

Raimati nodded. She took out a magazine from a plastic cover and handed it over to him saying, 'I picked this up for you.'

'Oh, Hindi?' laughed Pusu. Pusu was from Telangana but he did not come from those areas where he could have learnt Hindi. Though he had been working in Bastar for many years, he still did not have much grip on the language. He listened to the Hindi news, read the Hindi newspapers and the party magazines published in Hindi. That was all.

'Of course, because it is in Hindi,' said Raimati laughing. 'No Pusu, you must get a better grip on the language. This is a magazine published by our mass organisations in North India. The language is lucid. That is why I selected this for you,' she added.

In fact, Pusu was one of the few comrades who learnt Koya language the fastest. After he was transferred to Dandakaranya (DK), in the earlier days he would particularly spare time to sit with elderly persons like Somaru *dada* to learn the authentic Koya language that is not adulterated with Telugu, Marathi or Hindi words. He used to tease the new generation Koya young-sters saying – 'What's this Koya that you people speak? The real Koya is with the older generation.'

Pusu remembered how Somaru *dada*'s eyes had lit up when he said this and now a smile played on his lips.

'Somehow I am not able to concentrate on Hindi. Maybe because of the fast growing responsibilities, I cannot find time...' He got into the habit of defending himself over this lapse with such arguments. So without thinking much he blurted out the same in this half sentence.

'I always think of sparing some time. But there is always something to attend to...'

'You are an educated man and if even you hesitate, what can one say? Your responsibilities are increasing. If we want to organise all classes of people in the areas we are working in, learning Hindi is compulsory. How many more times are we going to write in our reviews that there are lapses in organising vast sections of people? You tell me. Whatever you don't understand, you ask me, at least during my stay with you,' said Raimati firmly as if brushing aside any or all excuses. 'If you don't learn, this time you will be tasked with writing that review,' she added teasingly.

'Oh, she caught me at my lie.' Pusu smiled shyly. He called Sukku who was talking with Raimati's guard Siyabatti sitting a few feet away and gave him the magazine.

'Enquire if Sukki and others who have gone into the village are back,' he told Sukku. Before he could finish, Sukki appeared.

Sukki handed over a cloth bundle made from a big handkerchief to Pusu. He opened it and saw leafy vegetables.

'See, I told you, if we search earnestly we will find everything but you were like – where *dada*, where would we find the greens?'

He called Siyabatti and handed over the bundle to her. 'You and Sukki have a daily duty to perform. To whichever village we go, you should go in search of greens, collect them and cook them without chilli and with very less salt for Raimati *didi*. And you are forbidden to say – 'where *dada*, where would we find them?'

If you say so, I will come and show you where to find them and everybody will laugh at you both,' said Pusu laughing.

As they had been born and brought up in the forest, Sukki and Siyabatti felt amused that he was challenging them both and burst out laughing.

'And tomorrow it is to Sukki's village that we are going,' reminded Sukku.

'Fantastic! So you will know what all will be available and where. See if you can get some bitter gourds. We can dry them under the sun and store them too. People say eating bitter things is good for stomach ailments,' said Pusu.

All the three younger PLGA comrades nodded their heads and took away the cloth bundle with them to pluck and prepare the greens for making curry the next day. Raimati was a bit embarrassed but watched these happenings with a smile. She had an infection in her intestines and her health was seriously affected. Almost nothing was suiting her stomach. So she was forced to take some precautions regarding her food.

'Did Sukiyari instruct you?'

'Yes, but even if she didn't, I know it too..'

Raimati who never liked her health being a discussion point did not let him finish and changed the topic asking, 'Sukki's village means Rainu's village too, right?'

'Yes, and tomorrow we will be meeting Rainu's father Somaru *dada* too...'

Raimati was silent for a few seconds and asked hesitatingly, 'Are you tired?'

Pusu looked at her, surprise written on his face. Raimati understood. 'There is no question of my being tired when there are things to be done' is what it meant.

'No, it is just that I do not know in detail about that incident where you slapped Rainu. We were all discussing very important things and then there was the pressure of the meeting, so I did not get the opportunity to ask. So if you can sit for some more time, I would like to listen...'

Pusu lowered his eyes. He was silent for a few seconds contemplating where to begin.

'Rainu and Sukki belong to the same village. Both of them worked in the militia. There is not much age difference between them too. It's almost as if they grew up together. Both of them became full-timers. Both of them started working in the same squad. Rainu had a liking for Sukki. So Rainu proposed to Sukki but she did not accept the proposal saying she had always thought of him like a brother. Everybody knows this story. Everyone thought that from then on, he would withdraw.'

Pusu stopped speaking and just sat like a statue. He was not even aware that he stopped speaking.

After waiting for a long time, finally Raimati prompted, 'And on that day...?'

Pusu came out of his trance and said, 'Oh yes, on that day I was with their squad. Sukki and Rainu were on joint sentry duty. I do not know what he thought, but he began pressuring her to rethink. It was a mistake to talk during the sentry duty. Moreover, pressurising her when she had already refused was another mistake. Sukki could no longer bear it and approached us after threatening him that she would inform everyone. By then, he must have realised what he had done and must have been scared. He placed his weapon near the sentry point and ran. It was night time and everyone was asleep. The commander and I were awake because we were discussing something. As soon as Sukki came and informed us, the three of us ran to catch him. We could hear him running. We could even see him in the light of the torch. We asked him to stop, but he didn't. I was very tense and angry with what Sukki told us and by the fact that we had to chase him by lighting the torch in the midst of such state repression. Finally, I caught him. Even then he tried to wriggle out and run. It became impossible to get him under control. So I lost control and slapped him once. Only then did he stop. By then the commander had arrived too and both of us brought back Rainu to the *dera*. I have been going through self-criticism sessions precisely for this – losing my temper and slapping Rainu.'

Both of them were silent for a few moments.

'How many days after this did Rainu quit and go home?'

'He accepted his mistake and apologised to Sukki and to the Party. He said he would change. This time, we felt he was sincere. He realised his mistake. But what we did not understand at that time was that he had already decided to quit. He waited with the hope that Sukki would accompany him. But as things turned out in this manner, he did not stay for many days. He said he wanted to go home and quit. I have known him since his childhood and the family is also very close to us. So I spent a lot of time and energy trying to convince him to stay. I had already criticised myself for slapping him. He said he would work for the movement while staying in the village. When we go there tomorrow, we will know to what extent he is working. I haven't had any reports lately.'

'Huh, in spite of our giving so much education about respecting women's opinions, one or two such incidents keep coming to our attention. The strongest impact would be that of our women comrades' resistance to such things. That would be the biggest anti-dote, don't you think so?'

Pusu nodded.

'I wonder what the real reason was behind Rainu's decision to quit.'

'That is what I still do not understand. Some of our comrades say it may be because there is more discipline here than in the militia. It seems he had problems with following discipline even there. People say he had changed a lot by the time he joined the squad.'

'Without discipline, how long can anyone continue even in the militia? That too in the midst of such severe repression! There may never be one single reason for quitting, Pusu! Several factors influence it. Anyway, why am I explaining this to you?'

'It is okay *didi*, please do. Just because I have been working for some years doesn't mean I can understand everything. After some days, some new angle always crops up. Your experience is far superior to mine.'

'Anyway, what's there to discuss afresh about something that had been reviewed in the committees. You people must have discussed it from all angles. The reason for my asking is not just with a curiosity to know...'

Pusu understood.

'No *didi*, now I do not think that he quit because I slapped him. Earlier I thought so and was troubled a great deal because of it. We have reviewed....'

Raimati did not ask him why he was feeling so disturbed to meet Somaru *dada* if that was so. But he could see that question in her eyes.

'Are my feelings reflected in my face like in a mirror? Then it was Sukiyari and now Raimati. Or Sukiyari must have told Raimati. Yes, that is what must have happened,' thought Pusu.

But he was not in a position to talk. He was himself surprised at his feelings. What could he explain to her?

'Okay *didi*, I will leave, don't be awake for a long time, we have to walk such long distances tomorrow," said Pusu, getting up.

Raimati wanted to discuss things for some more time with him. But she hid her disappointment and said, '*Ingo.'* And she had no intention of sleeping yet. She pulled the translation papers towards her. 'If I don't finish this during the journey, I will not find time later.'

Pusu lay down on his *jhilli* but sleep eluded him.

In the past few years, they had been recruiting full time members into PLGA after assembling the entire village, informing them about it and also taking their opinions about the recruits. This has become the practice. They followed the same procedure when Rainu, Sukki and others got recruited from that village too. On that day the happiness on Somaru *dada*'s face was something to be seen.

Somaru *dada* had been a comrade who had stood firmly with the Party since its activities began in that area. He was very active in the DAKMS[4] in his younger days. As old age advanced, he retired. Now he was a pillar of support for the Kranthikari *Janatana Sarkar*, and a most reliable comrade for the Party.

There was also the bond that developed between Somaru *dada* and Pusu, who had worked as a commander in that area and later continued his work as the Divisional Committee Member (DVCM) in the same area. It is true that communists do not have any private property or families. However, the kind of bonds that developed between them and some families and some persons in the areas where they had worked in their early days or as commanders go very deep. It would almost seem as if only those who had experienced it could gauge their depth. It was because those bonds are closely intertwined with the development of those comrades.

The bond between Pusu and Somaru was similar. As Pusu was also present on that day of recruitment, Somaru *dada* had shared with him the pride and happiness he felt at Rainu getting recruited as a professional revolutionary. In the village meeting too, he gave advice to Rainu and those who were getting recruited along with him by reiterating several times that the Party was like a mother to them and that they should not quit the struggle till the poor gained political power. And the villagers pointed out Rainu's lapses in matters of discipline. Everybody was so content that the meeting went so well.

At the end before dispersing Somaru went to Pusu.

'Did you decide where Rainu would be posted?'

'No *dada*, it will be decided in the meeting.'

'Would you send him too far?'

Pusu felt amused and also had sympathy for the old man. In an attempt to lighten the atmosphere he teased him with familiarity, 'In the meeting, you encouraged them so much and now you are worried that he would be sent to far off places. Tell me, dear *dada*, how will we win the war if we don't expand our movement?'

'Good heavens! That's not the reason for my asking. They have to go wherever the Party sends them. I am not worried about it. I just feel he may turn out good if he is posted near you and works under your supervision ...'

'Any of our comrades would put a good effort to develop the newer comrades, *dada*...'

'No, no. That is not what I am saying. You know Rainu since he was a boy. He is a good lad, but sometimes suddenly something goes wrong within his head and he goes out of control.

That is why even the villagers spoke about his lack of discipline...'

'As far as I know, there is no plan of sending him anywhere. But you know very well how the needs of the movement influence decisions. That being so, any of us would have to go wherever we are sent. As far as possible, the Party allows the persons to work for one or two years, assesses them and only then transfers them to other places.'

But Somaru *dada* was not yet satisfied. His face reflected it clearly.

'Oh *dada*! Rainu is not going anywhere, nor am I. I will keep a watch on him not with one eye but both eyes. Just don't worry. He will develop into a good comrade. But you should also realise that all this is a collective effort and is not achieved by individual efforts alone. More importantly Rainu should feel internally that he should develop into a good comrade and serve the people selflessly. You had listened to the philosophy class, did you not? You know no chicken would be hatched by sitting on a stone....'

It was only then that Somaru *dada*'s face glowed. He even laughed at the idea of hatching a stone.

'*Ingo*. I understand. My only wish is he should develop to be like you,' said Somaru *dada* and happily shook hands with Pusu and with a *Lal Salaam* took his leave.

Whenever he thought of Rainu these days, all these things had been going around in Pusu's mind in a confused manner. Though he had explained about collective effort and internal causes to Somaru *dada*, he had actually accepted in his heart a responsibility for Rainu. In fact, he felt a responsibility for every comrade. However, as he had slapped Rainu, this had become more of a personal issue for him, however much he tried to avoid it. Reviews, assessments, discussions with Sukiyari were all done, but somewhere in his heart of hearts he thought – 'I have not kept my promise to Somaru *dada*. And I contributed to Rainu's decision to quit the Party'. He was not able to get rid of that thought.

'If Somaru *dada* also thinks that my slapping Rainu had contributed at least a bit to his decision to quit the squad then what?' This was the question gnawing at Pusu's mind.

'If he really thinks so, what explanation can I give him?' It is one thing to review with Party comrades, but it is quite something else to explain things to *dada*', he thought. 'What can I say? *Dada* wanted Rainu to develop so well inside the Party, he was so confident that I would help him in that task!' This was the thought to which Pusu returned to repeatedly.

When Pusu was transferred to DK, comrades had informed him right during the initial days that Adivasi women and men look after their children with a lot of love and that they don't beat their children. Whenever he found men carrying toddlers on their hips and going about their chores just like women, Pusu used to be fascinated. Though Rainu's issue was completely different, he was reminded of that too. There were moments when Pusu also felt that he was thinking in an individualistic manner but he was not able to overcome it.

After all those events, Pusu was going to meet Somaru *dada* for the first time only now.

He thought, 'Maybe that is why I am feeling like this, once I meet him and talk and present my self-criticism to him, this burden I am carrying will become lighter.'

His mind wandered to his partner Neela.

'When she needs me, I am not present, and when I need her, she is absent. What to do? I wonder what she's doing now? I won't be meeting her for another two months....'

Thinking of her with some disappointment and some love, he tossed and turned and finally slept at around 2 a.m.

By the time Pusu and others returned from their dump job the next day, it was already evening. When they approached the *dera*, they came across Sukki who had come there to collect the cut pieces of bitter gourd that she had kept there to dry under the sun.

'Oh, so you succeeded. What else did you get?' asked Pusu, walking alongside Sukki.

'Greens'

'Did *didi* eat?'

'She ate along with some gruel.'

'Good. So what did you cook for the evening meal?'

"We had collected a lot of greens. There is a lot of extra curry, so we kept aside some for you too.'

'No, I don't need it. But Rajesh, who came with us, is down with a fever. Send it to him. And yes, *didi*'s curry does not have any chillies, so put some chillies and heat it. With his fever, he may not feel like eating without chilli.'

Sukki nodded and left. Pusu found some villagers near the *dera*, so he went and shook hands with them. After some small talk, he and Sukku went towards the kitchen to wash their hands and feet. And there they found Somaru *dada* sitting on his haunches and sipping black tea. As soon as he saw Pusu, his face opened up like a flower and he got up to greet him. Both of them shook hands. As always a feeling of great warmth spread itself inside Pusu as soon as he saw *dada*.

'How does he manage to love all comrades from such depths of his heart? Half my tiredness is gone, seeing his smile,' Pusu could not help wondering.

'Prepare black tea for Pusu *dada* and others,' Somaru *dada* was encouraging PLGA comrades who were decades younger than him. Then he turned towards Pusu and asked, 'How many of you are there, *dada*?'

It did not seem like the squad's *dera*, nor did he look like a villager who came to visit it. It looked like it was his home and the squad members were his guests. It seemed as if a father or a grandfather was asking them to do some chores. It wasn't at all surprising. This was just one of the several such scenes one naturally encounters in several villages of DK.

'Twelve,' answered Sukku.

'No, it is eleven. Rajesh has a fever and I told our squad doctor to prepare some milk for him,' said Pusu.

Mangli was on kitchen duty and saying, 'Ingo,' she poured water into a vessel for the decoction.

By the time Pusu and Sukku came back after washing their faces and feet, piping hot decoction was ready and they filled their mugs. A bit of decoction was left. So Mangli poured it into her mug and gave it to Somaru *dada*. He protested, but she said affectionately, 'It doesn't matter, drink again, it is winter,' and he relented.

'*Dada*, come, let us go to our *dera*,' said Pusu and made him get up.

'Sukku! Don't forget my mug. After *dada* finishes drinking, bring it back to me,' shouted Mangli behind their backs.

'*Ingo*,' replied Sukku and Pusu at the same time. Even after so many years Pusu never let go of a chance to say '*Ingo*'. He was fascinated by the manner in which this word jumped out of their mouths so involuntarily. He also liked to observe the various meanings this word acquired on different occasions, apart from the usual 'Yes' and 'Okay'.

They went to the place where their 'covers' were located and spread their *jhilli* nearby. They were anyway going to start their march after eating, so there was no need to make any sleeping place.

'How is Budri *didi*? How are you? How is your health?' Pusu enquired.

'We are good. But nowadays I am not able to see so well after dark.'

'Oh, that's bad. Our doctor is nowadays testing eyes and prescribing glasses. But he is not in our area now. If he visits, I will ask him to conduct eye tests and prescribe glasses for you. But we do not know when he will come, it may be late...'

'It is better than nothing.'

'If he comes, bring Budri *didi* also to him for tests.'

Somaru nodded. After some such small talk both fell silent. They needed those silent moments to come to the real topic.

'How is Rainu doing, *dada*? How is he?' Finally Pusu asked, breaking the silence.

'He followed our comrades' advice and is working in the militia again. He is being good at home too, doing his chores, helping. We also made him talk with Sukki's family. They too advised him to be good and were good to him. If you had come earlier you would have met him. Their entire team went patrolling and for sentry duty outside the village just before you arrived.'

The difference between what Somaru was feeling and what his words were expressing was apparent. His voice betrayed his disappointment. If it was just disappointment, Pusu would not have been surprised. But there was a feeling of guilt in it.

That went beyond Pusu's comprehension because he was waiting for Somaru to get angry with him, accuse him, question him or demand an explanation from him.

Just then Raimati arrived and Pusu introduced them to each other. Usually when a higher committee member came to the area, Somaru used to talk and get acquainted with them with a lot of enthusiasm. Due to his experience even they would sit with him for some time, ask about his past experience and the details of the movement in his days which he happily narrated passionately. But today none of it was there. This was breaking Pusu's heart.

'*Dada*, do you know how everything happened regarding Rainu...'

'Yes, our comrades told me. I expected he would develop well. At least he could have stayed in the squad after he admitted his mistake. But no, he had to come home.'

Maybe Raimati also felt his disappointment unbearable. She intervened and said in a tone offering solace, 'It is not impossible for him to join again after working for some days in the militia, *dada*; there have been some past examples.'

Somaru slowly nodded his head, but his heart was not in it. It was very clear that he did not have much hope about such a thing happening. It was just a remote chance in his view.

'Will it happen soon? Would I be able to see it? Not very likely.'

Pusu was still trying to find a way to bring up the topic of his slapping Rainu if Somaru doesn't bring it up. It was obvious that *dada* was not much bothered by it. Pusu was now in a dilemma whether he should mention it or not.

'No, how can I not mention it? Unless I place my self-criticism in front of him, I won't find solace' he thought.

Unless Rainu's topic got out of the way, even Raimati felt there was nothing she could do to turn the conversation to other topics. So she also kept quiet.

Finally it was Somaru who said, 'It has been six months since Rainu came home, I have been waiting for you...'

'*Dada*, you know how our work is; even I wanted to meet you so much....' Pusu felt a lump rising in his throat.

'I have become old. All these days, I thought Rainu was there to work in the Party. But since Rainu came back, I have been thinking that I made a mistake. I felt first of all I should have got recruited. If I get recruited now, will you accept me? My Party membership is intact. You give me tasks that I am capable of fulfilling and I will carry them out. I have discussed this with Budri too.'

Raimati and Pusu were shocked to hear this proposal that came out of the blue in such an unexpected manner. 'Did he discuss it with Budri *didi* too? Does it mean that this is a serious proposal?' The same questions arose in both their minds.

But Somaru was looking at them very anxiously. Pusu was till then only thinking of how to bring the topic of his self-criticism into the conversation, so it took him some time even to grasp the real meaning of what Somaru was saying. He sat there just staring at *dada*.

Raimati understood his state of mind and said, '*Dada*! You live in the village and are like a pillar of support for the Kranthikari *Janatana Sarkar* and this is in no way to be underestimated. The experience of your generation of people is very valuable to the next generations. It is not that everybody should join the squad. You have done whatever you could in your time. It is never valued any less. And then Rainu is not your only child, just look at the squad comrades here. They, the *Janatana*

Sarkar and the mass organisation activists are all like your own children. You must share your experiences with them. You should teach them why it is important to be with the Party and the struggle and to not abandon them, ever. This is a very big task,' Raimati explained, trying to soothe him.

Somaru *dada* now turned towards Pusu as if he understood that it would be difficult to convince Raimati.

'Pusu! You tell our people to recruit me. I will do whatever work you give. I will go wherever you want me to go. Where is Naaranna? You tell him, he knows me from my earlier days, he would definitely accept,' Somaru *dada* was pleading.

It was then that Pusu came out of his reverie and said, 'No *dada*, don't take so personally what Rainu had done...'

Somaru *dada* intervened before Pusu could finish. 'No, no. It is not like that. Whatever I thought was not because of it or only concerned with it. Maybe I cannot run around like you, as actively, but definitely there would be some work that I would be able to perform. You are the leaders, you think and tell me. Where is Sukiyari *didi*? She is also closely acquainted with me, she will definitely recruit me...'

Somaru's voice was shaking. Even as Pusu and Raimati were looking at him, tears rolled down his wrinkled cheeks.

Whatever preparations Pusu had been making all these days to face the situation now turned utterly useless within seconds. And the explanations he wanted to give? Words, they are nothing but mere words, which are worth nothing. Somaru *dada* had turned everything upside down. Somaru *dada* was causing a tumult with his words.

Pusu slowly got up, sat near Somaru *dada* and held him close to his bosom. As always, solace led to more tears. Pusu felt as if those tears were pouring over the innermost recesses of his heart without sparing even the remotest corners and washing away all kinds of murky things left over there.

Pusu looked at Raimati through the tears welling up in his eyes. He did not find any sign that she was trying to control herself like him.

Translation of Amulyam (First published in Arunatara, March 2017)

Translated by the author

Notes:
1. Division Committee: a Party committee
2. Dump: a safe storage space for ammunition or papers or any other critical material.
3. Cover: the place where each comrade is supposed to take her/his position to fire on the enemy in case of an attack, usually a boulder or a tree trunk, something that can offer 'cover.'
4. DAKMS: Dandakaranya Adivasi Kisan Mazdoor Sangathan, the peasant-laborer organisation

The Story of an Arrest
Bharati

I t was the first week of June. The day was cloudy and it started to drizzle lightly. The squad had set up small tents among the trees. Everyone helped with tasks like gathering firewood and lighting fires, and collectively completed the cooking.

'We will have a collective study session after everyone has eaten,' said Comrade R.K.

After eating, everyone cleaned their guns and gathered for the study session. Ideally, they would study together for two hours every day, but sometimes it wasn't possible. On that day, they sat together for a longer time. The light rain had turned into a heavy downpour, making it hard to hear what was being read because of the noise on the tent. The collective study session ended up feeling like a farce.

'Comrades, we have an appointment in the evening. After that, we will head to the plains,' announced Comrade R.K., who was a member of the Warangal district committee and was with our squad as part of his duties.

Some people studied on their own, while others lay down to rest.

After the area committee meeting, the squad commander said, 'There is an appointment at 4 p.m. in a village, after which we'll move from here. Nakshatra, you need to change into civilian clothes and go to the village I mentioned.'

I changed into civilian clothes and set out to the village. It took me half an hour to reach it. When no one showed up for the appointment, I came back. By then, the squad had descended from the hill, and I met them at the base. It was around 6 p.m.

'Hurry up and change your clothes; we'll cook after crossing the road,' said Commander Ailanna.

The drizzle continued lightly. The day remained dark with overcast skies, and cool wind was blowing. The trees, which had shed their leaves, were now sprouting fresh shoots. The smell of the wet earth was pleasant, and the squad members were enjoying it, each in their own way.

'Do not talk while traveling,' warned the commander.

We crossed the Jaakaram road and halted close to the nearby village, Sriramulapalle. The wall around the well where we halted was gravelly but the field was muddy.

'Nakshatra and Suseela, both of you go into the village, get some rice cooked, and bring the *Sangam* members along. We will stay here until you return,' the commander instructed. Suseela and I bade farewell to everyone with a *Lal Salaam* and walked towards the village. It was almost 8 p.m. by then. Commander Ailanna pointed out a school as a landmark in case we lost our way and told us to signal when we returned.

'Don't get scared in the night! Be careful, there are dogs in the village!' Comrade Shyam said teasingly.

Ignoring his words, Suseela and I walked confidently towards the village. We went to the house of the *Sangam* members. The *amma* and *akka* of the house greeted us with *Lal Salaam*. 'Have some food, child,' said *amma*.

'We are 15 people, *amma*, could you cook some rice and dal for us to take?' I asked. The mother and daughter quickly cooked rice and dal. The *Sangam annas* had gone to work till late in the evening and it didn't look like they would return any time soon. It was almost midnight. We decided it was time to leave, and said our farewells to the mother and daughter. I balanced the bundle of rice on my head, while Suseela carried the steel can of dal.

'Be careful, children. The village dogs have been barking a lot,' *amma* cautioned.

We walked slowly along the muddy road soaked by rain, and reached the school. If we turned around the corner near the school, we would reach the squad.

Suddenly, someone materialized out of the dark, asking, 'Who is there?' He had a .303 rifle slung over his shoulder, and it was clear that he was a policeman. He grabbed the bundle of rice from my head, asking, 'What is this?'

Both of us had a grenade in hand. I hinted to Suseela to place the grenade on the nearby wall, as I did the same. Suseela got my hint and placed her grenade on the wall as well. The policeman didn't notice this because of the darkness. We regretted not being able to use them.

'What's in the bundle? What's in the can?' he shouted. We just stood silently.

'Get up, get up, the squad is nearby. They are taking food to the squad, hurry up!' the policeman shouted. We realized then that a complete police team was there. We were caught by the enemy and were certain we would die. The enemy didn't understand that our squad was nearby. Determined not to give away the squad's location, I held Suseela's hand tightly. She understood my thoughts and squeezed my hand reassuringly.

All the policemen sleeping in the school[1] quickly got up and came towards us. They gathered around us, opened the food bundle, and poured out the dal. They patted our shoulders, checking if the skin there was calloused from carrying the gun for a long time. It was still drizzling lightly.

'Where are you going?' one policeman shouted loudly.

'We are crane workers. There's no electricity till nightfall. So, our men are at the well, trying to operate the crane through the night until dawn. We came for food," we replied.

"Where is the work site?" he asked.

"On the Jaakaram side," we answered.

They didn't believe us. Two policemen went and woke up the nearby house residents and asked them about it. Those people said that crane work doesn't happen during the rainy season and it's not currently being done in that village. The policemen returned and relayed this information.

Immediately, one policeman called on his cell phone, 'Sir,

we have detained two women. They are taking food and curry, sir.'

On getting instructions from the other side, he said 'Let's all go outside. Take us to where you were taking the food and curry.'

Thinking that we needed to make a big scene to alert our people, I started crying loudly, 'Please Sir, we don't know anything. Don't take us anywhere, we haven't done anything.' Suseela also began to make a big fuss.

'You claim you don't know anything, yet you are taking food to the squad. They won't listen like this, bring a stick,' one policeman said. Another brought a thick stick and hit both of us three or four times. We cried out loudly in pain. They stuffed cloth into our mouths to silence us.

One policeman came close to us and said, 'You are making a scene on purpose. Tell us where you were planning to go, and we won't do anything to you. Which squad are you from?' With the cloth stuffed in our mouths, we could only shake our heads and couldn't speak.

The commotion was starting to draw the attention of nearby residents. 'Everyone, stay inside and go to bed!' the policemen yelled, driving them back indoors. It was pitch dark, and the dogs were barking loudly. We had to find a way to mislead them. We decided to take them towards Jakaram road, as the spot was already exposed. It was a semi-forested area there. The police, about 25 of them, were making us walk in front, following us closely and walking in parallel. They took a prone position at any small sound. When we stopped in confusion, they whispered, 'Sit down, sit down.'

'Take us directly to them. We don't want to die unnecessarily. So tell us when we are close, and signal us before you speak. We will fire on them, and then let you go,' one policeman said in a low voice.

Their fear made us want to laugh. Poor fellows, they didn't realize they were aiming their guns at people fighting for the likes of them, for the poor and downtrodden.

The fields had been ploughed once, making the ground sink to knee level. The policemen were bending and walking through the fields. Meanwhile, the Sub-Inspector's cell phone lit up. 'Sir, we can't see anything, it's all fields, and it's drizzling lightly,' he said.

'Find a spot to sit in the field. We will move at dawn. Sir said they would come. Set up sentries in all the directions,' the S.I. instructed.

Our hearts were pounding. We didn't know what happened to the squad. We were leading the police, making them believe that the squad was on this side. We had no idea what the situation would be by dawn. It started raining heavily. The policemen, scared, kept their guns ready and waited for dawn. When they saw fireflies flying around, they said 'looks like your people are coming. Give the signal.' We didn't respond. They said the same thing again, so we gave the signal.

'Hey, is this the correct signal? Are you sure? Is it something else?' they asked.

We told them that it was the correct signal and whistled twice like birds. There was no response from the other side. We waited until dawn. Gradually, rays of light began to appear. 'Let's go, let's go,' everyone said as they got up. We took them to the well where we always stop. The well was next to a path used by carts and it ran alongside a row of green trees. The police looked around the well. There was nobody there nor were there any footprints. They asked us to call out. I shouted 'Oh Rajanna' twice but there was no sound from any side.

'These bitches lied and brought us here. They fooled us until the squad escaped,' they said, and started to beat us with sticks. The first two or three blows made my body burn. After that, I didn't feel anything. Cursing us, they went on beating us as they pleased.

'You lied to us and got us drenched in the rain all night,' they said, venting their anger.

For a while, I couldn't speak. They poured water on my face, lifted me, and kicked me hard, making me fall far away.

They lifted Suseela and beat her severely. They made us walk some distance.

After a while, the Deputy Superintendent of Police from Mulugu came with many people. They took us into the forest from the place where we were beaten and kept us in separate places.

I was wearing a saree and blouse, while Suseela was in a skirt and jacket. They gave us guerrilla uniforms and told us to wear them. They made us stand in one place. We thought we were going to die. We looked at each other. We communicated with our eyes, deciding not to say anything we knew. They gave us caps to wear, so our heads wouldn't be visible.

They took Suseela away. Following the DSP's orders, four men beat her again with sticks. They kept saying, 'Tell us now and you will live. Otherwise, we will kill you here.'

'I don't know, sir,' she wailed.

Then they took me to the DSP.

'You saw what happened to your comrade. We will strip and beat you too. You tell us, or we will 'encounter' both of you here. You didn't tell us last night and let the squad escape. Where is the squad headed after having their meal?' he showered me with questions, cursing intermittently.

'We don't know, sir. We are new, sir,' I said.

'Don't tell stories. Would you carry food without knowing? Where were you taking the food?'

'They asked us to bring it here, sir. We were supposed to stay here.'

'She will not talk like this. Strip her clothes off,' he said.

'No, sir, we don't know anything, sir,' I wailed. They beat me with sticks again till the sticks broke.

'This is the last time I'm asking. Where would the squad go after eating?' the DSP asked.

Pretending that I am unable to bear the pain, I finally said, 'They planned to stay on the hillock beyond Jaakaram, sir,' revealing the place we had already passed.

'You aren't telling the truth, I know. How many people are

there?'

'There are ten people, sir.'

'You are lying. Why would you take so much food for just ten people?'

'The leftovers are for the morning, sir,' I said. They kept asking the same questions for about an hour. The DSP left in between, talking on the phone and returned, cursing. 'How old are you? Aren't you ashamed? You joined the Naxalites to bring revolution, eh? Hold them separately,' he ordered and left.

By then, the rain had stopped. It was about eight o'clock. Our bodies were swollen and we couldn't sit or stand. They sent for food and brought it on leaves for us after everyone had eaten.

'We don't want it,' we said. 'Eat the last meal before you die,' they said, leaving it there. We drank some water but didn't eat the food.

Three new officers arrived.

'Give us information now and you will live,' they said.

'We don't know anything, sir,' we replied.

One of the officers said, 'There is no point in asking them. We should just shoot them and send them to hell to meet their squad.'

Another one said, 'We should strip them, tie them to a tree and beat them mercilessly.'

Various thoughts ran through my mind. They might leave us here and search the nearby villages, claiming an encounter occurred if they found any of our people. The squad might have realized we were arrested. They might have heard the commotion when we were arrested. At least the sentry might have heard it. Who knows where they went in the rain?

The police discussed among themselves for a long time. After a while, two jeeps arrived with the DSP from Mulugu. Everyone stood up and started to move around quickly. One of them said, 'Bring them.'

It must have been 10 in the morning. We started walking towards Jaakaram with the two of us in the middle, and batches of police in front of us and at our back ... People herding sheep and goats passed by.

My trousers were loose and slipping down. A policeman gave me a belt. They also put a cap on my head. It was difficult walking with a swollen body. Two policemen held my hands and helped me walk. Two batches of police walked parallel to us, ensuring we weren't visible to any passing farmers.

We crossed Jaakaram road and lake. There is a small forest and plantation next to the lake. We skirted the villages and went through the forest and came to a *thanda*[2]. There are fields and wells next to the *thanda* and a stream flowed through the fields. The police stopped near the stream and asked us if the squad said it was going to come there. We replied in the affirmative.

They went along the stream for some distance looking for the squad but couldn't find anyone. They talked to the farmers working in the fields and all of them said they didn't see anyone. One of the officers asked the farmers to give them water to drink. After all the policemen drank water, they also gave us some and then we were taken to the hillock in front of us.

The DSP came to me and said, 'Now tell us, and you will live. You have made us wander around for a long time. You said the squad would come this way.' They separated me and Suseela and questioned us again about the squad for another half an hour. Later, I heard the sound of gunshots. Three rounds were fired. I thought Suseela was martyred.

The DSP came to me and said, 'Give us information at least now; that girl is dead. You heard the gunshots, didn't you? No one knows you are in our custody. By morning, the papers will say an encounter took place, and two women died. Tell us, where was the squad planning to go?' I replied, 'I truly don't know, sir.'

He said, 'You are very young. You have a life ahead. You are unnecessarily dying at our hands. She is already dead,' and loaded the pistol and said, 'You go back.'

I replied, 'Why should I go back, sir? If you want to kill me, kill me. We don't know anything. I am not lying, sir.'

Two people came and pushed me aside. 'It's up to you, sir. We don't know anything,' I said as he fired a shot next to me. I thought he aimed at me, and I thought I was dead, but he fired next to me. He fired one shot and stopped. As he walked down the hillock, he said, 'Take her and finish her off where we shot the other one,' and they started leading me.

It was getting close to six in the evening. 'Bring her to the lake bund,' the DSP said. As I walked on the bund of the lake, my steps were slipping.

If they killed Suseela, why didn't they kill me too? If they had to kill, they should have killed both of us, right? My mind was filled with various thoughts. Since they didn't find the squad, they might take me back to the forest again. So far, I haven't admitted to being part of the People's War Party. If tomorrow the newspapers publish statements from our Party, they might kill me. Suseela must have suffered a lot before she died. She became a martyr at the age of 17. She didn't reveal anything to the enemy.

The vehicle got stuck in the mud and came to a halt. It wasn't starting again. They tied it to a van and tried to pull it, but that didn't work. It seemed like the battery was dead. We were stranded for quite some time, and the police were furious.

'All this happened because of these bitches. They made us roam the whole night for nothing,' they muttered angrily.

'It's getting late. We are taking three policemen with us. Go to the village and bring some farmers and try to pull the vehicle with ropes. Or else we can get it later. Wait for some time and see.'

Saying this, the DSP started to leave. After a few steps he stopped and turned back to look at me. 'Eh. You come with me,' he said.

Until we reached the bus stand, my stomach was churning

with the thoughts of Suseela. I felt like crying with the pain of the loss and fear. I didn't know what to do. By the time we reached the Jaakaram bus stand, another batch of police were already there waiting for us and I saw Suseela in their midst.

When I saw her, relief washed over me. So they didn't kill her. They just threatened me, that's all.

She had changed her dress. Even my belongings were with her. 'Ask her to change her dress,' the police told Suseela. She came and handed me the dress. She also thought that the police killed me. Tears welled up in her eyes. We moved a little bit aside and I changed my clothes. We didn't know where they were taking us now. They took us to the bus stand but there were no buses at that time. They stopped a lorry that was passing by. We were asked to get into the lorry along with some of the policemen and we got down at the Mulugu police station. Perhaps they were not going to kill us. They pushed us both into a room and locked us up and gave us food.

'Eat. You'll need it. We'll take care of you tonight,' they said.

We thought they might beat us a lot that night. I got a high fever and headache. I didn't feel like eating. They gave me a tablet. Then they asked for our real names, our villages and said they will inform our families. We told our village names. After a while, they locked us up again.

The lockup room was pitch dark. The smell was nauseating. There were police crates stacked in front of the room. The two of us sat there, gripped with fear. We quietly started talking.

'The police said you were dead. They said you were shot. My heart nearly stopped. I can't tell you how happy I was when I saw you at the bus stand,' I said.

'They even beat me with sticks up in the hills. Did they beat you too?' asked Suseela.

'Yes, they did. After they caught us, more batches of police must have been dispatched. I wonder when our squad figured out that we were caught and what difficulties they faced,' I said.

We were sitting and talking like this, uncertain about when the police would come and beat us. Every time the sentry changed, they kicked the boxes in front of the lockup. Hearing that sound made our hearts sink with fear.

Dawn broke. The two of us sat in a corner. A constable came and said, 'The newspapers say you've been arrested. Which party do you belong to?'

We didn't say anything.

'The DSP has come. Now he'll ask us to bring them,' the constables were talking outside the lockup.

Our hearts raced, fearing that we'd be beaten again. No matter how much they hit us or questioned us, we thought we shouldn't say anything. Just then, a constable came and unlocked the door of the lockup. 'Come on, they're waiting for you,' he said sarcastically, smiling, and took us to the DSP's office. Our hands and feet were trembling. Words barely came out of our mouths due to weakness.

'Are you joking with me? Don't I know if you lie to me? Tell the truth without me having to ask, or else I don't know what I might do!' he yelled angrily.

He seemed ready to act. We thought he wouldn't stop even if we resisted. At that moment, a constable entered and said, 'Sir, it's ready in that room, sir.'

Immediately I said, 'We lied out of fear, sir. We belong to the People's War Party. My name is Nakshatra, and her name is Suseela. Our commander is Ailanna.'

The DSP, seated in his chair, stood up and kicked me, asking, 'Then why didn't you say so before?' I was thrown to a corner of the room, and Suseela collapsed. He hurled abuses that I cannot describe. He was furious.

'You made fools out of us. We kept searching here and there until dawn, thinking the squad would be found. We waded through filth. Whatever we do to you now is justified. Take both of them to that torture room,' he ordered.

They took us both to the adjacent room. There was a stick tied with a rope. A constable said, 'They should be given electric shocks.' Another was preparing the wires.

They tied Suseela's legs and hoisted her up, so that her

hands and legs came together. She screamed aloud, 'I don't know anything, sir!' she cried out. They did the same to me, and a terrible fear gripped me, as if my life was about to end. They were showing us hell. My nerves were taut with pain. My head spun, and after being lowered, I felt completely disoriented, as if my life had left me. They beat us without any consideration for us being women. The fear I felt at that moment was indescribable, even greater than the fear of death. When they hit with the ruler stick, blood clotted into thick, red patches. My face was swollen. They didn't give me electric shocks, but they took Suseela away. However, they brought her back without giving her electric shocks.

The DSP then said, 'We know your names and your party. Whatever we ask, you only repeat what's in the papers. When we ask other questions, you say you don't know. They know everything but won't tell us. Take them away from me.'

'Now, if you tell the truth, you might survive. Sir is a good man. If you don't speak, he'll continue beating you,' said the constable who took us outside. 'Wash your face,' he instructed as he led us to a tap in the midst of filth and stains from discarded pan spit. The police station was as filthy as the minds of the policemen.

Half an hour later, they brought us out of the lockup. There was a jeep waiting in front of the station, with the DSP seated in the front. A few policemen got in, and they covered our faces with sheets and made the two of us sit by their feet. Breathing was difficult with the cover over our heads, and sitting hunched over made our backs ache. We had no idea where the jeep was headed.

It seemed more than an hour had passed before the jeep finally stopped. Everyone got down, and they told us to get down as well. When they removed the sheets from our faces, we saw policemen everywhere, and police quarters around us. People were coming and going. They made us sit on one side. We assumed we were brought to a police camp.

A jeep pulled up and stopped. Everyone stood up at

attention. Another jeep arrived, and three men who looked like officers got down. They placed chairs near where we were sitting for those three.

'What are your names?' they asked. We told them.

'Don't lie to us. If you tell the truth, we'll let you go. We haven't officially announced your arrest yet. Keep in mind that we could still do an encounter right now.' They asked us the same questions the DSP had asked before.

'Are you married?' one asked. I said, 'No.'

'Really?' he asked again. 'Yes, sir, really,' I answered.

They asked a variety of questions, like, 'How does your squad operate? Who all are in the group? Who are your contacts in the villages? What are their names? Have you set up any organisations? Where? Who are the RYL (Radical Youth League) people in your area?' To all these questions, our only answer was, 'We don't know anything. We're new recruits.'

'Why did you join the Party?' they asked.

'If we want to do some good to the society, it's possible only in the People's War Party,' we replied.

'You are talking about many things but not telling us anything about your squad,' the officers said.

'We really don't know because the decisions regarding where the squad will go are taken on the spot. They don't share every matter with all the members,' we replied.

They asked the same questions for a long time. We had no information to give, and we had nothing more to say. At one point, they even brought us tea. They kept hitting us intermittently. By then, it had been three days since we were arrested. We didn't have a female constable with us. Only a male constable was accompanying us, even when we needed to go to the bathroom. Due to the beatings, our legs and arms were swollen and we were in a lot of pain.

The officers left. Again, we were put in a jeep and taken to the Mulugu police station, where they locked us up again in the rundown cell. After a while, someone brought painkillers and rice and told us, 'You have to eat the rice to get the painkillers.'

We tried to eat the rice but couldn't, so we threw it away and took the painkiller.

We talked quietly until dawn about the innumerable people who died in fake encounters[3], about those who were tortured and killed in police custody, about the leaders of mass organisations living in villages who have been harassed and tortured mentally and physically by the police. We told each other that our troubles were small in comparison. By then, it was the fourth day since our arrest, but we had no idea about the situation outside. We heard the police talking among themselves that Buchanna of Narsakkapalle, the in-charge of area RYL, set fire to a bus in protest against our arrest and he died in the action. Two female constables came, and after they arrived, they took us out of the lockup. One of them escorted me to the bathroom and told me the news from the papers.

They brought us out of the lockup and made us sit. Every police person who came to the station, regardless of their designation, asked us the same questions, and we kept repeating the same answers until we felt we were going mad.

Seven days passed like this. One time, they took me alone to the Mamunoor camp. There was a high-ranking officer there.

'Are you married or not? Tell the truth,' he asked.

'Honestly, I am not,' I replied.

'If you were married, what should we do with you?' he continued.

'I am not, sir,' I answered.

Without saying anything else, he said, 'Call Prasad. We'll discuss this with him.'

I didn't know that Comrade Prasad had been arrested. My heart nearly stopped. They brought Prasad, who also didn't know about my arrest. He looked at me with surprise.

'What is her name?' the officer asked him.

'Nakshatra,' Prasad replied.

'Is she married?'

'Yes,' he said.

'To whom?'

'To R.K.,' Prasad answered.

'Take him away,' the officer ordered.

My situation became dire. He told the female constable to leave the room.

'You bitch! How many lies will you tell? You lied about the squad? When the squad was on one side, you made us go around the entire Jaakaram side. When I asked if you were married, you said no.'

He called two policemen and asked them to bring sticks. They stood on either side of me.

'Now tell me the truth. What is it?'

'I don't know anything,' I replied, and each time I said that, I got hit on my back. My whole body was aching from the blows. A slap landed on my cheek. Tears welled up in my eyes, and my face turned red.

'How long has it been since you got married?'

'It happened in April.'

'So, three months. Where did you hide the dumps?'

'I don't know,' I started to say, but before I could finish, I was struck on my back with lathis.

'Was R.K. with the squad when you were arrested?'

'Yes, he was.'

'Why did you lie?'

'I was scared, so I didn't tell you.'

This questioning and beating continued for an hour to an hour and a half. I was getting really angry. He was asking me things I truly didn't know. Just because I was R.K's wife, would I know about money or dumps? The party has its procedures. It felt like my whole body was burning with headache and fever. The officer kept asking the same things unrelentingly.

'Give them both tablets and take them to all the places they've been,' he said and walked away.

They put me back in the jeep. The female constable with me said, 'Why are you taking these beatings? You could just tell them, right? You're getting beaten unnecessarily,' she said, trying to give me advice, which made me really angry. While they were hitting me, she could have spoken up, but now she was advising me. They took me back to Mulugu in the night. I told Suseela that Prasad got arrested too and he told the police that I was married to R.K. The next morning they put me in a jeep without a female constable and took me to Jaakaram. There, as we walked through the forest, the path and the hillock, they kept asking me about the squad and the dumps[4] and I kept telling them I didn't know anything. At about 7 p.m., they brought me back to the station.

In this way, we stayed in the foul-smelling lockup at Mulugu station for 15 days. One day, after taking our signatures and handprints, they took us to Warangal. They placed handcuffs on both our hands. Since our hands were thin and the cuffs kept slipping off, they tied cloth around them. Everyone was looking at us. That day, we went to the jail.

In the jail, we were looked after well by all our people who were already there. They brought medicines for our pain. For a month, the bruises on our bodies didn't fade. For many days, we couldn't get up or walk. Our *akka*s in the jail took care of us with a lot of affection. Comrade Kattanna was in jail (he later became a martyr in a fake encounter). When he found out we had arrived at the jail, he arranged a meeting and talked with us.

'They beat you badly. Will you go to the hospital?' he asked.

'We're taking medicine here,' we replied.

He told us about the jail routines and how we should conduct ourselves. 'Stay strong. Soon, you might be able to go out on bail,' he said.

He told us about what happened with the squad on the day we were arrested. That day, they had been near the well keeping a watch for a long time. Due to the rain, they hadn't gone anywhere. Early in the morning, they went up the hill. They had heard the commotion when we were arrested. But they thought, 'It's the Moharram festival; maybe the kids are making a ruckus.' Around two or three in the morning, they went to the village and found out we weren't in the village. Then they went to the people who had given us food, and they told them that a lot of time had passed since then. When they heard the dogs barking loudly, they assumed we had been arrested and left.

Hearing all this, the two of us cried.

'We shouldn't cry; what we need to do is take a stand. When we stand by the people, the government and the police subject us to brutal torture. Torture is nothing new for communists. When I was running from the police, they fired at me. I was hit in the leg and fell; then they caught me. They know that the only ones doing good for the people are the People's War Party, so they shoot us dead for fighting against the government. They subject us to all kinds of torture. Will a revolution come just like that? Every morning, every evening, people are killed in police shootings, and no one knows who dies and when. The state conducts encounters daily. We know how many of our leaders were killed in fake encounters. In these circumstances, we must remain brave. The struggle continues even in jail. We must confront jail authorities about our issues here. If you want to confront them about any problems, do it collectively, as a group. Or, we can decide together the plan of action when we meet during visiting hours,' explained Comrade Kattanna in detail.

By then, the guard announced that time was up. We shook hands with everyone and left. A letter had arrived from Comrade RK, which made us very happy. Suseela and I sat down to read it.

"Dear Comrades, wishing for your well-being with red salutes. We are all doing well. Kattanna must have told you everything. We were there for a long time on the night you were arrested. We heard a commotion, but thought it was just a regular noise from outside, as it happens during festivals when they immerse the deities in the well. Three of us went back to the village when you didn't come. By then, they had already taken you from the school. The villagers told us they saw the police come to the school after you had entered the village. Be brave. Try to read books. If you're not well, get permission to go to the outside hospital. Take medicines. If possible, we'll meet again through letters. We'll discuss everything in detail when we meet."

The sisterhood and support we received in the jail, the meeting with Kattanna after two days, and Comrade R.K.'s letter after ten days gave us immense courage. It was our first experience in jail. Comrade Kattanna talked extensively about the jail conditions, the struggles here, and our health. As soon as we entered jail, the *akka*s received us warmly and took care of our needs. Perhaps this is what it means to have class solidarity.

At first, life in jail felt new, but soon it became routine. When we first came to jail, we had two visits per week, but things changed later. Anyone who came to see us was grouped together, so Suseela and I had one joint visit. Our schedule changed according to the jail timetable.

As soon as the morning roll call was done, they'd count the inmates. After using the bathroom, we'd get tea along with some rice and soup. Most people didn't eat the rice, but everyone drank tea. At ten, we'd get rice again. Then everyone would study or read on their own. In the afternoon, we'd bathe, have dinner in the evening, and then walk a little, chatting with each other.

The remand prisoners would come and talk about their cases, families, and the troubles they were facing. We went on a two-day hunger strike, demanding that the jail provide prisoners with basic necessities. After the superintendent promised to meet the needs, we broke our fast.

Later, when hunger strikes were organised in jails across the state, a letter with 42 demands came from the Hyderabad jail. On December 6, relay hunger strikes began. Thirteen of us from our barracks joined on the first day while all the men from their barracks joined. We didn't feel much hunger on the first day. We sang songs for a while and held a meeting.

'Why are we on a hunger strike? How can we achieve our demands? We must continue the hunger strikes until the government concedes. Everyone should remain determined. Some of us might be taken aside and persuaded to abandon the strike. They may try to weaken us, but we must stay strong.'

These were our common thoughts.

Two of the women in our group were mothers of infants. After two days, they could no longer produce milk for their babies, who cried all night. Because of this, we decided that these two mothers should end their fast. We submitted a petition to the superintendent stating that they wanted to end the strike for this reason.

For the first two or three days, it wasn't too difficult, but then intense hunger, thirst, and weakness started setting in. It became very hard. The doctor would come and tell us, 'You should eat. Otherwise, your health will deteriorate. Your male comrades are also participating in this, so you can stop. At least have some water with glucose powder.'

We replied, 'If the government meets our demands, we will eat food. Why should we drink water otherwise?'

Comrade Kattanna is a thin person and the hunger strike made him thinner. They brought him to the hospital in the middle of the strike and tried to give him glucose water but he refused to take it. We heard then that his condition was serious. After the futile attempts to give him IV (intravenous), they took him back to the barracks.

Every morning and evening, we were given rice, curry, and milk, which we set aside and discarded the next morning. We didn't receive any newspapers for 11 days and were not allowed visitors. We had no idea what was happening outside. Every morning and evening, the superintendent and doctor would visit us, saying, 'Eat, otherwise your health will suffer. We will give you glucose. You should negotiate with the government, not with us.'

On the 11th day, around 8 p.m., the superintendent came and said, 'The government has agreed to your demands. The government has discussed this with your leaders. We have just given lemon juice to them, and now we are bringing it to you too.' He offered us lemon juice, and everyone accepted it. We were all given glucose in IV (intravenous), and for two days we drank just porridge.

The following week, we were allowed to meet with our comrades and discuss everything that had happened during those eleven days. We saw it as a meaningful experience.

Going on hunger strike for various issues, followed by the authorities conceding, and then breaking the fast – political prisoners in jail continue to fight for their rights in this manner.

After six months, we were granted bail. We thought we were happily heading home. However, that happiness did not last long. The moment we stepped out of the jail gate, two of us were made to get into a police jeep. We couldn't understand what was happening. The jeep stopped near the Matwada police station. The Circle Inspector, Venkata Narsayya, asked, 'Where are you going?'

When we asked, 'We were supposed to go home. Why have you brought us to the police station?' he replied, 'We know a lot about you. We know where you are going.'

I was kept at the Matwada police station for 17 days. Four more cases were filed against me, and I was sent back to jail. Suseela, who was with me, was sent home.

After another six months in jail, bail was granted and I was released. In total, I spent one year in jail.

We witnessed the suffering of hundreds of people. Some died because they couldn't withstand the extreme tortures. Women were subjected to unspeakable tortures, and there were also those who faced encounters.

This is not just our experience...

There are many women like us across the country who are fighting every day, enduring the same experiences. We are two among them.

Translation of 'oka arrestu'. (First published in the collection "Two Struggles" – Jan 2014)

Translated by P. Aravinda

Notes:
1. In the movement areas of erstwhile Andhra Pradesh, the police used the school buildings as a camp site when they went for combing, as there were no other bigger places for the force to stay put. While they were

in those schools they used to harass the people and loot their small earnings etc.

2. Thanda: hamlet, mostly of nomadic tribes
3. Fake encounters: In innumerable incidents the police kidnap the revolutionaries or catch them alive, torture and kill them and later announce that there was an exchange of fire between them and the Revolutionaries in which the latter died.

Encounter

Vannada Vijayalakshmi

I t was probably around seven in the evening. Busy working on the computer, I looked up when I heard someone say, 'Hello Officer, how are your tasks coming along?' It was comrade Gangadhar. 'Don't call me "officer," comrade! Why! Don't I look like a guerrilla?' I said, turning away. Laughing, he explained, 'I said that because, in the army, all the senior officers get only pistols. They don't carry AKs or SLRs.'

'All right Comrade, the magazine work is done. When will you review it? Won't you give your feedback and suggestions? First tell me, how did your final exams go? Did you pass?'

'Wait, comrade! Why are you shooting off questions like it's a quiz? Let me answer! I put in so much effort into preparing and teaching. Wouldn't it be better to ask those who attended my classes? How can I say?' said Gangadhar.

'Comrades, the food is ready. You can continue your discussions afterwards, but go and eat now,' came Budri's call. I grabbed a plate and dashed off to the kitchen. By then, a discussion was going on – some were saying, 'Those aren't stars, it's a torchlight,' while others insisted, 'No, those are definitely stars.' I hadn't slept for five days, so with my bleary eyes, I ate quickly and slipped away from the kitchen.

Around 9 o'clock in the night, the comrades who went to get vegetables returned. Just then, two *dada*s from Ramguda village also arrived. 'A man came to meet the squad. He's in the village. Should we bring him here?' the *dada*s asked the local comrade.

The local comrades brought this to the notice of senior leader, Comrade Samar *Dada*. The message also reached the senior leader, Comrade Rupesh *Dada*. Both of them pondered over the visitor. 'Why did he come here instead of going to the designated APT[1] location? And that too at this hour...?' Both of them reflected on the visitor and sent word to the Ramguda *dadas*: 'Let him stay with you for tonight.'

As usual, the kitchen duties began at 1 a.m. At 4:30 a.m., all the comrades got up and brushed their teeth. I too got up, but the cold inhibited me from moving out of my *jhilli*. I don't know when Rupesh *Dada* woke up; but he was still writing by the light of his rechargeable lamp. It was 5 a.m. and the comrades were having tea. I got up, brushed my teeth, had tea, and got ready for the toilet. Just then, the Platoon comrade returned from patrolling and said, 'The situation looks normal'. So, I headed towards the hill where lights were said to have been spotted the previous night.

Along the way, a female comrade advised me, 'Why are you going alone? Take someone with you.' Smiling, I moved on. When I returned, I heard the roll-call whistle. Two minutes later came the sound of a gunshot. I thought it might be an accidental fire. Immediately, it was followed by the sound of firing continuously from an automatic weapon. It wasn't an accidental fire; it was the police, for sure. Even before I could reach a conclusion, I sensed people running and trees shaking behind me. I started running swiftly. It wasn't easy for me to descend the hill while running. I tripped and fell a couple of times, got up, and kept running. It felt like the police were on my tail.

I made my way down the hill and reached a bridge. The sounds of gunfire pierced the air, filling the camp and the surrounding areas. There was no time to think about what to do. Once before, I had ended up alone during a gunfight. I resolved that this time, it should not happen; somehow, I had to get back to my section. No sooner had I taken a few steps on the path towards the camp from the bridge than I saw the police forces, firing salvos, surging towards the river. Meanwhile, ten or fifteen militia comrades came running from the camp towards the bridge where I was standing. There was a blaze of shots inside the camp area. It was clear that I couldn't go to the camp.

All I could hear was the barrage of bullets and nothing else. I ran along with the militia comrades. The police forces on the riverbank targeted us, increasing their pace. They continued to advance in the firing position. But, they couldn't reach us because of the large canal between us. However, that didn't stop them from firing countless numbers of bullets. All the militia comrades running ahead of me were unarmed and I had a pistol. Struggling with breathing problems, I thought I would load the pistol once I had slowed down. We all reached Ramguda village. I had fallen behind by then. I sat down in front of a house, thinking I would catch my breath before moving on. No militia comrades were visible. All the villagers were in a panic. People's movement was all I could sense. I couldn't hear any other sound. My ears were still ringing due to the sound of the echoing gunfire. Where should I go? Since the police noticed us, it was clear they were proceeding toward the village. I decided not to stay in the village at any cost and got up immediately. But, I didn't know where to go. All the safe escape routes were now under police control.

Whichever direction I took, the river was in the way. So, I ran towards the river. Two young militia members were starting the *donga*[2]. I went up to them and asked, 'Comrades, let me come with you. Take me along.' But they refused. The police on the other bank were watching and firing at us. When they refused to let me join, I turned back and took barely five or six steps when the two comrades on the boat disappeared from sight. I couldn't hold back my sorrow. I ran, crying, with the faces of those two I had spoken to just a moment ago, fixed in my mind.

After walking some distance, I ran into the man who had come to meet Comrade Samar *Dada* the night before. I knew him because he came to meet the squad earlier. Upon seeing me, he asked, '*Akka*, are you all right?'

'Yes. But why are you here at this hour?' I asked.

'I came to meet Samar *Dada*. While talking to him in the village, the firing started, so *Dada* and others left,' he said. While talking to me, he was taking a video of the firing on his tablet.

'Why on earth are you recording a video at a time like this when the firing is so intense? If you stay with us, they will definitely kill you. It's too risky to delay any longer; let's leave,' I urged him.

'No, *akka*! I won't come. I can't keep up walking with you. Where will you also go? You too, stay in the village,' he replied.

'Have you lost your mind? Look behind you – there are so many police! They would have already entered the village. The sooner we leave this place, the better it is. Don't argue; let's go now,' I said firmly.

'I am scared, *akka*. I'll go to them and surrender. I'll raise my hands; they must already know that I came to meet you,' he stammered, showing cowardice.

'What have you learned after all these years of relationship with the Party? How can you say you'll surrender? We should be ready to lay down our lives in times like this. Are you going to betray the Party that trusted you? If you surrender, they'll interrogate you about the leaders you know and why you came here. Betraying the Party means betraying the people. Think about it,' I said and left.

I climbed down a small hill and went closer to the river. I loaded my pistol. I found cover among some bushes near the river and crouched there. I couldn't sit for long on my knees, so I stood up. No one was in sight. On the other bank, I saw villagers, but how could I call them? If I called out loudly, the enemy might hear and come, but if I didn't, this chance might slip away. Then I heard footsteps on the hill. I thought it must be the enemy, and stood up, alert. If it was the enemy, I would fire. On three sides, I was surrounded by the river; on the other, enemy forces. Retreat from that position meant going into the water with no other way out. So, I resolved to shoot and die if the enemy closed in. However, the steps didn't come down my side. I exhaled in relief and approached the river. I called out to the villagers on the other side. They all looked over, but no one came over to help. I stood by the river for half an hour. Frustrated by the lack of response from the people despite their watching me, I paced along the bank. Earlier in the morning, the police fired at the boat, which might have been why they were afraid.

Just then, I saw two men going on a boat. I ran and shouted, '*Dada*, please take me with you.' They only sped up. I stopped in disappointment. As soon as they crossed the river, another *donga* came towards me. 'Get on quickly, *didi*,' said the *dada*, stopping the boat in front of me. I climbed in immediately. As soon as we reached the other bank, they told me to get down fast. As I disembarked, my pistol accidentally went off. Oh no! What a mistake I made, I thought in regret. If the enemy hears this gunfire, it'll endanger both me and the villagers.

As I was thinking, 'What now?' The local people quickly advised me, '*Didi*, it's better if you leave this place and go somewhere else. If the police heard the sound of firing, they might come. The sooner you get out of here, the better.' They helped me get into another *donga*. After about ten minutes, I looked back. Along with me were two other militia comrades who I assumed had died in the police firing. I was surprised to see them safe. I asked them how they managed to escape. They replied, looking pained, 'As soon as the police fired on the *donga*, we jumped into the river, clung to the *donga*, and swam out. We didn't take you with us because we thought you might get into trouble, *didi*.' I was relieved that they had escaped and were alive.

It must have been around 10 o'clock by the time I reached the house where I took shelter. Upon arrival, the *akka* of the house gave me some civilian clothes, while the *dada* of the house took my shoes and pistol and hid them somewhere. Holding the clothes she gave me, I stood there. Just then, I heard two gunshots. Standing still, I wondered who had been shot. I didn't even try to put on the saree. *Akka* saw my state and came and helped me wear the saree. She and the other family members prepared food for me and the militia comrades who had come with me. She gave me a new bar of Santoor soap, saying, 'Go bathe, *didi*.' I was restless. So I went and sat in the verandah instead. The family members served the food on a plate and pleaded with me to eat. I didn't have any appetite. I couldn't ignore their pleas, so I started eating.

I don't know how long it took me to finish eating. I could barely swallow, as I had no appetite. All I could think about was the firing, wondering how everybody in the squad was, who had been injured and how badly they might be injured. As I thought of all these things, tears began to roll down my cheeks into the plate. In my distressed condition, I hadn't even noticed when the militia comrades had finished eating and left.

What could I do with that food? How much must these people have toiled to grow this plate of food? I remembered the words of advice of the comrades to those who used to throw away food in the camp. But this time, I couldn't bring myself to eat. So, I went to the back of the house, threw the food on the ground, washed the plate, and sat in the courtyard looking towards the river. Around half-past twelve, the head of the house came over after listening to the news on the radio. He told me, '*Didi*, the news says that 21 of our people have died,' and upon hearing that, I broke down. The whole family and the neighbours gathered in the courtyard, grieving over the firing. Some said they had never heard of so many casualties before; others insisted that the firing took place based on precise intelligence. Some of the young men were filled with anger, swearing to avenge our fallen comrades. Right around one o'clock in the afternoon, the sound of a helicopter made us all alert. '*Didi*, go inside the house,' they urged me, worried. The helicopter landed by the river, near where the morning's firing had happened.

Only then did I realise the camp was clearly visible from where I was. Another helicopter hovered in the air, and I understood it was patrolling. Only the river separated us. The helicopter finished its task in about fifteen minutes and ascended back into the sky. I sat there, watching in the direction of the camp and crying. 'A *dada* has come from another village,' said the woman of the house. I came out of my oblivious state and spoke with him. 'Some of our comrades are there in a nearby village, *didi*,' he said. He didn't specify who they were, but I was eager to meet them at the earliest. Right at three o'clock, a letter arrived from Samar *Dada*. I read it. The letter said, 'Come with the comrade who gave you this letter. We will talk about everything when we meet.' One line in that letter filled me with a great deal of courage. I got up immediately, saluted the family that had sheltered me and prepared to leave.

They stood there watching me go, saying, 'Be careful, *Didi*.' My heart swelled with gratitude for the generosity of the people. When I saw Samar *Dada*, I felt overjoyed as if I was meeting the entire squad. He was with guards and local comrades, including Rajanna. Samar *Dada* asked me, 'How did you escape from the firing?' I briefly recounted my retreat and journey.

Around four or five in the evening, the two helicopters came again, just as they had before. One landed, and the other patrolled the area, leaving after about fifteen minutes. From this, it seemed they had brought in a new batch after sending back the firing squad. We all sat silently for a while. The news had confirmed that among the more than eighty of us at the camp, 21 had become martyrs in the firing. But, what was the state of the others? Samar *Dada* continued making efforts to gather more details about all of them through the people.

In the meantime, a comrade who had escaped the fierce firing reached that village and described what he had seen. 'During the second round of firing on the camp, as we were moving from one hill to another, Prasad, Munna, Lata, Mamata, Tata, Madhu, Kiran, Daya, Jyoti, and Rajitha all were martyred. I don't know about the others, but some were injured. Rupesh *Dada* was hit in the leg.' The news of Rupesh *Dada* being alive gave us some relief. But the loss of the others filled us with sorrow.

The comrade continued, '*Dada*, the injured are bleeding heavily and suffering a great deal.' On hearing this, Samar *Dada* got details of their location and decided to move them from that dangerous place. He weighed all options and after careful planning, he reached the place where wounded comrade Rupesh *dada* and the others were present. By then, it was eleven o'clock at night. He brought back Rupesh *Dada* and five others. Seeing Rupesh *Dada* alive brought overwhelming joy and filled my heart with courage. I wanted to ask him how they had countered the enemy. However, they were discussing our losses and the enemy's encirclement. Leaving aside my thoughts, I joined the others. Each one of them had been hit by bullets, and blood was still seeping from their wounds. Even though they had tied their handkerchiefs tightly around their injuries, the bleeding hadn't stopped. Rajanna began treating everyone with the medicines available with the local people. When he asked for my help, I went closer. The sight of their injuries frightened me. This was the first time I saw grievous wounds like this. One comrade's thigh was severely mangled; another had a large hole below his lungs as a bullet had gone through his ribs. The rest were hit above the knees, in the thigh area. Rupesh *Dada* had a bullet lodged below his knee. Considering that they had defied death despite such severe injuries, I resolved to overcome my own fear. I began assisting Rajanna in treating the wounds. We walked throughout the night, reaching a different camp by dawn.

It was just the beginning of the winter season. The Balimela River flowed next to us. We were around thirty. Having lost everything during the firing, we had nothing left to spread on the ground or to cover ourselves. Knowing how fierce the winter cold would be, the people gave us shawls and blankets. But those meagre coverings were no match for the biting chill. We spread leaves on the cold, hard ground and laid on them, wrapping ourselves tightly in the shawls. Yet, the bitter cold seemed to gnaw at our very bones. We had no choice but to light fires and we gathered around them. That night remains etched in my mind – a bitter, unforgettable and tragic night. All of our thoughts were about Ramguda, and sorrow hung heavy on every face. The haunting images of the firing flashed relentlessly through my mind.

I must have dozed off for a moment when I thought I heard someone calling, 'Vasudha, sentry duty.' I woke up with a start but didn't see Gangadhar among the comrades by the fire. I assured myself, 'He must have retreated safely by now.' But there was still an uneasy feeling within me. I wanted to believe he had retreated safely. I imagined telling him everything that had happened, especially about my retreat. If only I could see him now, I would pour out all my pain, let the tears flow freely, and release the heavy burden that has been weighing on my heart. Although he disliked tears and even got angry at the very mention of crying, I felt he was the only one to whom I could open my heart freely and fearlessly. I recalled many memories of him. His words, 'Crying is cowardice,' echoed in my mind, yet tears kept coming faster.

I kept thinking that nothing should happen to Gangadhar and that he should meet me soon. Various thoughts occupied my mind. Comrade Jagan who was with Gangadhar during the firing said he called out to him, 'Gangadhar, come, let's go.'

'You go on, I hurt my leg. I'll be there shortly,' was his response to that.

I was torn, not knowing if Jagan's words were real or not. If it was true, then he must be injured but alive. I hoped with all my heart that he was alive.

'Isn't it cold? Come closer to the fire,' someone called out, but I couldn't see who. I walked nearer to the fire. The cold had numbed my ears with pain, but that pain seemed nothing compared to the agony of our recent losses.

It was about five in the morning. None of us slept well, but dawn had already arrived. We had no utensils and no provisions, so the people brought us cooking utensils and provisions for two days. In mainstream society, when a family member was in trouble, their relatives or kin would come forward to fulfill their needs and support them. We had neither of these; instead, people who loved us and are related to us by class arranged everything for us. Swallowing their grief, everyone went about their duties.

It was eight o'clock. Like the day before, helicopters were flying in the sky, heading in the direction of the previous day's firing. Immediately after, the sound of firing echoed as though someone had fired from an automatic weapon. No one could understand what had happened or to whom. During that day's roll call, a team of three doctors was announced, and I was one of them. Immediately, I remembered Lathakka and Tata. As soon as he entered a village, Tata enquired about the people's health issues, and provided Ayurvedic treatment. Lathakka enquired about the women's health problems, advised them on hygiene related to health, and provided them with allopathic medicines. Both of them offered considerable assistance to people with their medical services. All the injured comrades had too many bloodstains, so they went and washed them-selves. Along with Rajanna, another comrade and I offered treatment. As soon as everyone finished their tasks, they would remember the martyrs, mourn, and weep. They spoke passion-ately, discussing the cruelty of the state and its atrocities. Dark-ness fell. Engrossed in our thoughts about the incidents of the previous day, none of us paid attention to what was happening. That night, the sound of firing rang out again, leaving us uncertain about who had fallen. The night passed with double the sorrow we felt on the night of the 24th. We got to know the number of martyrs only through the news. The police searched for our people in the areas nearby the camp, and upon finding them, subjected them to brutal torture and even mutilated the corpses.

On the 26th, we heard on the news that Comrade Gangadhar had died in an encounter and that his funeral would be held that evening. Until then, we had hoped he might have retreated and was hiding somewhere, but now we realised he had become a martyr. Immediately, I thought of my father. After I lost my beloved father, I looked for him in Gangadhar. I learned so much from him about revolutionary life that I hadn't known before. He was a revolutionary mentor who taught me about guerrilla life and how to adapt to it. I had hoped to talk about all these incidents with him and the radio news filled me with unbearable sorrow. I wondered how this agony affected those who knew him outside, how much pain it must have caused to his life partner. To the many women in this patriarchal society who had lost hope in life and believed death to be their only refuge, Gangadhar gave assurance about life. Gangadhar's martyrdom must have been a profound shock to all those women, leaving them shaken and bereft. My thoughts turned to all those in mainstream society.

Later, we reached the site of the incident along with the people. On the right side of the path to the camp, we could smell a dead body. However, we could not see anything. As soon as we entered the camp, we saw our cooking utensils lying there. When we went past them, we saw all our belongings piled up in one spot and set on fire. They had burned everything so thoroughly that not a single item was in a usable state. We went in the direction from which the enemy had first entered the camp. It was an old path, a direct path leading to the camp.

If one came in about a hundred metres from the tar road, they would reach our camp. It was clear that the enemy must have charged in, using the cover of the nearby sections, where the roll call was on at the time. Then, we climbed the hill from where lights had appeared by taking a path next to the canal by the kitchen. At the exact spot where the lights were seen, there was a handbag and two packets of glucose. Many comrades got martyred while crossing this hill. Comrades who were witnesses to the entire firing and escaped reported that Com. Prasad had been shot and martyred by bullets coming from a hill in the opposite direction as he descended. They also told us that Comrades Daya, Kiran, and Birsu had retreated towards the left side of the hill while descending, so we headed that way. In the spot where Comrade Birsu became a martyr, we found many bullet casings, and at the place where Daya was martyred, we saw bullet casings along with the shattered frame of a pair of glasses. We were told that Kiran had been martyred a short distance from Daya, but we couldn't find any traces of him. After descending the entire hill, there was a *ganja* (marijuana) field. A majority of comrades lost their lives in that empty field. Comrade Munna, who took cover and fired there in the *ganja* field, was martyred in the process of protecting the leadership. Comrade Erral, who was retreating with his AK, was killed about two feet away from Munna. Several comrades lost their lives while climbing the hill during their retreat, as the enemy forces who were stationed in a firing position on the surrounding hills, fired without a pause from their automatic weapons. This resulted in the martyrdom of the comrades Mamatha, Latha, and Tata. Comrades Madhu, Rajesh, Budri, Manjula, Rajita, Jyoti, Kamala, and some militia comrades, who took the SLR of a martyr and were retreating, faced the bullets from the enemy and spilt their precious blood at that place. Comrade Madhu's SLR was taken by another comrade who retreated, and Comrade Jyoti's .303 rifle was also picked up by another comrade. Despite the heavy rain on the day before we went to the scene of the incident, the place where most of our comrades laid down their lives still bore red-stained marks of their blood on the soil. It seemed as if the red-stained clods of earth were reminders to us of their ideals and were showing us the way forward in our battle with the State.

One of the wounded comrades told us that five or six others who retreated with wounds had been hit by bullets there. Comrade Gangal, the guard for leaders, who was on sentry duty, must have been coming towards the camp. Judging by the condition of his backpack and the dried, blood-soaked ground, it was evident they had tortured and killed him there. On the return path, we reached a bridge, and we found Comrade Gangadhar's cap nearby. The hole at the centre of the red star on his cap, which would have been at the centre of his forehead, indicated it was a bullet hole. The comrades who saw him said he was wounded initially in the leg. Later, he must have been captured, tortured, and killed. I myself had sewn that cap two or three times. When I suggested to him, 'You could get a new cap,' he replied, 'Communists are supposed to use every item until it's completely worn out; we should follow this principle as much as possible.' His words echoed in my mind. Clutching the memory of his resolve, I swallowed my grief and stepped across the bridge, carrying an unbearable weight in my heart.

About ten steps later, the stench of death surrounded us again. This was the same place we had detected the odour as we entered. We searched the surroundings to find its source, and we found the dead body of Militia Comrade Loykal! The body was decomposed beyond recognition, missing one leg and an arm. About twenty metres away, we found grenades and boots with an in-sole from Flamingo Company, which confirmed that they belonged to Comrades Gautham and Naresh. Villagers informed us that on the same hill, in the direction of the village, Comrade Chilaka, who was unable to move due to injuries, had been tortured and decapitated in order to make the body unrecognisable.

Two years ago, the Central Committee initiated the 'Campaign for Bolshevisation[3],' encouraging comrades to rectify their non-proletarian tendencies and adopt proletarian discipline (such as quitting tobacco, improving political study, and giving priority to collective tasks). These comrades who had died had been making progress in that campaign, and their martyrdom would leave an irreplaceable loss for the Party and the people. These were comrades who had mentored lower-level comrades, and taken the Party ahead with their strategies; who had excelled in military, medical, agricultural, and technical fields; who had been advancing into leadership positions with their many new skills; who despite being newcomers, were learning party discipline. All these comrades with diverse skills had taught us many lessons in waging the struggles.

The area where the helicopter had landed, and the river banks were littered with wrappers of fruits, buttermilk, water, rice, liquor bottles, and non-vegetarian curry packets – left half-eaten and reeking of the contents discarded all around.

A few days after we returned from the camp, all of us who had retreated from the encounter met together. Days passed by. Some had lost blood relatives in the tragic incident; others had lost life partners. Some had managed to retreat safely from various encounters, while other experienced comrades taught lessons of struggle to the new recruits who knew little about the movement. Some comrades provided succour to those struggling emotionally and helped them stand strong in the Party. Others left an indelible mark on many hearts with their revolutionary songs. Subduing their grief, with heavy hearts, everyone was moving forward, immersing themselves in their respective tasks.

I was truly amazed when I saw the women who had lost their partners. Outside the guerrilla life, I had seen women sink into despair, believing life was over once their husbands passed away; many would spend their remaining years consumed by memories of their husbands, their health deteriorating over time. What about these women guerrillas? They were immersed in their tasks. Didn't they love their departed comrades? Didn't they have feelings of sorrow that torment them? Their practice is the answer to those who have such questions. These were not ordinary women – they were people's guerrillas bound by the ideology of Marxism-Leninism-Maoism. They lived on the battlefield. They understood clearly that war was, at its core, a relentless struggle against death. Long ago, they had left behind their parents, siblings, and friends to pursue the ideas of the liberation of the oppressed and transformation of society. They had picked up arms to overthrow the powerful armed enemy. They had internalized class consciousness at the core of their beings for this people's war to establish rule by the oppressed.

That's why, fuelled by the ideals of their fallen comrades, they march on with determination against the enemy forces for the seizure of power by the oppressed. Beholding these women guerrillas filled me with pride. Indeed, how noble is the people's war!

I spoke with Comrade Rita, who had lost her partner. 'Amid the firing, when I was retreating, Ramana, who was wounded and unable to move, called out to me, 'Rita, take me with you.' I ran back to him immediately. He had been shot in the hand and leg, and was bleeding profusely. I couldn't carry him entirely. So, I held him by hand and helped him walk for a short distance. There was heavy firing from the hill opposite to us. 'Rita, I can't go on. I won't be able to walk even with your help. You go ahead; if you delay, we'll both die. I don't want you to die because of me. Don't waste a single second. Go quickly,' he said firmly. I left him behind in that condition and retreated, firing. Not being able to save Ramana, who was dying, is an unbearable pain that haunts me to this day. But I know that Ramana took up the gun for the Adivasi people, and gave his life for a proletarian State. As long as I'm alive, I will fight to make his dreams a reality. I'll speed up my work on the path that will fulfil his vision.' Even though she spoke through tears, her final words, 'I will fulfil his dreams,' inspired me tremendously.

The agility of all the comrades in their work, the steadiness of comrades who lost partners, and the anger against the enemy in the party ranks and file – all these comforted my saddened heart after the martyrdom of thirty comrades. It deepened my faith in the Party.

The police, the lap dogs of the oppressive ruling class, spread false propaganda. They boasted that they had turned the AOB (Andhra Odisha Border) region into a Maoist-free zone, that not a single Maoist remained, and that they had finally eradicated the Maoist party. Meanwhile, they forcibly took away village youth, killed them, claimed they were part of the militia and blamed the militia's deaths on the Maoists. Further, they claimed that this was told to them by the families of the militia members themselves. They spread these lies in the media. While they were carrying out this propaganda, we were present in those areas. I often wondered how the people, and the families who lost their children, would respond to the Party after the encounter. But soon enough, I learned that they were remarkable people. Many of them took great care of us while we were grieving over the loss of so many comrades. As soon as we reached their villages, they carried out sentry duties, and patrolling, they collected food and fed us. They comforted us over the losses and gave us courage.

When our comrades asked the people, 'Were you scared after the Ramguda incident, *dada*?', they replied, 'No, *dada*. We only thought about all of you. We were worried about the party members – how and where they were, and how many had died. Don't be afraid, *dada*. We are here for you,' they assured us with confidence. I felt that their warm reception was a very favourable thing for the movement.

The roll call whistle sounded. We all stood silently in rows. 'Now, we will go and speak with the families of the martyred militia comrades. They are grieving the loss of their children. So, even if they rebuke or strike us, we must not react hastily. Let us speak with utmost sensitivity.' With these words, the commander ended the roll call.

Yet, I felt very nervous. Even after witnessing the warm reception from the people, I felt uneasy about how they would respond in their grief over losing their children. I recalled the police propaganda published in the newspapers claiming that the parents of the militia comrades allegedly said that 'the Maoists took our children away and killed them.' I kept thinking of all these things as I walked, and soon we arrived at the village we planned to reach.

The dogs, sensing our arrival, began barking. Realising our presence, the people gathered, along with the *Sangam* members and the parents of the martyred militia comrades. A local comrade greeted us with '*Lal Salaam,*' and we all shook hands. The area commander started speaking and as he narrated the events of the encounter, the visibly moved people responded passionately, '*Dada*, we're not just grieving for our children. So many of your party members have become martyrs, too! They came from places we don't even know – not from this state, not from this district, but they gave their lives for us. Why would we be angry with our Party, *dada*? Our children didn't die just for you; they died for many like us, for all poor people, to change our lives. We do understand you, *dada*!' They spoke with such clarity, shedding tears and giving an impassioned explanation of the politics they imbued. Was this real? Or, was I imagining this? I questioned myself. Their response was the opposite of what I expected. Witnessing this scene in person, I felt proud to be among such pure-hearted people. My love for the wretched of the Earth who are making history grew even deeper. Truly, the consciousness of people is on a higher and nobler plane!

Translation of 'Encounter'. (Written in December 2016, first published in Arunatara, December 2023)

Translated by Vimal

Notes:
1. APT (appointment): As the guerillas work underground and are constantly moving, appointments are fixed for squads or individuals who have been away on errands to reunite with their formation or when a meeting is necessary with another formation(s) in other areas. The appointment is fixed before leaving the squad or before the squad leaves its current location. If an appointment is missed for any reason the squad or individual still will go to the rendezvous point (RV place) fixed for it for that day.
2. *donga*: a small boat, usually round in shape, used for transportation over rivers
3. Bolshevisation campaign: Bolshevisation is a campaign conducted in the Party from time to time to impart the cadre with a spirit of steel discipline, democratic centralism and determination to overcome the odds and repression. The word Bolshevisation was coined from the 'Bolshevik spirit' of the Russian Communist Party.

She *is* My Daughter
G. Renuka

'My daughter...that's my daughter...Oh God, that's my daughter...Sukki...' From among the women looking at the dead bodies, Bhime fell on top of one of the bodies and started weeping. She would be about 50 years old.

Everyone looked at her amazed. Then Adime came up and sat down beside her and said, 'It's not Sukki, it's Kosi.' Adime was Bhime's neighbour, of approximately the same age.

'No, no, it's my daughter...it's my Sukki,' Bhime said, weeping inconsolably.

'No aunty, it's not Sukki, it's Kosi; look at her closely,' said Kamli, who stays in the same lane as Bhime.

Bhime continued sobbing, in no position to listen to anyone.

'That's right aunty, it's not Sukki,' added Lakke. Few others joined in the chorus. Bhime did not heed any of their words.

'Sukki also looks the same. She also has a similar boyish haircut. Poor thing that must be the reason she is mistaking her for Sukki,' said Somvari.

'The body is also swollen, and the facial features can't be recognised,' said Kamli sadly.

The twelve bodies were those of the revolutionaries killed in a police attack, in the Adivasi village on Chhattisgarh-North Telangana border. The village is part of Dantewada district under the Kunta block. So the bodies were brought for post-mortem to the hospital in Kunta block.

Of the twelve killed, seven of them were from north Telangana. Their relatives, members of *Amaraveerula Bandhu Mitrula Sangham*[1] (ABMS) and a few from other rights groups came across the state border to accompany the bodies back. Rest of them were from the nearby villages of Kunta block. But in reality, the situation was not conducive for those from Chhattisgarh to go to claim the bodies because the government was treating all those who were not in the camps as naxalites and enemies. So, approaching the police was akin to voluntarily entering a lion's den.

However, after coming to know that a lot of people had come to claim and accompany the dead bodies from Telangana, about 50-60 middle aged and old women from the nearby villages of Kunta block also reached Kunta to claim the bodies of their own kith and kin. They came to know exactly who the dead were because the neighboring villagers who carried the dead bodies told them about it.

It has been three days since their death...and in addition to that, it was summer. The stench from the decomposed bodies was unbearable. The whole scene was pathetic, with the heart-rending sobbing of near and dear ones and those consoling them. The situation was tense with the curses and slogans of the gathered people, who were incensed that the police would not even ensure safe storage of the dead bodies.

It was only after they reached the police station and recognised the dead bodies that they came to know who exactly was killed. Police did not make any clear statement about who died. Newspapers carried vague stories speculating the names of those who might be among the dead. Hence, many people went to the police station on suspicion that it could be their kith and kin. After seeing the dead bodies, some of them were relieved that their people were not among them. They looked sympathetically at others who lost their loved ones, looking tearfully, in compassion, at those who were inconsolable in their grief, feeling as one with them. It became clear only then that seven were from North Telangana and only five were from Chhattisgarh. There was only one woman among those five. She was identified as Kosi. All except Kosi's family were present. Some of the women from Chhattisgarh could speak and understand a little Telugu. They spoke to the ABMS and requested them to help them with the handover of the five bodies from Chhattisgarh. So, the efforts were underway to claim eleven of the bodies.

At this juncture, Bhime started sobbing over the body of the woman claiming that was her daughter. She continued to weep pitifully and would not listen to anyone, or accept that it wasn't her daughter.

Having heard that there was a dispute regarding the twelfth body, Ajitha, leader of the *ABMS*, came along to enquire. Upon seeing her, Bhime appealed to her to handover the body as that is her daughter's.

'Are you sure it is your daughter? Did you take a good look at her?' asked Ajitha sympathetically, placing her hands around Bhime's shoulders.

'Yes, it is my daughter, my daughter only...my Sukki....'

'No, it's not Sukki, it is Kosi...Kosi is also from our locality. They used to move around like sisters. Sukki also had similar hair. So, my aunt is mistaking her to be Sukki. Also, the body is swollen now,' said Kamli.

'Shut up, as if I wouldn't recognise my own daughter? And you would?' yelled Bhime. She turned to Ajitha and asked her, 'You tell me – wouldn't I recognise my own daughter?'

Ajitha was puzzled. She asked Kamli, 'Did Kosi's parents not come?'

'No, they do not stay in our village anymore,' Kamli said, and was about to continue when Bhime interrupted her. 'No, no, please believe me, it is my daughter only. I carried her in my womb and brought her up with my own hands,' she said tearfully.

'Ok, we'll hand over your daughter's body to you,' Ajitha got up, convinced.

'But everyone is saying that it's not her daughter. Maybe the old woman is making a mistake,' said Sajaya, a Civil Rights activist, walking along with Ajitha.

'So what if it isn't? If it is Kosi, her parents have not come till now. And they won't dare come after we leave. Even if they do come, the police will definitely not hand over the body to them. They will bury her somewhere. Instead, it's much better if Bhime takes her back to her village where, among the revolutionary people and with revolutionary fervour her cremation will be completed. If her parents come later, at least they will be able to visit her at the place of her cremation. Otherwise, her parents will be deprived of even that,' said Ajitha thoughtfully, looking at Sajaya.

'You're right. Already the bodies are decomposed. We can't request that her body remain till her parents show up...'

Five bodies tied to yokes were carried by women. They had to be taken to five different villages. But since the villages were close by, they were all going together. There was a heavy atmosphere of grief. Some mothers were still crying, unable to control their emotions. It was summer, so even though it was evening it was still hot. And that was adding to their fatigue. Some of them had tied a cloth to their noses, to escape the stench from the dead bodies. Even then, it was still revolting to the stomach. In a situation of such heart rending tragedy and grief, there was also contentment. They were content that the bodies of their loved ones were not left unclaimed, like orphans.

The women stopped for a short rest. They carefully put down the yokes with the bodies, wiped their faces and drank water from the containers they brought. Kamli, Lakke and others' minds were in turmoil...was Sukki safe somewhere? Why does Bhime have to go through this trauma in case she was alive?

Since Bhime was incensed with anyone saying it was not Sukki no one dared to say anything further. But, Lakke couldn't help herself. 'Don't worry aunt, it is not Sukki...,' she said to Bhime.

'You poor things...how can I not recognise my own daughter...I know it's not Sukki...'

Everyone looked in wonder at Bhime. Two or three of them said in unison, 'then why did you say it was Sukki?'

Bhime said, 'If I didn't say it was Sukki, do you think they would hand over the body to us? I kept insisting it was Sukki and you dumb things kept saying it was Kosi. I was terrified in case the *Judum*[2] thugs heard you. If they did, wouldn't those thugs go to Kosi's parents to verify?'

'What if they had verified?' asked Lakke. A few others had opened their mouths to ask the very same question, but were now waiting eagerly for the answer.

It seemed as if some of them understood.

'How can you ask such a foolish question? However evil they may be, any parent would come to claim the body. And they would take Kosi and throw her in the cremation place. Do you think anyone who knows her would gather at her cremation? Will there be any well wishers of hers in that place? Would they cover her body with the red flag? They would dispose of her body as they would a dog. Did she die like a dog to deserve that kind of treatment? She died a valiant death like a tiger cub. That day, how she had pleaded with her parents and brothers not to join the *Judum*! How she had cried! Don't you people remember? What did she say that day? "I am not your daughter anymore if you join the *Judum*. If I die, do not lay your hands even on my dead body". Did she not say that? Yet, they didn't pay any heed to her. They joined the *Judum*. Her brothers turned into thugs, raided the villages and started spying on the villagers. Do such people have any legitimacy to claim her body? She grew up right in front of us, roamed hand in hand with Sukki...it is for our sake that she gave up her life. So, let's only take her. Let us only give her the final farewell in the place where she played, sang and learnt to be a fighter.' Bhime's voice became hoarse with emotion. Overwhelmed with emotion, others too blew their noses and wiped their tears.

Translation of 'Naa Biddane!' (First published in *Mahila Margam*, March – June 2010)

Translated by P. Anuradha

Notes:
1. ABMS *(Amarula Bandhu Mitrula Sangham)* : In the late 1990s, after an encounter, the police refused to hand over the bodies of martyrs to their relatives. Instead, they started burying the martyrs themselves. To oppose this and claim the bodies of the martyrs, and offer them a respectable homage and burial, in 2004, a committee was formed in Telangana and Andhra Pradesh with friends and relatives of the martyrs – the *Amarula Bandhu Mitrula Sangham* (ABMS) It soon evolved into an organisation. ABMS has been working with the same mission for the past two decades.
2. *Judum*: *Salwa Judum* (literally meaning "peace march"), a vigilante force that was mobilised and deployed as part cf counter insurgency operations in Chhattisgarh, India, aimed at countering Naxalite activities in the region. The force, consisting of local Adivasi youth, received support and training from the Chhattisgarh state government and was criticised for its violations of human rights and its criminal activities.

Three Mothers
Padmakumari

At the Bhadrachalam government hospital, a group of women crossed the Out Patient (OP) wing in the hospital and were walking towards the mortuary. The hospital was unusually chaotic. There was anxiety in the eyes of the people walking in the hospital corridors. Starting from the main gate, there were police everywhere in the hospital. Going ahead, the women spotted loads of bags and rifles on a platform under the shade of a tree in the hospital compound area. There were some Greyhound[1] police dozing next to these rifles while a few others were dispersed all around the hospital with rifles in their hands. The hospital looked almost like a battleground.

Noticing them walking towards the mortuary, around fifty-sixty Greyhounds rushed towards them. The atmosphere around the hospital turned tense resembling a war zone with the clattering of their boots against the ground and the rifles in their hands.

'Who are you...where did you come from...why are you here?' they asked without a pause.

Vasantha, who was walking hurriedly towards the mortuary, answered without stopping, 'we are from Hyderabad.'

A police officer confronted her and asked her sharply why they had come. As they questioned them, there was agitation in their eyes too.

'We are here to see the dead bodies,' replied Vasantha.

'You can't go just like that. Come here first,' the police officer took them aside.

There was the usual routine of unending questions. They

had to answer several ridiculous questions in a terribly tragic situation when they could barely talk. They answered with anger and resentment mingling in their voices. One could answer all the questions, but how does one answer the difficult question of one's relationship to the dead persons? How does one express the relationship of the living with the dead? What sort of an answer would satisfy them? Certain questions are difficult to answer. They are ours. They belong to families like ours. Will such responses satisfy them? Will it suffice if we tell them that we are here to comfort the families, who lost their loved ones like we once did, and have the same heart ache as we do?

Vasantha showed her identification cards to the police officers. She went on to explain who the others were. She talked about two or three and then weariness due to sleeplessness overtook her. She couldn't proceed anymore. So, Janaki took up the task.

Vasantha, observed the situation around her. The previous night they stayed at a house that's right next to the mortuary. They got information about the encounter just the previous afternoon. A few opined that getting the dead bodies out of the forest could be difficult and it would take at least a day or two. But there were also rumors that helicopters would be used to transport all dead bodies. To be on hand when the bodies arrived, they left for Bhadrachalam immediately and reached in the evening on the same day. Thankfully they met a journalist there.

'They brought the dead bodies. But because it is too late in the night, they will only allow people to go inside tomorrow,' the journalist said.

An Adivasi friend of theirs also met them.

There was so much commotion in the town as the infuriated policemen took out processions in protest as some of their colleagues had been injured in the encounter. It looked like the entire town was under the control of the police. It was difficult to stay in the bus stand and staying in a lodge wasn't safe either with the eagle eyes of the police on every one.

'Where should we stay tonight? We are a total of ten people. No house can accommodate these many people.' As Vasantha was struggling to figure out what to do, the Adivasi friend said, '*Akka*, stay in our home. It is a tiny house though, so you have to adjust'.

That is more than enough, Vasantha thought to herself.

'*Akka*, in fact the mortuary is right next to my home...it will be easy for you to go there early in the morning,' he continued. His family of four stayed in a house that had a kitchen, and two tiny rooms. That night, the ten of them who travelled to Bhadrachalam managed to share the house with his family of four.

Sharada, who had come from Warangal, asked Vasantha innumerable times, '*Akka*, did you get to know any names?'

How would Vasantha know the list when none of them did? It is not that Sharada didn't know that, but her severe anxiety made her ask that question. Vasantha understood the pain of a mother behind Sharada's quivering voice.

Vasantha came out of her thoughts and found that the police had finished writing all the details of the people in their team.

Everyone turned their heads when they heard the sound of a jeep that had just entered the hospital premises. Around ten Adivasis got down from the jeep, four of them being women.

Police rushed towards them as soon as they saw them. The Adivasis said something in their language to the police. Noticing that, Vasantha also went towards them.

Two of them were explaining to police that they were the heads of the village and were there because the police had asked them to come. Yet the police continued with their questioning – where were they from? Were they really who they claim to be? They responded to the police questions in a mix of Gondi and Telugu.

The rest of the people who alighted from the jeep were looking fearfully and suspiciously at the police and the surroundings of the hospital. The women began crying softly. Their faces looked like they had been crying for a long time.

Controlled grief clouded the faces of men too.

Vasantha and Sharada approached them. Initially, the Adivasi mothers hesitated to talk to them. Vasantha held them close and her touch instilled confidence in them. Holding their heads in their hands, they began crying loudly and saying something in their language.

The police rebuked them angrily. Yet, they continued to beat their chests and say something in their language. The police couldn't stand that, so they ordered Vasantha and Sharada to move away from them.

They did not pay any heed to those orders. Instead, they held the four Adivasi mothers tightly, as a support in their sorrowful times. The Adivasi women continued speaking in their language and Vasantha and Sharada couldn't understand anything. But they understood their pain and grief and tried to console them as best as they could. One language that is certainly understood universally by all humans is grief.

The police were vexed with the crying of the women and snapped at them. By then, the Adivasi men had given the police all the required details.

All of them started walking towards the mortuary.

Vasantha was very anxious about seeing and identifying ten dead bodies. A dead body may mean a person without life, but entwined with them are relationships and memories that are alive. Vasantha felt the same anxiety and sadness every time she had to do this despite going through the experience hundreds of times. The police did not clearly announce the names of those dead yet. Only a few names were announced. What is in the names anyway? They are such great people and it was unbearable to have to see them like that.

While waiting near the mortuary, Vasantha looked into the eyes of the Adivasi mothers. They all held their breath, their eyes conveying their worry and fear that one of the dead bodies may well be their child.

Janaki and Bhagya requested the police to announce the names once again.

They were announcing: Ravi, Soni, Rajitha..Bandi..Badri...

Listening to the list, Sharada held Vasantha's hand tightly. Her ice cold hand conveyed her state of mind. Vasantha pressed Sharada's hand reassuringly to give her some courage.

Noticing all this, Janaki had come closer to Sharada and Vasantha. She put her hand around Sharada's shoulder and said, 'don't be afraid all the time .... as if you are always anticipating the worst.' All of them had been telling Sharada since the previous day to stay calm, but to no avail.

They opened the door of the mortuary. Vasantha helped the four Adivasi mothers to go inside the room.

On one side, there were dead bodies in the freezers with numbered cardboard pieces stuck to them. Why would they murder people and transform them to mere numbers? This brings to mind the mother in Mahashweta Devi's novel 'Hajar Churashir Maa[2]' who had to look for her son among the dead on the basis of a number. These mothers put so much of their care, time, and strength to raise their kids and at the end they were reduced to mere numbers. Those who come looking for their children, spouses and parents among the dead are disquieted by these numbers. They had to check if the number announced by the police and the one present on the freezer matched. Amidst tears and with a heavy heart they had to search for and identify their dear ones among the bloodied and nearly unrecognizable bodies. What kind of a system is this that turns a blood relationship into mere numbers?

Meanwhile a police officer had come inside with a bundle of papers and asked who Warangal Rajitha's mother was.

That sent shockwaves across the room.

Sharada collapsed on the bloody, wet, dirty ground crying her heart out. Janaki hugged Sharada to give her a semblance of support.

Nobody there said explicitly that Sharada is Rajitha's mother. But the police understood. They continued reading out the names and the corresponding numbers.

'Dear child, I had to come here today to see your dead body...' Sharada was sobbing her heart out.

For the past ten years, Sharada had been going to the places of encounters and mortuaries to check if her daughter was alive or not. She would see her child's features in all the women killed, but would realize that it wasn't her child. Even though she was relieved that it wasn't her child, it was still someone else's child and sadness would envelop her. Her relief was short-lived though because she would start looking for Rajitha in every incident and every mortuary.

Vasantha hugged Sharada tightly, feeling terrible about the situation wherein a mother had to find out in this heinous manner that her own flesh and blood was brutally murdered by the police.

This was not the time to talk to her and comfort her. She should cry her heart out. Sharada, who identified the bodies of several martyrs and helped people perform the last rites of their near and dear ones, was today in a state where she had to identify her own daughter's body in a numbered bag. While her daughter's body was lying all night on this side of the wall, Sharada spent all night on the other side in their Adivasi friend's home worrying about her child.

Meanwhile, two Adivasi mothers identified their children's bodies. They collapsed near the bodies and were wailing. Vasantha got up and walked towards them. The dead bodies were tied tightly with only their faces being visible. Their faces were not very recognizable either. They might have died a gory death in the hands of these Greyhounds. Where could one search for their sensitive hearts, kind eyes and radiant smile amidst such bloody body bags? The Adivasi mothers identified their flesh and blood children without knowing the aliases and numbers that the police read out. Those things make no sense to them.

There is no language to comfort these mothers. One could only give them assurance through their touch and expression in their eyes that they understand their pain and everyone feels things the same way, no matter which language each of us speaks.

Sharada got up and walked towards the freezers.

By then Rama and others already identified Rajitha. There was a big injury on Rajitha's face. Her body was tied tightly in a polythene cover. The blood that flowed from the corpse was frozen on one side.

Everybody present there knew Rajitha since she was a small kid. She would call them all by her relationship with them and used to play with their kids. She would always accompany her mother to their houses and meetings. Yet none of them could see her likeness in this battered face. Sharada saw her child's face, and just collapsed to the ground staring into her face. She remained in that position for a long time.

Vasantha pulled herself together, gave Janaki the responsibility of taking care of Sharada, and got up to walk around the mortuary to console other mothers. The scent of blood has made the mortuary unbearable. Perhaps because of that, or perhaps because of the sight of several weeping mothers, Vasantha's head was beginning to spin slightly.

By that time, the police had still not disclosed the names of seven other people killed in the encounter. The rest of the Adivasi women were still not sure if their children were dead or alive. Vasantha noticed that. She approached the police who were moving to and fro with their guns.

"Are you still not going to tell us the rest of the names?" she asked angrily. They were utterly indifferent to her question and did not bother to respond. Meanwhile two police officers walked in with a sheet of paper.

They declared that Rajitha and two others were the only non-Adivasis. The rest of the killed were Adivasis. They read out the names of the other two non-Adivasis: 'Ravi, alias Sudhakar, and Khairunbi, alias Soni.'

Vasantha suddenly remembered something as she heard these two names. She ran towards the dead bodies to see their faces. It was her, without a doubt!

Vasantha couldn't stand. The grief weighed her down, literally and physically. It was Soni in the last box and in the box next to her was Ravi. They were together even in death. Vasantha gently touched the foreheads of Soni and Ravi, weeping slowly.

Bhagya came to Vasantha and requested her to come to the other end. Vasantha mustered all her strength to get up and go with Bhagya. At the body numbered 2, an Adivasi woman was crying, beating her head. Vasantha couldn't understand her language but it seemed that she was saying it was her son. She turned towards Vasantha and gave her son's name and the Adivasi men confirmed it. However, the police claimed that it was not the body of that person as the name they had was different from that given by the Adivasi woman. That mother was scared that the police wouldn't let her take her son's body home.

'If the mother recognized, who are you to decide if it is her son or not?' asked Vasantha.

'They are giving some other name and even the village name is different. We won't accept that,' said the police.

Trying to decipher this conversation happening in Telugu and Gondi, the Adivasi woman approached Vasantha to again plead with her to make the police understand that it was indeed her son. She said in Gondi, although Vasantha did not fully understand, 'that is my son, can't I recognize my own son?'

The police did not bother.

Sobbing with anxiety that the police wouldn't let her take her son home, and trying to convince everyone else in the room that it is indeed her son, she uncovered her breast and pointed at her son's dead body as if to say 'My son ... the one who drank my milk and grew up....' Vasantha felt as if somebody was twisting a dagger in her heart. She burst into tears, hugged that mother tightly and covered her breast with her saree.

'It is your son, you will take him home. Don't worry,' Vasantha said, comforting her. If Vasantha did not give that assurance in that situation, the Adivasi mother would have collapsed. Apart from the grief of her son's death, she was shivering with the fear that her son's body would not be handed over to her.

On the one hand, Sharada unexpectedly saw her daughter as a corpse. On the other hand, even when this Adivasi mother recognized the body as her son's, the police refused to accept it. The remaining men and women were crying over their children. What was to be done? Should Vasantha cry like others? Or pull herself together and console them? Or focus on the tasks to be completed? There is nothing more unbearable than having to fight back one's sorrow.

Janaki asked Kamala to take that Adivasi mother out and make her sit because she was unable to stand. Kamala and Bhagya tried taking her out. Suspicious that she would not be allowed to take her son, she sat beating her head and refused to move from her son's body. Later, some of the Adivasi men escorted her outside the mortuary.

Soni had told Vasantha all about her brother. With a big family in poverty, it was her brother who strove very hard to help everyone else in the family. She described all the torture he had endured at the hands of police after she left and he had been utterly scared since then.

Sitting under the palash tree as the morning sun beamed on her face, Soni told Vasantha many things about her personal and political experiences. Even though she looked a little unhealthy, she was still good looking with her fair skin, and thick hair.

Later, she told Vasantha about Ravi. They decided to move to the forests because it was becoming difficult to work in the plains due to repression. Ravi was at a meeting an hour away that day, but Vasantha couldn't meet him. But Soni talked so much about him and his life that Vasantha almost felt that she had always known him.

'He is always worried about my health. He tells me that health impacts our thoughts and actions. So he always encourages me to take care of my health,' Soni told her.

'You know, Ravi has two mothers! They are sisters. Since the older sister did not have children, the younger one gave Ravi to her in adoption. Ravi is pained that he couldn't meet and talk to his mothers for years. But this is all routine for us,' she said laughing. Vasantha recalled this conversation with Soni from twenty years ago and wiped her eyes.

Vasantha tried reaching out to both their families based on the details that Soni had given her that day. Even the police were trying to get in touch with them.

Vasantha received a call from Ravi's mothers. It was difficult to console them, especially over the phone.

'We are old now. We were worried that he may not even know when we die. Still, we hoped that he would perform our final rites. We prayed to many Gods to let us see him at least once before we died. And now this news!! We did not expect that he would be gone while we are still alive,' they said crying.

Vasantha gave them the location and the directions to come to the mortuary and asked them to come as soon as possible. Two hours later, she called them up to ask how far they've reached.

Ravi's brother took the call this time.

'Sorry, Akka. We love our brother, but we can't take the dead body. We have other problems and we can't face them...' he said.

True. There will be a lot of problems in taking the bodies of Naxalites and conducting the final rites. However, if one reasons and cajoles, there have been instances when the relatives agreed to take the body home. Vasantha tried convincing Ravi's brother but he showed no signs of courage and interest. Mothers cannot simply let go despite the difficulties. So, she thought speaking to them would do some good.

'Could you please let me talk to your mothers?' Vasantha pleaded.

He said he would get them to call her back in a short while but she did not hear back from him. Later, when she tried calling, the calls did not even connect.

Meanwhile, Soni's brother and relatives arrived.

They were in a hurry to take away Soni's body. On the other hand, there was no sign of Ravi's relatives. Vasantha did not know what to do about it. She talked to Janaki, Rama, and Bhagya about the same. They came to a decision and talked to Soni's brother.

'Whether or not we like it, Soni and Ravi chose each other, lived together, and died together. If the last rites can also be done together, it'll be better. We will take Ravi's body also to your village and conduct his rites also there,' Vasantha said.

Soni's brother didn't utter a word. They had come all the way here only with the help of their village *sarpanch*. They were not ready to come on their own. Soni's brother talked separately with the *sarpanch* and his relatives. The *sarpanch* told him he could not help him with any problems that may arise if he took Ravi's body also along. His relatives also did not agree to the proposal, maybe due to religious reasons. "We will only take our Soni's body,' declared Soni's brother.

Vasantha understood that there was nothing more they could do on that. The only thing left to do was to get the political leaders of Ravi's area to talk to the police to hand over Ravi's body to them.

It was afternoon and they were conducting post-mortem on the bodies.

Vasantha thought that Ravi's dead body would leave the world unclaimed and orphaned. Unlike ordinary people, Ravi was a person who had developed relationships with hundreds of people. Will he now have nobody to mourn him in death? She felt rather low and tried calling his mothers once again. This time Ravi's mother – the one who gave him birth – took the call but she wasn't in a position to talk.

'It is okay, *Amma*. It is fine if you cannot take the dead body with you. But at least come and see him one last time. Otherwise, you will regret not seeing him. Because you won't get to see him ever again...' Vasantha pleaded.

At this, the mother sobbed her heart out. She seemed to have fallen down while continuing to cry. Vasantha then heard a commotion in the background over the phone and the call got disconnected.

There was no chance their family was going to claim the body. So, she approached the police along with Janaki, Rama, and Bhagya.

She informed them about their family situation. 'Give me his dead body,' she asked the police.

If their blood relatives don't claim the body, we will perform the last rites but we won't give the bodies to anybody else, the police said. They all argued a lot about this. By then, Soni's dead body was taken away by her relatives. Some of the villagers too left with two of the Adivasi bodies. The mother of dead body number two and others were still waiting for the police to release the body for them to take home.

The police said they were conducting enquiries and if nobody else came to claim the body, they promised to give it to the mother sitting outside the mortuary. That gave her some hope and she sat there waiting.

At around three o' clock, the police approached Vasantha with some papers and asked her to sign it, and then take Ravi's body. The paper said: "Ravi, alias Sudhakar, who is killed in the encounter is my friend. I am giving it in writing that I know him very well. Since his blood relatives did not come to claim his body, I take the responsibility of performing his last rites." Vasantha signed on it immediately.

She experienced strange emotions that she never felt before as she signed that paper. She went into the mortuary and stood near Ravi's dead body. The post-mortem was yet to be done. She could see his feet and one of his hands. With grey hair and a bony face he looked like a prematurely aged warrior. She touched the feet, hands, and the forehead of this soldier who had sacrificed his youth and life to help others. It felt like she was touching a small baby. She had only heard of him, never met him before. And yet, he became related to her after his death. 'Did he die? Or is he being reborn in my hands? One mother gave him birth, the other raised him.... his bond with them that got cut off is now tied to me after his death' thought Vasantha.

Vasantha ran her fingers on his head as though he was her child. The maternal feeling in her expressed itself in her tears.

Janaki interrupted her thoughts and said 'Akka, what is this? Pull yourself together. It is getting late. We have to think about what to do with Ravi's body. Let us talk to Sharada and take his body to Paidipally along with Rajitha's.'

The sun was beginning to set. Not only the people from this village, but people from nearby villages too joined the procession and it was a sea of red flags. Sharada had recovered a little from her sorrow. She stood with a red flag in her hand on the tractor that was carrying the bodies of Rajitha and Ravi. Amidst the sadness, she was also raising slogans along with the hundreds of people surrounding the tractor.

Vasantha was on the tractor too.

Rajitha – someone she knew from her childhood. Ravi – she had only heard of him but never seen him until now...

Although physically present, Vasantha's mind was wandering. She couldn't think of anything or anybody but Ravi's mothers. They shared equally the responsibility of giving birth to and raising Ravi. Soni's words were resounding in her ears, 'Do you know, Ravi has two mothers?'

How could these old mothers bear this loss? On top of that, to not be able to see their son one last time ...she was worried about them.

The procession continued. It was getting darker. The only light for navigation were the red flags.

Amongst all that sound and sloganeering, someone ran towards the tractor. That person tried to tell Vasantha something but she could not hear anything. He repeated his message and went back. As they couldn't hear the message, Vasantha and Janaki looked at each other blankly.

Meanwhile the procession reached the middle of the village where there were memorials for the martyred revolutionaries. It was the custom of the village to bury the bodies of the martyrs and build memorials there. Vasantha spotted two women struggling to get to the tractor while pushing aside the people blocking their way. The man who just gave the message to Vasantha was showing them the way.

Those women looked alike – like, twins or sisters – with grey hair and plain sarees. They were elderly women from a middle class family. As they approached closer to the tractor, Vasantha became very emotional. She was waiting for these mothers to come. She couldn't reconcile to the situation that Ravi would leave the world without their seeing him one last time and bidding him goodbye.

It was the family relationships that stopped them from claiming Ravi's dead body. Vasantha thought that at their age, they had no choice in the matter and they wouldn't be able to come at all. Eventually, their wish to see their son emerged victorious over the objections from their family.

But how did they manage to come now? Vasantha wondered.

Immediately she deflected this thought because that was not very important now. They were here finally, to see their son – for the last time.

The tractor halted. With great difficulty both of them entered the tractor. They were too old to get on the tractor all by themselves. Vasantha and Sharada helped them climb up and showed them Ravi's body.

They fell on his body and cried incessantly, pouring their hearts out. It was difficult to know who had given birth to Ravi and who raised him.

Ten minutes later, they turned to Vasantha and asked if she was in fact Vasantha.

'One of us carried Ravi in our womb for nine months. The other raised him for twenty years. But on his last day, you were the one to take him into your lap. And you handed him back to us again,' they said as they hugged Vasantha. 'You have given some space for our son along with your daughter, we cannot thank you enough,' they told Sharada. Sharada understood the longing and grief of these mothers who waited for years to see their son only to see him as a dead body.

Vasantha just stared at these mothers silently. She couldn't utter a word. She just wiped their tears.

They made arrangements to bring the bodies down.

They brought down Rajitha's body first. Sharada held high the red flag in her hand and raised slogans with a raised fist.

With Janaki's help, Ravi's two mothers stood firmly and raised their fists, while wiping away their tears.

Translation of 'Mugguru Thallulu' (First Published in 'Arunatara' June 2019)

Translated by P. Aravinda

Notes:
1. Greyhounds: The Greyhounds are a militarised police unit of the Andhra Pradesh State Police that the state has trained specifically for operations against the guerillas.
2. *Hajar Churashir Maa*: (No. 1084's Mother) is a 1974 Bengali novel written by Ramon Magsaysay Award winner Mahasweta Devi. It was written in the backdrop of the Naxalite revolution in the Seventies. It was also made into a film in Hindi.

The Forward March of History

V. R. Chaitanya

"People burning the effigies of Maoists."

While reading the newspaper headlines on her tablet, Sudha zoomed in on that news. The photo beneath the news showed many BSF (Border Security Force) police with black clothes wrapped around their heads and a few people. Some of those people were holding placards that read, "Maoists, do not come to our villages!" The photo depicted two men in plain clothes holding aloft human-like effigies made of straw, dressed in olive green clothing, that were set on fire. She tried zooming in further to see if she could recognize those two men, but the image was too blurry to make out who they were.

Another news headline caught her eye: "People hoist a tricolor flag on a Maoist memorial." Where is this memorial located? It's quite a large memorial. She removed her glasses, cleaned them, and put them back on to get a clearer look. In front of the memorial were some police and a large crowd of people. None of them looked familiar. When she delved into the details of the news, she understood. It was a memorial for the martyrs, built collectively by the villagers with voluntary contributions. It was built during the time when talks took place between the People's War party and the Andhra Pradesh government. Back then, there was no police camp. Five years ago, after the BSF camp was established, the police hoisted the tricolor flag on the memorial. Why are the people hoisting a new flag now? A weekly market takes place next to the camp. The people coming to the market were likely forced to stand in front of the memorial to make a grand show for the media on August 15[1]. The burning of the effigies might be a similar drama, she thought, feeling frustrated as she moved on to other news stories. That's when she came across another news article.

"Seventy Maoist members surrender in Manjari Panchayat, a stronghold of the Maoists. These individuals had been working as Maoist cadres, mass organisation leaders, and militia commanders. The government has already announced a reward of one lakh rupees per head for those who help in capturing them. The total number of surrenders has now reached seven hundred." As she read the news, she zoomed in on the photo. It showed the DGP (Director General of Police), SP (Superintendent of Police), ASP (Assistant Superintendent of Police), BSF Battalion Commandant, and other officials. Their faces radiated pride as they sat confidently in their chairs. The SP appeared to be saying something to the reporters, holding a microphone in his hand. What might he be saying? It would be – 'Due to the development programs initiated by the government and the police, these people have become conscious and have chosen to surrender, opposing the Maoists. The government will provide employment opportunities to all of them.' It was the same old story, the same tune they always sing.

She zoomed in to see the people standing behind the police officers. There were many men and women, all familiar faces. Among them were people who, unable to participate actively in the movement, left it a long time ago, but had refused to surrender to the enemy and continued to work in the mass organisations and militias. There were members of the *Jana-tana Sarkar* Committees, the people's alternative power organs, as well as party area committee members and Platoon Party Committee members. Also present were militia commanders who had repeatedly instilled fear in the enemy with booby traps and ambushes, making it terrifying for them to enter the area. There were women who would tell the men to stay behind when the police entered the village, while they stood at the forefront with knives, axes, and chilli powder, surrounding the police and preventing them from taking even a single step forward.

They would confront the police like tigresses, snatching their guns away, tying their hands, and rescuing their men. Among them were the *akkas* from the women's organisation, who, no matter how busy they were, would run to the squad the moment they entered the village, warmly greeting them and offering them whatever they had saved – whether it was dried mango, jackfruit pulp, roasted corn, or at least a guava from their trees. There were also the leaders of the women's organisation, who shared their personal problems with the squad as they would with their parents, and who awakened and organised the women in that area and solved many of their problems.

Now, all of them were standing helplessly. It was difficult to discern any emotion on their faces. Sudha noticed someone at the end of the line, in the corner, who looked like Lakmo. She zoomed in on the photo. It was indeed Lakmo. Her head was slightly bowed. Sudha stared intently at her face, trying to imagine the inner turmoil she might be experiencing at that moment. 'When my husband was around, you would think twice before coming into our area... Unable to capture him in the village, you took the help of some greedy traitor and ambushed him when he went out on some work, and broke his legs and arms. Then you threatened us, saying you would kill him if we didn't all surrender, forcing us into this surrender. What cowards you are.' Lakmo must have definitely thought along these lines.

Just ten days ago, the police had arrested Lakmo's husband, Birsu, subjected him to severe torture, and planned to stage a fake encounter[2]. As soon as the villagers and his family members learned that he had been caught by the police, they, along with the entire *panchayat*, issued statements to the media and held protests in front of the police station with knives and axes. With no other option left, the police used their final weapon, 'If all your regional leaders surrender, we will release him; otherwise, we'll kill him.' This led to their forced surrender, and only then did the police present him in court.

As Sudha read the recent news in the papers, her heart ached. Involuntarily, tears welled up in her eyes. She thought about the immense mental pressure that people were subject to. The distress of not being able to meet them during this time and the pain of not being able to do anything troubled her deeply.

She set the tablet aside, took off her glasses, and gently pressed her temples with the tips of her fingers. She checked the time on her watch. 'Oh! Is it already eleven?' she thought, glancing to the side. Everyone in the tent was fast asleep. Someone was snoring softly. Although it was the beginning of October, it still felt stuffy for some reason. She thought stepping outside the tent for some fresh air might help. She switched off the tablet, turned on her flashlight, put on the boots that were by her feet at the end of the *jhilli*, and walked out of the tent.

'Who's there?' asked the comrade on sentry duty.

'It's me,' she replied, taking two steps forward, and then asked, 'Are you on sentry duty?'

'Yes. Haven't you gone to sleep yet?' Kosi, the sentry, asked.

'No! I was reading,' she said and mentioned that she was going to attend to nature's call and walked ahead.

On her way back, she asked, 'Kosi, who's on duty after you?'

'Mangi is next. My sentry duty is for another half an hour,' Kosi replied, checking her watch.

'Everything's fine, right? Is your gun loaded? Don't fall asleep,' Sudha said as she returned to her tent. But for some reason, she didn't feel like going inside. She didn't feel like reading that news again, and she wasn't sleepy either. She sat down next to the tent on a large rock leaning against a big tree, resting her head against the tree, and closed her eyes for a moment. She immediately opened them again and looked up. The round, cool moon was shining brightly in the sky through the tall trees. It was probably a full moon day. The cascading moonlight seemed to join the sky and the earth. A gentle breeze touched her face, bringing a sense of comfort.

Kosi, standing on sentry duty taking the *Maddi*[3] tree as cover with gun in hand, was also clearly visible in the moonlight. Because they had set up camp on the edge of the forest, there was an open field to the right of the camp. The village was on the other side of that field, at some distance. The occasional sound of dogs barking could be heard faintly. During the day, a large solar panel, supported by four poles, would be set up in that field for charging the battery and every evening, it would be taken down. But for some reason, it hadn't been removed today. The moonlight was reflecting off it, making it sparkle. Cicadas were making a loud noise. They were supposedly very small insects, but their noise was so piercing. Sudha had often wanted to see what they looked like, but she hadn't had the chance yet.

The moonlight falls equally on cities, villages, towns, plains, forests, hills, trees, flowers, fields, and the huts of Adivasis without any discrimination, doesn't it? Is it possible for the rich to steal even this moonlight from the poor? The strange thought made her smile.

"There's some inseparable connection between the light of the full moon and love. Moonlight evokes emotion," she recalled reading somewhere. But, what emotion? With her head splitting from the headache, she wondered if even moonlight might become unbearable.

Suddenly, she recalled the words of her life partner who said, 'Our emotions shouldn't take flight in fantasies, detached from material reality.' Where might he be now? What might he be doing? Is he also looking at this moonlight?

Thinking of her partner, who was working in a distant place due to the responsibilities and needs of the movement, brought a smile to her lips. But it didn't last long. The news she had read in the paper once again occupied her mind.

'Mangi... Mangi... It's time for sentry duty, wake up!' Kosi said waking up Mangi. Mangi got up and went to take her place on sentry duty.

Clear moonlight falls on the high mountains, the rocky outcrops, and the Adivasi villages in the Manyam[3] forest just as it does here. The hearts of the Adivasis are just as pure as this moonlight! The enemy is plotting so many schemes to poison and corrupt these innocent people, who know nothing of deceit

and trickery. How should we prepare them to face this psychological warfare? Various thoughts troubled Sudha's mind.

Sudha's bond with the people of the Manyam forest
spanned two decades. She had worked in that area since she
joined the squad. Has it really been twenty years already? she
wondered. Did she ever imagine she would survive for so many
years? When she first joined the squad, she thought she would
last only two or three years, or at most ten years in the midst of
the war with the State. Oh, ten years seemed too ambitious, she
remembered thinking back then, which made her smile now.
She thought all the additional years were a bonus.

She spent twenty years in the lap of her parents, and
another twenty years in the lap of the forest. Whenever those
who joined the revolution after her, those younger than her,
and those who walked along her side in the revolution became
martyrs in front of her eyes, a deep, inexplicable sorrow twisted
her heart.

Over two decades, Sudha witnessed numerous developments in the revolutionary movement and her personal life.

She realized through experience the truth that matter is
always in motion and that quantitative change leads to qualitative change. In Srikakulam, Vizianagaram, Visakhapatnam and
East Godavari districts of the Manyam region; and Koraput
and Malkangiri districts of Odisha where she worked – she
directly observed the culture, lifestyle, determination, and
the vigour of the struggle for land, forest, identity and self-respect of the Adivasi communities like Savara, Jatapu, Kuvvi,
Bhagata, Koya, Gadaba, Kondareddis, Nookadora, Vaalmiki,
Rana, Poraja, Didoy and others. She saw their sacrifices and
learned a great deal from them. Each time the people protected
the squads during encounters and attacks as if they were their
own, Sudha silently vowed to dedicate her life to these people
who had given them a new lease on life.

Her experience seemed insignificant compared to the experiences of these Adivasi people, who were born in these forests
and had endured generations of exploitation and oppression,

relentlessly fighting against it. The service she rendered to these people felt like a mere drop in the ocean. Memories from the past flooded Sudha's mind.

'Sudha, you haven't slept yet? Why are you sitting here? What's wrong?' Lalitha, who had gotten up to answer nature's call, asked in surprise and with concern.

'Nothing! I just went to answer nature's call and sat down here,' Sudha replied, and Lalitha, understanding, informed the sentry and went for her nature call.

'Come on, Sudha, go to sleep,' Lalitha urged again, leaving Sudha with no choice but to get up and go inside the tent.

She lay down in her *jhilli* but couldn't sleep. Thoughts kept flooding her mind. For the past two years, the enemy had intensified brutal attacks on the movement. Continuous combing operations, encounters, martyrdoms, arrests, surrenders, forced surrender campaigns, misinformation campaigns, and the rapid establishment of police camps, roads, and mobile networks as part of carpet security were hindering the squads' ability to meet the people and maintain organisational structures as they had in the past. The party and the people had faced such situations before, where enduring severe repression and losses, squads stayed close to the people, organizing them, and launching waves of mass struggles. They had dealt significant blows to the enemy with proper tactics and regained the upper hand.

But what should be done now? How could they meet the people in the current situation? As her thoughts raced, Sudha's favorite song, "Hum Dekhenge," set as an alarm, began to play on her cell phone. Surprised by the alarm, she picked up her phone and realized that she meant to set it for 12:30 p.m. to check the news, but had forgotten to set it for p.m. That's why it rang at midnight. Laughing at her mistake, as she was about to turn off the phone, she saw the date on the phone.

It was 13 October. Has it already been a year since Comrade Saketh (a central committee member) became a martyr? Her thoughts turned to Saketh. How much had she looked forward to meeting him? She remembered how her heart stopped for a few moments when she heard the news of his martyrdom, just when she was about to meet him in a few days.

The words of Saketh echoed in her mind: 'Revolutionaries must possess an optimistic perspective that allows them to see even the faintest light of fireflies in the darkest of times.' She also remembered another instance when, during a class, he said, 'We must have the resilience to remain unfazed even if the heavens fall on our heads. But that doesn't mean we should be indifferent to things like a buffalo standing in the rain! We should also have the agility to respond with the speed of lightning.' The memory of everyone in the class bursting into laughter at his comment brought a smile to her face.

Once, when a military camp was going on and the class hadn't started even at 2 p.m. Saketh, who was passing by on some errand, walked into the classroom and wrote a quote on the board: "Shape your body to be tough, and your mind to be civilized." His smiling face as he walked away and his thin figure flashed before her eyes.

She vividly remembered the situation ten years ago during the brutal government crackdown to suppress the "Narayan-apatna" people's movement. The enemy's propaganda had confused the people, with the landlords in the villages spreading rumours that the Party was killing Adivasis under the pretext of them being informers. Villagers were so frightened that they shut their doors when the squad approached, refused to offer food, or cooperate in any manner. In some villages, people even ran away at the sight of the squad. Despite these heart-breaking situations, the squad members persevered, going hungry but patiently writing letters to the people, putting up posters, and staying outdoors in the villages all night, and explaining the truth to the people in the daylight. Eventually the same people, who had once been afraid of the squad, finally embraced it with tears in their eyes. Upon listening to all such experiences of the squad, Saketh's heart was filled with compassion for both the people and the comrades of that squad.

Saketh's eyes sparkled with determination when he said, 'If we stay close to the people during tough times, we will surely win! The people are our teachers, the people are invincible. You must definitely write about this experience. We will publish it in our 'Bolshevik' journal.' Sudha couldn't forget the gleam in his eyes when he said that.

'Many of us become confused when the movement faces difficult circumstances. We start doubting if we can win. At such times, we must look back at history and understand it from a dialectical perspective. We should recall the victories achieved by the people in their heroic struggles. In history, all the just wars waged by people were won. We too shall win! Defeats and setbacks are only temporary. Every defeat is the mother of victory. We must find opportunities even in adversities.' The sharp, incisive words from Saketh and the recollection of the experiences of oppressed people throughout history gave Sudha immense courage and mental solace. As plans began to take shape in her mind and as she found some resolution to her thoughts, Sudha drifted into a peaceful sleep.

'Tubri... Tubri! I'm heading to the redgram field. You cook the food and bring the porridge to the field,' Dasu said, grabbing his axe and heading out of the house. As he stepped outside, he saw Gasi and Kaathru from a neighbouring village walking towards his home. Wondering why they were coming so early in the morning, Dasu stopped at the threshold of his house.

'Where are you off to, *anna*?' Kaathru asked as they approached.

'To the redgram field, but why are you here so early?' Dasu replied, puzzled.

Hearing voices, Tubri, who was in the kitchen, came outside.

'Come inside, *anna*, have some black tea before you go,' she offered, handing them a jug of water.

'No, sister! Our youngest son Chinna said he would call from college today. We gave him your husband's number.

If we're late, he might leave. We'll stop by on our way back. Let's go, *anna*. We will get a signal in your field, right?' Kaathru said, and the three of them started walking towards the field.

'*Anna*, we got a letter!' said Kaathru as they walked.

'What letter?' Dasu asked, stopping in surprise.

'It's from 'our' people,' Kaathru replied, carefully pulling a letter out of his shorts pocket, which he had worn under his *lungi*, and handing it to Dasu. They had reached the field by then. Dasu looked around to make sure that no one else was there in the neighbouring fields. The three of them sat on the stone slabs placed under the jackfruit tree.

'I'll read it, but you both keep an eye out,' Dasu said as he unfolded the letter.

'Okay, okay,' they agreed, but their eyes were fixed on the letter, eager to know what it contained. Dasu too, was not in a state to notice anything else; he was equally anxious to read it. Slowly, he began to read.

"Dear village organisation leaders and people, *Lal Salaam!*"

The familiar handwriting and greeting made it clear who had written the letter. "We deeply regret that due to the obstacles created by the enemy, we have been unable to meet directly for the past year. We know how much you've been waiting for us. Many changes have taken place during this time. Many comrades have become martyrs. Others have been arrested and are bravely enduring severe torture in jails. Some, however, have lost faith in the people and defected to the enemy out of cowardice. The government, police, anti-people elements, and landlords in our region are extensively spreading the lies that the Party has been completely wiped out from the Manyam forests, and that it no longer exists, and will not return. With this propaganda, they are trying to break the spirit of the people and are forcing them to surrender through intimidation and threats. We saw the news in the papers about the surrender in your RPC (Revolutionary People's Committee) pocket as well. We can understand the immense pressure and hardships you must have faced…"

Dasu paused and remained silent for a while. Memories of the attempts, threats, and coercion by the village head, *sarpanch*, and the police to make them surrender flooded his mind. He recalled how, during that time, they made attempts to meet the party and believed that it would somehow contact them. However, unable to withstand the pressure, he too surrendered along with the villagers. With a heavy heart, Dasu resumed reading.

"No matter how much pressure the enemy exerted, you should have avoided surrendering. This is the time when we must stand firm and courageous. This is the time to protect the forest, the land, the power, and the victories of the struggle, won by the blood of many martyrs..."

Dasu's voice quivered with pain as he read. 'Damn! We shouldn't have surrendered. We should have held on,' he muttered aloud, regret evident in his voice. Gasi and Kaathru, listening intently, nodded in agreement.

"Comrades, we have only two paths before us. Should we surrender and live as slaves, as labourers? Or should we fight with determination to protect our forest, our land, and the power of our people? Think about it! The Party is not just individuals. The Party is the invincible people's power, shaped by the guiding principles of Marxism-Leninism-Maoism. People's war is not a war waged by individuals. It is a just war fought by all the oppressed people for their rights. Therefore, it is impossible for the enemy to completely eradicate the Party or the people's war. Individuals may die, be arrested, or surrender. The enemy may deploy countless soldiers and carry out severe repression on the people. But none of this can destroy the power, aspirations, and just rights of millions of oppressed people. Today, we may be weak, but these defeats are temporary. This repression is temporary. Our *Manyam* people have a long history of defeating even more severe repressions..."

The letter continued to emphasize the importance of perseverance, courage, and unity in the face of adversity, urging the villagers to remain steadfast and committed to their cause despite the overwhelming challenges they face.

"So, do not despair. We must once again assess the enemy's conspiracies accurately, gather our strength with the right strategies, and work secretly. We must keep an eye on the enemies of the people, detect the weaknesses of the enemy, and strike when the opportunity arises. For the sake of fulfilling the just aspirations of the people, for our right to the forests, and for power to the oppressed people, we must move forward in the people's war with courage and determination, overcoming any number of obstacles..."

By the time the letter was finished, their hearts were heavy with mixed emotions of pain, sorrow, and joy. They felt as though the squad itself was standing before them and speaking, giving them courage. Any lingering doubts they had about how the party would understand or perceive their surrender had completely dissipated. They began enthusiastically discussing how and who and when to convey these points made by the Party, who to keep an eye on, where to accommodate the squad safely the next time they come to the village, how to provide them with food, where to station sentries, and so on. However, they stopped their conversation when they noticed Tubri climbing the hill, carrying a pot of gruel on her head and her child in her arms.

'Did Chinna call *anna*?' she asked, placing the pot on the ground with both hands after handing over the child to Dasu.

'Yes, yes, he did, sister. He needs money to pay the fees. Tomorrow, your sister-in-law and I will go and give it to him,' replied Gasi to Tubri. Then both Gasi and Kaathru got up saying, 'We'll head out now, *anna*.'

'Oh! Have some gruel before you go, *anna*,' Tubri said, pouring some into bowls. Gasi and Kaathru drank the gruel given by Tubri and descended the hill recalling the discussions they just had and the tasks that needed to be done. Dasu watched them with satisfaction.

✳

'*Akka!* I am sending newspapers of the past ten days and other downloads. Please copy them and return the pen drive.' After reading the letter sent by Vennela, the computer operator, Sudha checked the size of the pen drive, copied the files onto her tab, and wrote a small note saying, 'Thank you for sending the downloads,' and sent the pen drive back to Vennela.

Although Sudha was eager to look at the newspapers she had copied, she was told that there was a meeting at 5 p.m. Thinking it might be to discuss the planning for tomorrow's program, she looked at her watch. There were only ten minutes left. She turned off the tab, grabbed her pouch, slung her gun over her shoulder, and called out to her guard, 'Lalitha! We need to go to the meeting. Let's head towards headquarters.' Lalitha closed the book she was reading and accompanied Sudha.

The meeting lasted until 8 p.m. Lalitha had already eaten and placed food in a container for Sudha. When Sudha returned to her tent and was about to take out her tab to read, Lalitha, out of concern that Sudha might skip dinner due to her habit of getting engrossed in reading, said affectionately, 'The food is already cold. You can read after you eat, right?' Smiling, Sudha replied, 'All right, comrade, I'll eat,' and put the tab aside, washed her hands, and finished the meal Lalitha served her.

Feeling a small sense of pride and joy that Sudha ate immediately after her suggestion, Lalitha took out her book and sat down in her corner to read. She set the torchlight next to her ear so that the light would fall on the book and tied it securely to her head with a scarf. 'Why tie a light to your head like Singareni miners and read this late? It's 9 p.m. now. Why don't you sleep, Lalitha?' Sudha asked with a smile.

Lalitha looked up and asked innocently, 'How do Singareni miners look?'

Laughing, Sudha said, 'They tie lights to their heads like you.' She then sat down in her corner and opened her tab. Lalitha asked curiously, 'Do they also read with lights on their heads?'

Sudha burst out laughing and said, 'Oh dear, it was my mistake to rake up this topic with you. I have some work now, but I'll tell you about Singareni miners tomorrow.' Lalitha returned to her book without asking further questions.

Sudha started flipping through the newspapers, one by one, in chronological order. The state assembly elections were approaching. The newspapers were filled with articles about the ruling party's politicians and the MLAs (Member of Legislative Assembly) conducting the *'Gadapa Gadapaku'* (Door-to-Door) program. One particular news story caught her attention: "MLAs faced obstacles at every step while trying to conduct the *'Gadapa Gadapaku'* program amidst tight police security in the Manjari Panchayat, an area with significant Maoist influence."

Until then, she had been casually flipping through the papers, but now she started to pay more attention. Headlines like "People obstruct the *'Gadapa Gadapaku'* program by burning effigies of the Chief Minister and MLAs," "Villagers questioned the ministers who came for the *'Gadapa Gadapaku'* program, asking what development they had brought to their villages during their tenure," and "Women protest with brooms and empty pots" made Sudha look through the news with excitement.

"In Nathavaram Mandal[5] of East Godavari district, people from five panchayats sat on the road in protest against the transportation of bauxite under the guise of laterite in the name of proxy owners. The people set fire to five tippers and seven tractors." Another headline in bold letters read, "Attack on Chitrakonda Police Station." Startled and unable to believe what she was seeing, Sudha widened her eyes and zoomed in on the paper. Attack! Who attacked there?

The paper continued, "Nine Adivasis were injured when the police lathi-charged the people who took out a rally on their issues. Angered by the incident, the people stormed into the Chitrakonda police station, destroying chairs, tables, and files. They also set fire to six bikes parked in the compound." The photo clearly showed the Chitrakonda Police Station board, half-burnt and hanging upside down.

The next headline read, "Clash between the police and the people while attempting to stop a protest by the people against China-clay mining in Araku Mandal. Two constables were injured in the clash, and the local Sub-Inspector (SI) fell into a mud pit." The reporter had clearly captured a photo of the SI lying in the mud. Sudha remembered past incidents in the same area where people had confronted MLA Kidari and later punished Kidari and Siveri Soma in front of the public on the same road.

As Sudha read these reports, she felt an overwhelming joy. With difficulty, she suppressed the urge to wake up those sleeping next to her and share the exciting news.

The fire smouldering beneath the ashes was slowly igniting. Who could stop it? This will turn into a great blaze. A small spark can create a wildfire. History always moves forward... ever forward! Who can turn back the wheel of time? Who can prevent a quantitative change from transforming into a qualitative one? With such thoughts racing through her mind, Sudha was filled with excitement and joy. She cannot sleep when she's too happy, so she set aside the tab and stepped out of the tent.

It was probably a new moon night, as it was pitch dark outside. Fireflies were glowing here and there in the dark. The stars in the sky were shining brightly. On a full moon night, they would fade away, but that doesn't mean they don't exist! People are like that too. Repression only leads to more rebellion. People will build their own bright future. The task of the Communist Party is to awaken the people with the MLM (Marxism-Leninism-Maoism) ideology and fan the flames of this smouldering fire! Thoughts that could spark a people's revolution were sharpening in her mind. In the dark, a smile spread across Sudha's face.

Translation of 'Charitra munumunduke'. (First published in *Vasantha Megham*, December 1, 2023)

Translated by N. Ravi

Notes:
1. 15th Aug 1947 – Indian independence day
2. Fake encounters: In innumerable incidents the police kidnap the revolutionaries or catch them alive, torture and kill them and later announce that there was an exchange of fire between them and the Revolutionaries in which the latter died.
3. Maddi: large Indian laurel Tree (Saaj in Hindi)
4. Manyam: Srikakulam, Vizianagaram, Visakhapatnam and East Godavari districts of Andhra Pradesh state
5. Mandal: Administrative sub-unit of a district

Glossary

T = Telugu · H = Hindi · G = Gondi

Akka (T), *Didi* (H) – elder sister, but this term is also used by people to address female comrades

Ambali – gruel

Amma (T) – mother

Ammamma (T) – grandmother

Anna (T), *Dada* (H) – elder brother, but this term is also used by people to address male comrades

Arunatara – a monthly magazine in Telugu run by Revolutionary Writers Association

Beedi – local hand-rolled cigarette

Bharmar – a muzzle-loading gun. Adivasis have been using bharmars for hunting since almost the time of the British occupation. They are made locally and also used by the militia.

Bolshevik – is a political magazine run by the Andhra Orissa Border Committee (AOB) of the Maoists

Dera – dwelling place; in a camp *dera* usually refers to a tent

Dharna – sit-in protest

Dump – a safe storage space for ammunition or papers or any other critical material [of the Party]

Gotul – community place in the village for meetings and cultural activities

Ingo – Gondi word for saying Yes and Okay

Janatana Sarkar – the People's Government

Jawan – soldier/policeman/woman of the lower ranks

Jhilli (H) – polythene sheet

Kolimi – a Telugu literary online magazine

Krantikari Adivasi Mahila Sanghatan (KAMS): is the revolutionary Adivasi women's organisation. KAMS was initially established in Gadchiroli district of Maharashtra. It later expanded to the Bastar region of Dandakaranya. The KAMS took up the task of educating against and opposing the Adivasi customs that are oppressive for women, for example, they carried out an active campaign against forced marriages as a result of which, forced marriages became rare in the areas where KAMS is active. KAMS has also actively participated in the anti-famine protests, in election boycott campaigns and in developmental activity in the villages. Representatives of KAMS are also part of the Revolutionary People's Committee, wherever they are formed. At KAMS's annual conference, every person attending would bring a number of small sticks, which represented the number of members in their area whom they were representing at the meeting. The sticks were then all counted together and until a few years ago, it totalled around 100,000.

Lal Salaam (H)– Red Salute

Lungi (T)– cloth wrapped around the waist, the two ends of which are knotted together

Mahila Margam – a women's magazine run by a woman's organisation, Chaitanya Mahila *Sangam*, in the Telugu language

Mahua – is the Adivasi name of Madhuca longifolia or Indian Butter Tree which is abundantly found in the areas inhabited by the Adivasi in the central Indian highlands, extending westward into Gujarat and eastward to the Chotanagpur Plateau. The mahua tree is not just a tree for Adivasis but emblematic of their very way of life as custodians of their lands and forests, including the judicious non-extractive use of forest produce for sustenance and livelihood. The flowering/shedding season starts about April for about three months, and the flowers and fruit are collected early in the morning when they are freshly fallen – usually the entire family/community is involved in this work during this season.

Militia – the auxiliary force of the PLGA. Formed with the local people armed with their traditional weapons, e.g. bows and arrows, etc. The militia members are not full timers, they have their own occupations, e.g. farming etc., but aid the PLGA whenever the need arises.

Nayana (T) – father

Panchayat – village council as per Panchayat Raj Act 1989

Party – CPI (Maoist) – Communist Party of India (Maoist)

PLGA – People's Liberation Guerilla Army

Porumahila – a women's magazine brought out in Dandakaranya in Telugu language

Salwar kameez – a traditional Indian women's dress comprising a long tunic and loose trousers that are gathered and tied at the waist

Sangam – a mass organisation such as women's organisation, workers' organisation, youth organisation etc.

Sarpanch – The elected head of a Gram Panchayat, the village-level local government institution in India, responsible for the overall development and welfare of the rural community

Vasanthamegham – a literary bi-lingual web magazine run by the Revolutionary Writers Association

Viplavi – a bulletin run by the women's organisation of AOB

Note: Though words like Amma, Naanna, Akka, Anna, Babai, Mama, atha, Tata, ammamma denote a familial relationship, the person being addressed need not necessarily be related. It is part of Indian culture to address even non-related people using familial relationships, especially in the rural areas. Hence the readers will find these words in almost all the stories though the story is not taking place in a family.

Martyred Authors

Comrade Chada Vijayalakshmi (aka **Karuna**) was born in Nawabpet, Karimnagar district of Telangana. In 1986, she became a full-time activist. She worked in Hyderabad in the party's technical work, while also taking a nursing course. In 1995, she worked in the Uddanam and Jhanjhavati squads of Srikakulam. She served as the secretary of the Korukonda Area Committee. She was the first woman to reach the Divisional Committee level in the East Division. In 2004, she became a member of the Women's Sub-committee formed in the Andhra–Odisha Border Committee area. She strengthened the women's movement in the East Division. She took part in military offensives such as the Koraput multiple raid. She also served as a military doctor. After two decades of revolutionary life, on 27 December 2006, the police captured her along with her life partner Vadkapur Chandramouli, a central committee member, while on their way to attend the Party Congress. The police subjected them to severe torture, and killed them. In the movement, she was popularly known as Karuna. She wrote two stories. The story 'People are the bulwark' is included in this anthology.

Comrade Uppuganti Nirmala (aka **Nitya**) was born in Kondapavuluru near Gannavaram in Krishna district of Andhra Pradesh. She worked for 42 years in the movement, under the name 'Narmada'. Between 1987 and 1994, she was involved in the publication of the party's Hindi journal 'Prabhat'. From 1996 onwards, she began working in the Dandakaranya (DK) movement and continued until 2018, mainly based in Gadchiroli. By the time she came to Hyderabad city for cancer treatment, the disease had already advanced. While undergoing treatment clandestinely she was arrested on 11 June 2019. She spent time in jail without treatment and was then later shifted to a hospice center with the government claiming that no further treatment could be provided. On 9

April 2022, she passed away in the hospice while still being in custody. She had been in charge of the publication of 'Poru Mahila' (in Telugu) and 'Sangharsharat Mahila' in Hindi since 1996. She played a key role in the writing of the book '30 Years of the Dandakaranya Women's Movement'. She wrote numerous stories, poems, essays and reports under the pen name Nitya. She wrote and translated mainly in Telugu, Hindi, and Gondi languages. She was a member of the DK Special Zonal Committee. The story 'Bali' is included in this anthology.

Comrade Gumudavelli Renuka was born (on October 14, 1970) in Kadavendi, a village in Devaruppala Mandal of Jangaon district, Telangana, a region known for its legacy of struggle. Kadavendi is a historically significant village – it's the birthplace of Doddi Komarayya, the first martyr of the Telangana armed struggle. She completed her Law course and practiced as a lawyer for a short while. She worked in the urban movement for nearly a decade fighting for the rights of women. Later in 2004, she joined the underground revolutionary movement and worked in different areas and in different level committees before rising to the state level committee. She was a member of DK Special Zonal Committee at the time of her martyrdom. She was a prolific writer even before she joined the movement and wrote 37 short stories. Seventeen of these stories were about the revolutionary movement. She wrote several field reports from the battle ground about Green Hunt, *Salwa Judum*, land Struggles in Narayana Patna (Odisha) and about the migration of Adivasis of DK. She worked for the Party's political magazines 'Kranthi', and 'Prabhat'. She was sick and taking shelter in one of the Adivasi villages from where she was picked up, tortured and shot dead near Indravathi River in DK on 31st March 2025. The stories 'Defiance', 'Punishment', and 'She *is* my Daughter' are included in this anthology.

Comrade Vannada Vijayalakshmi (aka **Bhumika**) was born in Vemulnarva village of Keshampet mandal in Ranga Reddy district. She did her post-graduation and also had a bachelor's degree in education and completed a law course before joining the movement. She was active in the student movement while studying in Osmania University, Hyderabad. She was an active participant in the separate Telangana agitation. She joined the underground revolutionary movement in 2014. She worked in Andhra Odisha Border area for a decade. She worked as Central Committee staff and was in charge of running the 'Bolshevik' magazine. She was shifted to DK to work as one of the staff members of the General Secretary of the CPI Maoist Party, Comrade Namballa Keshava Rao where she was martyred along with him and 25 other comrades, in Gandikot, Narayanpur encounter on 21st May 2025. She wrote 8 stories and several songs on Martyrs. The story 'Encounter' is included in this anthology.

 **Comrade V. R. Chaithanya** (aka **Aruna**) was born in a small village Karakuvanipalem, Pendurthi mandal in Vishakhapatnam district of Andhra Pradesh. Her father worked as a teacher. Her parents are progressives and their house used to be a centre for progressive people. Chaithanya is exposed to these political discussions right from her childhood. As a child she participated in anti-arrack campaigns by performing the songs of the struggle. She used to participate in street plays. As a teenager she joined the women's organisation and worked on women's issues. Later she decided to work in the revolutionary move-ment and went underground and joined the CPI Maoist Party. She worked in Andhra Odisha border area in different positions and became a member of the state level committee. At the time of her martyrdom, she was a member of Andhra Odisha Border Committee. She was killed in an encounter in Maredumilli forest in Andhra Pradesh along with Central Committee member Ganesh on 18th June 2025. She was constantly in the news for her heroic participation in many military actions like the Koraput multiple raid. She wrote 6 stories with different pen names. The stories 'Red Flag' and 'Forward March of History' are included in this anthology.

Notes on Translators

Anupama P. is a faculty member of Computer Science in University of Hyderabad. She is concerned about the direction and models of "development" currently being followed in the world. She is a fan of Carl Sagan, and very much in love with Earth, our only home in the universe. She believes that Indigenous people in all the countries ought to be our role models for their care of nature.

Anuradha B. is a revolutionary activist, writer and translator. She was an editorial board member of Mahila Margam for over a decade (1995-2005). She wrote 30 short stories and many articles and translated books, short stories and articles from English to Telugu. Some of her translations include 'The Prisons We Broke' by Baby Kamble, 'We also made History' by Meenakshi Moon and Urmila Pawar, 'Feminisation of Labour Relations' by Dr. M. Vanamala, 'Feminist Ambedkar' (Writings and Speeches of Dr. Ambedkar on Women). She compiled and edited 'Viyyuuka – stories by women revolutionaries' in six volumes in Telugu.

Anuradha P. studied agriculture but is deeply interested in literature, culture and politics. She worked for more than fifteen years as a part of the editorial team in Meghan-Kiffer Press. She reads extensively and does occasional translations. She lives in Hyderabad.

Aravinda P. studied engineering but has a keen interest in literature, economics and politics. She worked in the software industry for 30 years and left it to pursue her interests in other areas. As part of her current work, she is actively involved in translations of English works into Telugu and vice versa. She is also currently studying various thinkers and scholars to understand the intersection of caste, class and gender in India. She lives in Hyderabad.

Ravi N. is a revolutionary activist. He has been participating in revolutionary, democratic and progressive movements and is engaged in writing political and polemical articles from a Marxist point of view and translating from English to Telugu and vice versa. He has translated '30 years of Dandakaranya Cultural Movement' from Telugu to English (under the pen name R.V. Sridhar), 'Gujarat files' by Rana Ayub, 'Varna to Jati' by Naveen Babu, and co-translated 'Wretched of the Earth' by

Frantz Fanon and 'Critiquing Brahminism' by Ajith (K. Muralidharan) from English to Telugu. He has brought out his collection of articles 'Caste and Revolution' both in Telugu and English.

Rigobertha Prabhatha is an educational content writer. He did his masters in English Literature and B.Ed. Translation is his hobby. So far he translated 10 stories and 40 poems from Telugu to English. He is very passionate about writing reviews of movies and web series. He runs a website rigoberthareviewsmovies.com and YouTube channel 'Prabhatha loves movies'. He also writes for websites Primepost, Southfirst and Telepu TV. Some of the stories he translated that have been published include: P Satyavati (Here I am), Unudurti Sudhakar ('A Barber's Tale'), B Anuradha (Dheesali and 'Ek Chadar Mailisi') and Jeevani ('From a Death Hole').

Shaheeda is a revolutionary, a writer, poet and a translator. She published an anthology of her stories in Telugu named *Jajipoola parimalam*, and an anthology of poems in Telugu *Oka maata, oka sambhashana*. She wrote several books and articles, also translated several books, articles and stories. She translates from Telugu to English and vice versa under different pen names.

Vimal is a Revolutionary activist, and a translator. He wrote several articles on social change. He translates from Telugu to English. He translated several articles and short stories. A significant work among his translations is 'Janatana Rajyam' by Pani. Accused of being a Maoist, he was detained as a political prisoner in multiple states from 2011 to 2019.

Vipanchika S Bhagyanagar is a PhD Student in History at Purdue University, West Lafayette. Her areas of interest include Punishment, Prison Studies, Colonialism, Surveillance Technologies, Cartography, Social History and Gender/Caste studies. In 2024, Vipanchika received the Harold D. Woodman Graduate Research Award for investigating the binary of "ordinary" and "political" prisoners in colonial Indian archives at the National Archives of India, Delhi. She published book reviews in peer-review journals of Sage and Taylor & Francis and wrote to The Wire, EPW, among others. She translated short stories.

EU Safety Information

Publisher: Daraja Press, PO Box 99900 BM 735 664 Wakefield, QC J0X 0C2, Canada

info@darajapress.com | https://darajapress.com

EU Authorized GPSR Representative: Easy Access System Europe - Mustamäe tee 50, 10621 Tallinn, Estonia, gpsr.requests@easproject.com

For EU product safety concerns, please contact us at info@darajapress.com